Household Words

bloomers, sucker, bombshell,
scab, nigger, cyber

Stephanie A. Smith

University of Minnesota Press
Minneapolis
London

61463591   10-2-06

A version of "bloomers" was previously published as "Antebellum Politics and Women's Writing," in *The Cambridge Companion to Nineteenth-Century American Women's Writing*, ed. Dale M. Bauer and Philip Gould (New York: Cambridge University Press, 2001), 69–104; reprinted by permission of Cambridge University Press. A version of "sucker" first appeared as "Suckers" in the special issue "Eating and Disorder" of *differences: A Journal of Feminist Cultural Studies* 10, no. 1 (1998): 175–208; copyright 1998 University of Illinois Press; all rights reserved; reprinted by permission of Duke University Press (the current copyright holder). A version of "bombshell" appeared as "Bombshell," in *Body Politics and the Fictional Double*, ed. Debra Walker King (Bloomington: Indiana University Press, 2000), 152–77; copyright 2000 Indiana University Press. Part of "scab" was previously published as "Scab," *Keywords: A Journal of Cultural Materialism* 4 (2003): 12–16. A version of "cyber" originally appeared as "Der Verkauf von Cyber(gen)etik," *Genealogie und Genetik* (Berlin: Academie Verlag, 2002), 269–91.

Published by the University of Minnesota Press
111 Third Avenue South, Suite 290
Minneapolis, MN 55401-2520
http://www.upress.umn.edu

Library of Congress Cataloging-in-Publication Data
Smith, Stephanie A. (Stephanie Ann), 1959–
    Household words : bloomers, sucker, bombshell, scab, nigger, cyber / Stephanie A. Smith.
        p.   cm.
    Includes bibliographical references and index.
    ISBN 0-8166-4552-3 (hc : alk. paper) — ISBN 0-8166-4553-1 (pb : alk. paper)
    1. English language—Etymology.   2. English language—United States—Etymology.   3. Americanisms—History.   I. Title.
PE1571.S65   2005
427'.973—dc22   2005024488

Printed in the United States of America on acid-free paper

The University of Minnesota is an equal-opportunity educator and employer.

12   11   10   09   08   07   06   10   9   8   7   6   5   4   3   2   1

This book is dedicated to John Michael Murchek with love

The unmediated contact with actual reality—
that dream and weapon of bourgeois
philosophy and common sense alike...

—Francis Barker, *The Tremulous Private Body*

Contents

Acknowledgments

Household Words took a long time to complete, much longer than I had ever anticipated. Therefore, my first thank you goes to Douglas Armato, the director of the University of Minnesota Press and my editor, for remembering the project after I resurfaced from a family trauma. Thanks also to Andrew Levy, associate professor and Edna Cooper Chair in English at Butler University, for his comments; indeed, both readers for the University of Minnesota Press made this book that much better. My thanks as well to Gretchen Asmussen at the Press, who has been an absolute mainstay, and to my copy editor, Robin Whitaker, whose precision I appreciated.

Thanks are due the English department at the University of Florida, most particularly the chair, John Leavey, whose even-handedness has been much appreciated; the University of Florida for research money in 1998; my colleagues in the English department, in all their many ways, with particular note of Don Ault, Roger Beebe, Marsha Bryant, Jill Ciment, John Cech, Pat Craddock, Sid Dobrin, Kim Emery, Pamela Gilbert, Terry Harpold, Tace Hedrick, Susan Hegeman, Kenneth Kidd, Debra Walker King, David Leverenz, David Leavitt, Jack

Perlette, Robert Ray, Mark Reid, Malini Schueller, Pat Schmidt, John Seelye, Maureen Turim, Phil Wegner, and Julian Wolfreys.

To my dear friends Sandra Gunning and Peter Melville Logan, whose support since graduate school, through good times and bad, has been nothing short of miraculous; to my friends in the profession, Nancy Armstrong, Dale Bauer, Eva Cherniavsky, Dan Cottom, Walter Herbert Jr., Anne L. Kibbie, Elizabeth Langland, Dana Nelson, Carolyn Porter, Shirley Samuels, Susan Squier, and Priscilla Wald, for encouragement, support, and intellectual challenge; and to Houston Baker, for a brief and encouraging pep talk. Thanks also to my current and former students, in particular Joel Adams, Mindy Cordozo, Frank Hering, Todd Reynolds, Ralph Savarese, Nishant Shahani, Kylie Slavik, and Nick Tischuk.

Finally, for me writing takes teamwork. I must also thank my friends Keith Alexander, Michael Cunningham, Molly Gloss, Ursula K. and Charles Le Guin, and Vonda McIntyre; my track coach, 100-meter hurdler Damu Cherry, who taught me that being a champion does not necessarily mean winning; to my financial coach, Jennifer Hickman, who taught me patience; to my mother, Carol, my sister Jennifer, and my aunt Marge for being there when I needed them and for not turning their backs on me when I get ornery. And last but not least, though they cannot read, speak, or write, to my "best" friends Nadja, Sebastian, Shaddo, and Trudi, who sit with me patiently, for long hours, as I stare at the computer.

"bombshell." Photograph by the author.

Introduction
Forgetting How to Read

This book began when, on my way to lunch one day in 1992, I happened to notice that the sidewalk spoke to me. Well, perhaps not only to me but also to any passerby who could read English. Before the cement had set, someone had scratched the word *bombshell*, along with several women's names, into the sidewalk. At that moment, the word had no full-fledged narrative, no context, no explanatory notes; it was just there, etched in concrete, as many words are on other sidewalks, in other cities. Still it spoke to me. For who could come upon the word *bombshell* without believing she has some idea what the word means? Years later, as I neared the end of this book, I returned to that same sidewalk and photographed the word, for it had taken on a meaning and a depth I had never expected. *Bombshell*, for example, can make of a mere woman a deadly thing, a weapon of mass destruction. I'm joking, of course, but then again one of America's most celebrated bombshells begged reporter Richard Meryman *not* to make her either a joke or a thing in her last interview with *Life* magazine, even if the making of sex object "Marilyn Monroe" had been her life's goal.

Moreover, as perhaps befits a word inscribed in stone, *bombshell* seemed, at that moment in 1992, to speak of something that had passed away, a term for femininity made ridiculous, passé, a relic of the social upheaval of the late 1960s that made Marilyn Monroe obsolete. But the word came out of semiretirement to haunt the mid-1990s: as also befits a word written in stone, *bombshell* reappeared, its meaning seemingly unaltered, as permanent as the common sense about femininity to which it referred suddenly seemed. The return of *bombshell* brought me to reconsider the complexity of meaning, the historicity of language, and the powerful endurance of common sense.

Furthermore, it was this word—and as I went along, all the others included in this volume—that taught me the value of *forgetting how to read*, if "to read" should mean merely "to get a signal." When I encountered the *bombshell* in the sidewalk, decorated by women's names, as I said, I was caught by something I thought long gone. I had relied, in my reading, on a way of making sense about women in my world that was being revamped even as I read the word in the cement. *Bombshell*, and an accompanying common sense about femininity, came back from the grave and showed itself to be alive. Indeed, as I approached each "simple" word in *Household Words*, I was astonished to find embedded within each an obscured or semiforgotten "currency" that could be reanimated in any number of circumstances. This currency, as I will show, forges a picture of how an overarching common sense about persons and things threads itself into everyday life, down to the level of the sentence. And therefore each word has also allowed me to examine and critique common sense, with an eye toward dissecting the long-standing shared belief in the United States that an appeal to plain old common sense, expressed in plain, simple English, can resolve thorny questions when other forms of discussion fail. Because common sense always *appears* authoritative, it conjures up rock-solid reassurance, reliability, stability. It is simple, obvious, and certainly not hard to read or difficult to convey. Indeed, from Thomas Paine to more contemporary appeals for a return to "accessible" language, common sense appears so widely shared that it rarely requires justification and so intimate that it is as if everyone should know it deep in the bones, both a public sense and a private sense, half intuition, half cultural attribute. We all know that a bombshell, especially a blonde one, is a bit of a ditz, sexy, dangerous, or dumb; whatever else she is, isn't, or might be, a bombshell is not a lady, even if she is female. A lady, so called by a word that denotes both gender and class, does not "expose" herself or anyone else. A bombshell does— one just knows this. It's simple.

And yet, of course, not so simple. During the 1960s, the bombshell as a popular figure of womanhood went into a retirement that Monroe's death in 1962 only accelerated. Ideological conflicts about the signification of femininity had already begun, revising the "bombshell as sexy" to mean "sexist," although that particular ideological conflict, along with the sexual politics it entails, is by no means over, or else the role of a "First Lady" might have withered away by now. As critic Alan Sinfield says,

> Ideology produces, makes plausible, concepts and systems to explain who we are, who the others are, how the world works... [and] the strength of ideology derives from the way it gets to be common sense.... The conditions of plausibility... govern our understandings of the world and how to live in it, thereby seeming to define the scope of feasible political change. (806)

Of course, such observations about the effect of ideology as common sense are hardly new.[1] Yet, since the late 1980s a significant renewal of a popular faith in simple language or plain talk, as well as a faith in the efficacy and the benignity of common sense, has taken place along with a refusal of "ideology," as inflected by Marxist interpretation and post-Marxian thought. Commenting on this trend in her 1992 examination of the concept of ideology, *The Politics of Truth: From Marx to Foucault*, Michèle Barrett concluded that it might be high time to abandon the attempt to modify or mobilize the Marxist term *ideology* because

> the definition of concepts, like the definition of everyday words, is partly a matter of usage: one cannot legislate against other people's uses of terms and one cannot with any confidence lay out a new meaning of a term and expect it to stick.... In some ways, the work undertaken by the concept of ideology is often too shallow and too easy, by virtue of the history of the usage of the concept. Better, perhaps, that we point with more accuracy to an instance that might previously merely be labeled ideological: a partial truth, a naturalized understanding or a universalistic discourse, for example. Better,

> perhaps, that we oblige ourselves to think with new and more precise
> concepts, rather than mobilizing the dubious resonances of the
> old. (168)

But the dubious resonances of the old cannot, as even Barrett herself
appears to know, be forgotten or erased so easily if the definition of
everyday words is partly a matter of usage.

Looking back now, I can see that I actually began writing this
book at the same key historical moment in which Barrett made these
comments, just as the so-called culture wars of the first half of the
1990s came to a close. Since those years, it has become something of
a reflex for *both* the left and the right to claim common sense as their
own during debate, a claim that appeals to ordinary understanding,
expressed in simple English or plain talk (as opposed to the jargon
used in discussing ideology). Common sense, we are told, laid out in
plain English will give everyone equal access to power and knowledge. In this book, I beg to disagree, and disagree seriously. Since the
mid-1990s a critical common sense, if you will, seems to have taken
hold. This common sense assumes that language must somehow be
made into concrete, as if language needs to be rendered as concrete
as a "real" material object—a logic oddly seduced by the givenness of
objects, as if an object in material culture cannot give rise to as many
meanings as a word can. This common assumption is often accompanied by a sense of impatience or perhaps exhaustion with theory and
its so-called jargon or complexity, which has left once-theoretically
informed fields such as cultural studies dangerously bereft. I would
echo Karen Newman in her claim that in the United States as of
1996, cultural studies were "mounting an attack of the present on the
rest of time [that] threatens to obliterate not only the past but also
the possibility of reading and acting politically in the present." How
"we read the past . . . determines how we construct and interpret the
present" (*Fetal* 115), so that what is and is not thinkable or legible *at
all* is at stake in our reading. *Household Words* will both insist that the
historicity of a single word is rife with importance and argue that the
act of "reading" is, as it should be, full of possibility. Finally, the social
and critical battles waged since the 1960s over the question of identity have left behind a largely triumphant identitarian logic involving the assumption that an identity is the most valuable "thing" a

person can have, coupled with a deep cultural and academic distrust of psychoanalytic theory (except when used to discuss trauma that gives rise to identity).

Now, while it may seem as if these issues, like the bombshell, have passed away since the mid-1990s, I will show in this book precisely how a common sense about intellectual work (as sketched out in the previous paragraph) continues to haunt us. I will argue that to demand the material—say, to insist that language resemble concrete—in tandem with a rejection of complexity and of history was and is dangerous. To demand a commonsense language so "accessible" as to be stripped of ambiguity, so "common" as to be universally understood, or so "intimate" as to be transparent appeals to the most disabling form of universalism—one that denies the sociopolitical history of conflict in America (often embedded, as I will show, in the history of a word) and the key role language plays in the split structure of the psyche. This ongoing cultural refusal to "know" how language is *both* communal and cutting, democratic and discriminatory, social and psychological, this strange common sense about common sense itself, is precisely what allows common sense to persist over time and thus to stymie change and encourage stasis, to retard the growth and dissemination of new knowledge. Particularly given how feminism— which as a word also has a vexed, half-obscured, or misrepresented political and cultural history—has had, as one of my own teachers said, to reinvent the wheel with each succeeding generation, I wanted to understand what I have seen as the inability of historicism alone, new or otherwise, to address the endurance of what Americans call good common sense and the status quo it so effectively preserves. Researching, recounting, and interpreting historical change, if valuable, increasingly fail to grapple with the persistence of vision that enduring modes of common sense can achieve.

What I found in the course of writing this book is that the history of words and their usage can demonstrate how common sense is *both* stable and unstable, shared and debated, evident and elusive. No matter how obvious common sense might at first appear, it is, in fact, hard if not finally impossible to achieve complete consensus. So diverse a nation as the United States both can and cannot manage to achieve political consensus, along with a "sense in common," good

old-fashioned horse sense, one size fits all.[2] Still, common sense itself
assumes consensus, and of course both consensus and common sense
remain important to how Americans define themselves as American.
When Thomas Paine declared that the revolutionary "cause of America" (63) must be set forth "in nothing more than simple facts, plain
arguments, and common sense" (81), he articulated a desire for simple
facts and common sense (or for what Francis Barker called an "unmediated contact with actual reality" [36] in the epigraph to this
book), a desire that remains decidedly American.

In order to investigate how common sense works to achieve consensus, *Household Words* samples the history condensed in and the
cultural "work" performed by a handful of commonsense key words,
or "household words," that have had sharp political and cultural reso-
nance for domestic affairs in the United States since the mid-
nineteenth century.[3] Through these words, this book both examines
and explains the slippery substance of common sense. It shows how
each word, belonging to ordinary parlance as it did or in fact still
does, has served as a lightning rod for political and social arguments
regarding what has been assumed as just good old American common
sense. I focus not only on the specific historical moment of each household word but also, through the sampled word, on the composition
and contestation of common sense over time, exploring the long social
history in which each is embedded and how that history constitutes
both the limits and the possibility of justice and democracy in the
United States—*democracy* itself, of course, being a word whose meaning shifted dramatically during the eighteenth century, as Raymond
Williams points out. Once a term more coincident with the notion
of mob rule, "*democracy* and *democrat,* in their entry into ordinary
speech, record the effects . . . for what we would now call democratic
representation" (*Culture*, xiv, my emphasis). In the spirit of Williams
then, yet also in keeping with the much admired, much maligned
American critic and lexicographer H. L. Mencken, I seek to "prod
into national idiosyncrasies and ways of mind," because such prod-
ding is instructive and, as Mencken quips, "always entertaining" (5).

In fact, all of the words in this study—*bloomers, sucker, bombshell,*
scab, nigger, and *cyber*—belong to a common sense, have helped to
constitute common sense, and share the uncanny ability to render

the person to whom they refer a thing. Questions of embodiment, and the "objectification" of the subject, indeed, run right the way throughout this book. But I should add here that for all the outrage to which the process of objectification might initially give rise—since assigning a person the status of a thing is often presumed disabling if not simply wrong—I will argue that one must avoid any easy piety on that matter. As Lacan argued, the gaze is an *objet petit a*. The object is a necessary, if violent, condition for subjectivity, and as Karen Newman reminds us, one longs to be the object of the gaze, even as one inhabits the position of the subject ("Directing"). The binary of the subject/object should be treated far more dialectically than is often the case.

My six American neologisms each treat people as things and things as people, and they do so at that strange conflictual space where joking, ridiculing, demeaning, oppressing, resisting, and regretting converge and reroute one another. Indeed, this necessary slippage between persons and things, while referring back to the violence of slavery, allowed for a new common sense about gender, race, and labor to arise in the late nineteenth and the early twentieth centuries. The chapters of this book therefore return to that period, to show how this new common sense eventuated in an ideological rift between work and words (see particularly the chapters "bloomers" and "sucker"), which became wider as the workforce expanded to meet the needs of industrialization, mass marketing, and mass consumption. Such rapid expansion required the alteration of an earlier nineteenth-century common sense about the "working man," as women, immigrants, and African-American laborers joined the paid labor pool. Tensions brought about by such change mounted, requiring an ideological suturing of the past to the future. This suturing altered older and increasingly destabilized beliefs about absolute gender, sexual, and racial differences, yet left certain aspects of these beliefs in place. Therefore, rather than allowing for the possibility of any radical social change, this ideological suturing reconstituted gender and race boundaries in a new common sense about labor and sex. Old beliefs, based on nineteenth-century concepts of physiology, propriety, and even "blood" (say, for example, a common sense that a woman in public was tantamount to a public woman, or the idea that African-Americans were, by nature, lazy), became unsustainable as industrialized capital needed more consumers and more hands. Nevertheless, such beliefs were also *necessary* to the maintenance of a (white, capitalist) middle class that understood itself as having social status, cultural superiority, and political power. Thus while prior ideological certainties or commonsense knowledge(s) about emotionally charged aspects of social and political life, such as the proper gendered division of labor, the idea of raced capabilities, or the so-called natural tendencies of various ethnic groups, *did* change in order to allow for the expansion of both an industrialized labor pool and commodity consumption, the new common sense would see to it that some certainties would not change *too much*.

Household Words

To begin, let me take up the term *household word* itself. In political rhetoric, in economics, and in sociological understandings of America, the household (both as a fact and as a rhetorical figure) has been pivotal. Therefore, aside from the fact that the idiom *household word* exemplifies what it also names, I have chosen my title in order to indicate how common sense is forged in and by the language of American daily "home" life. For where more powerfully than in the household could *bloomers* come to be the watchword of a conflict between the commonsense belief that the health of wives, sisters, and daughters was important enough to warrant dress reform in the nineteenth century and the equally commonsense assumptions about femininity and patriarchal authority? What better emblem of a "sucker" than the housekeeper or homeowner who buys a vacuum cleaner or encyclopedia from a traveling salesman? Where did boys conjure shared fantasies of femininity if not in the whispered invocation of the "bombshell" as they surreptitiously gazed at pinups or centerfolds (whose covert presence in the household was as tacitly approved as guarantor of heterosexuality as their open presence was proscribed as offensive to standards of familial decency)? Where could the common understanding of race encapsulated in *nigger* be more intimately engaged than in bedtime readings from *Uncle Remus*? What would be more threatened by the menace of the "scab" than the home to which the union worker brought his precarious pay? And is it not the home computer's ability to change—to morph—not only us but also our concept of self that is locating us ever more firmly in the outer limits of cyberspace, even as we make home pages and work from the home?

My title also alludes, of course, to Dickens's mid-nineteenth-century periodical of the same name and, through it, to Shakespeare, specifically to the St. Crispin's Day speech in *Henry V*. That speech suggestively anticipates a tension my study will explore, a tension between a nation composed of households, where blood and descent bind members of families together and separate families one from another, and a nation analogically understood as a household, all of whose members compose a family. At the same time that King Henry grasps the nation as composed of households divided between the "gentle" and the "vile," in which the names of those who fought will be "familiar... as household words," he also addresses his troops as a "band of brothers," figuring the nation as one singular family (4.3.48–60). So although Henry promises that the upcoming battle will gentle the vile by making heroes of commoner and aristocrat alike, para-doxically the names the king cites in his speech are not the names of commoners at all but rather remain those of the blooded aristocracy. The notion of the household word straddles the breach between these two conceptions of the nation: the identity of a nation lives on the tongues of its *separate* households, all of which, nevertheless, might become like a single family through a sharing of the household words. The speech retains its power to inspire the ideas of nationalism and democracy: it is no accident, for example, that the makers of the 1994 film *Renaissance Man* chose the St. Crispin's Day speech as a patriotic linchpin that brings the outcast, multiracial, male and female "band" of U.S. soldiers together in one military "family," despite on-going conflicts over diversity and power in the United States, partic-ularly in the military.

This embedded reference in my title to anxieties about the com-position of a political and social body indicates another dimension of my project: I explore how common sense about such things as birth, breeding, and brawn is challenged by social, medical, and political changes. If once bloomers were thought to be both indelicate and masculine, by the 1890s girls adopted the costume to suit their grow-ing social mobility. By the 1960s, bloomers had become sexy hot pants, indicating shifts in commonsense attitudes toward dress, hygiene, and sexuality. And yet, even with the fading of a particular common sense, one that is tied to a historical moment, a revised but relatively unaltered version is reasserted in order to maintain stability, a famil-iar, commonsense understanding of the sociopolitical whole. Bloomers, after all, remain "feminine."

The words I've chosen for this project, then, are not only every-day words; each has also played a role in shaping, or continues to shape, how common sense constitutes both the limits and the possi-bilities of *e pluribus unum*. Each chapter explores the tense relations between the private (household) and the public (words) proposed by the senses of common, plain-talk Americanisms. From the branding irons of slavery to the brand names we live with today, "thingification" has gone hand in hand with United States history, and our relation to these reductions that make people things and give personality to objects is marked by shades of violence and degrees of laughter. To the extent that these common words objectify, they, by definition, also tend to hide from view the structures of relations that give rise to them. The chapters that follow attempt to rediscover those struc-tures of relations—linguistic, sexual, political, economic, and racial. Moreover, although the objectifying force of each word attempts to fix what it names with the unambiguous certainty that common sense so prizes, these words tend, like the contents of the dreams Freud analyzes, to have multiple, ambivalent associations that give rise to conflicting emotions and desires that give both pleasure and pain. And as with contents of Freudian dreams, my words give rise to chap-ters that are centered differently from the way you might expect, breaking with common sense, as dream-thoughts do. Thus the chap-ter "scab" takes me to *Sister Carrie*, and the chapter on the "N word" to F. Scott Fitzgerald.

Of course, it is not surprising that conflicted desire gives rise to ir-rational, yet deeply felt, fright. Such fright is the stuff of the uncanny. For Freud, the *heimlich* has always been the *unheimlich*, a concept appropriate to my work, because the words I've lighted on are, all of them, "household" words, making up that homely, everyday language thoroughly rife with menace, revulsion, and rage.[4] Perhaps, then, what distinguishes my account of the strength of common sense from other accounts of common sense is the degree to which this book delineates the uncanny structure of household words that perpetually threaten to unleash the knowledge they nominally keep at bay.[5] Finally, while I demonstrate how common sense is achieved through the creation and currency of what Americans understand as their simple day-to-day language, I also seek to demonstrate that despite its simplicity, our language, like common sense itself, is capacious, fickle, and invariably interesting; slang comes and goes, vocabularies shrink and expand, neologisms abound.[6] And while this too may be common sense, it is often overlooked or at least rendered tame by such things as, say, the *Reader's Digest* "build your vocabulary" feature.[7]

Scientia

Of course, a shift in meaning or a change of usage is difficult to chart with assurance, as Michèle Barrett has taken note. Yet we seek that assurance. Derek Attridge has termed this desire for authentic meaning "the romance of etymology." And it remains tempting to turn to etymology for something like scientific, authentic meaning: real knowledge. Yet words are plastic, or, as Attridge asserts, "the etymologist is more of a poet than a scientist" (194), even if, as F. O. Matthiessen warned many years ago, "poetry [has] tended . . . to become divorced from 'knowledge' which, with the drift of the nineteenth century, became more and more the special province of science. As a result, we have lost living touch with the great poetry of contemplation; we have almost forgotten in our own practice that poetry can deal with epistemology" (247). What I hope to keep in view across the length of this study is how knowledge *(scientia)*, no matter how "scientific," depends on language. Words make, unmake, and remake our world. *Household Words*, then, will show how common sense, as routed through our everyday speech, both changes and conserves, accommodating various needs for social and political alterations, and at the same time resists anything like a radical shift in what constitutes "knowledge" and the "truth," for which common sense so often stands. Or as Attridge notes, "a linguistic usage we may wish to see disappear because of its sexist or racist connotations" cannot be entirely dislodged, either by an appeal to an earlier form or by a revision (192).

Indeed, it is my ultimate intention in this book to show how the frequent demand (both popular and critical) for the common sense of an unambiguous, unconflicted, and inescapable legibility that became so prevalent during the 1990s regenerated what Lynn Hunt has called a new positivism: a strenuously renewed faith in hard, reproducible, scientific or material fact. Versions of this new positivism may vary, but most contest the supposed relativism of poststructuralist and/or postmodernist modes of interpretation.[8] This positivism in *both* representation and interpretation is bound to and by a violent, coercive, phenomenal real—a reckless and potentially violent form of positivism that I hope to argue *against* urgently, particularly in my conclusion, as a practice for the future. Such positivism, rather than enabling any production of truth, or *scientia,* or even communication, produces nothing but a lie, and a dangerous lie to boot. This demand for an unmediated real is the ravenous specter of the impossible reimagined as the necessary, and, like the bloodsuckers lurking at the edge of the chapter "sucker," this demand cannot *but* haunt the political economy of any democracy as indebted to humanism as the United States is. Despite those assertions about the actual, which seem appealing—despite, for example, political claims made on behalf of real humans with real problems—the real *must* remain the unrecoverable; the real *must* remain free to muse. For if meaning is not free and open to debate, that is, if meaning is frozen into an *always* predictable legibility—one meaning fits all—then truth itself will vanish into a lie so overarching and profound that it will have the power to destroy everything a democracy and a democratic culture should cherish and protect: the right to dissent, the search for truth, the need for justice, the freedom to be. If we continue to refuse to know that words, whatever else they can and will do, *must* be free, we will, indeed, have forgotten how to read.

BLOOMERISM—AN AMERICAN CUSTOM.

Bloomerism—An American Custom. From the Picture Collection,
The Branch Libraries, The New York Public Library, Astor, Lenox and
Tilden Foundations.

bloomers

Clothes-Talk

In 1851, when temperance advocate Amelia Jenks Bloomer adopted a shortened skirt worn over what were called, at the time, Turkish "trowsers,"[1] she had no idea that her married name would give to the English language a new plural noun: *bloomers*. As originally worn by suffragettes such as Bloomer herself, or Elizabeth Smith Miller, Elizabeth Cady Stanton, and Susan B. Anthony (among a host of other, less famous women and not always those sympathetic to the suffragettes) (Coon 9), they were regarded as a garment that could free a woman from the confinements of more traditional styles. In the 1850s, a woman's daily garb consisted of ten to twelve pounds of "starched flannel or muslin petticoats,"[2] stays, and a tightly laced corset of whalebone; these underthings were covered by full-skirted dresses "that reached to the ground, sweeping up dirt and debris from country roads and unpaved city streets" (Coon 9). Dragging in mud, heavy as lead, and hot as Hades, these confining clothes did not promote mobility; in fact, trousers, when considered merely as an *item* of dress, were generally thought to be far more comfortable and hygienic than women's wear. Certainly, trousers offered mobility, or as African-

American abolitionist and diarist Charlotte L. Forten (later Grimké) reported on Saturday, July 15, 1854, she donned the "'Bloomer' costume" so as to climb "the highest cherry tree. . . . Obtained some fine fruit and felt for the time 'monarch of all [she] surveyed'" (Grimké 86). And as Elizabeth Cady Stanton wrote, after wearing the Bloomer for the first time, "What incredible freedom I enjoyed!"[3]

Soon many of these women adopted the Bloomer Costume, not only for the mere physical freedom it bestowed, but also as a sign that they sought freedom from other, more binding social and political constraints. *Freedom:* one of the most cherished and debated household words in America. Both during the original heyday of bloomers, from 1851 through 1854, and in their later, more widespread appearance in the 1890s as an athletic or bicycle costume, these trousers were a visual reminder that the traditional (male, white) shape of emancipation in the United States might someday be subject to radical reform. The visual impact of these pants spoke—sometimes more loudly than words—about the current discontent of many a middle-class (white) American woman with remaining off the public stage, without a legal voice, a real juridical presence, or a vote in a democracy that claimed to provide equality for all while retaining slavery as part of its makeup.[4]

But if bloomers served as a reminder that the concept of freedom was being pressured from several quarters to reform in the United States during the second half of the nineteenth century, the costume also had the power to suggest that the natural might be unstable and subject to interpretation. Gender, generally understood as part of the natural order, might not be rigidly fixed. Since the dominant sex/gender system of most cultures is rendered legible, in part, through the language of clothing, tampering with clothing signifies the potential for change—tantamount, perhaps, to tampering with the natural order of things. In fact, although a number of women had for many years either worn or adapted trousers for a variety of uses (as play clothes for young girls, as underwear, as spa clothing, and as working clothes, worn mostly by working-class women),[5] "panting" in public still signified masculinity to the middle class. Exceptions might be made for a variety of reasons, but women in pants were generally considered lower-class, risqué, or shocking.[6] A lady would *never* wear such things. A lady was an ornament. The suggestion that she might have passions of her own or might work like a man was a suggestion to be squelched. A lady didn't labor, except in childbirth, but of course reproductive work is still not regarded as labor. Such firm associations among class, gender, and dress remain evident in lingering prejudices about dress or in commonplaces such as "who wears the pants in this family?"[7]

By wearing pants in public, the Bloomerites threw the door open to questions that had often gone unasked, the simplest of these being: if women could wear pants, what else might they do? Would such panting allow masculinity to be usurped, even destroyed? Weren't trousers on women indecent, unnatural? The very possibility that "natural" sexual signification, like clothing itself, might be altered or that their girls might start panting in public gave parents pause: what did it mean? As historian Gayle Fischer writes, "It is difficult to determine if the general public's resistance to female trousers stemmed more from the fear that women would seize male power or from the fear that pants-clad women would be unabashedly 'sexy'" (113). This potential for modification to which bloomers pointed, along with the prospect of overt female eroticism or gender confusion, rattled the middle class and flew in the face of accepted common sense.

Clearly, a panting girl meant trouble. She would have to be managed. Such management is evident not only in the historical vicissitudes and ultimate fate of the "New Costume" (Coon 11), as Amelia Bloomer's trouser set was also called, but also in the linguistic fate of a once familiar, once household word, *bloomers*. A highly public, publicized, and political "statement" when Amelia Bloomer first wore the design in 1851, bloomers were parodied, criticized, and finally ridiculed to death by 1854. According to Elizabeth Cady Stanton, the word *bloomers* itself had come into being as an epithet designed to belittle the women's movement.[8] However, as the historical record shows, many women adopted both the costume and the name "Bloomer(ite)" with pride and defiance in the face of such ridicule, just as women in the latter half of the twentieth century adopted with pride or abandoned in disgust the name "feminist." In fact, Amelia Bloomer held it as a point of personal pride to have given her (ironically) married name to the costume, and she wore the trousers until she retired from public speaking. But by 1854, other women in the movement had ceased to wear the garment as street wear, and so it vanished for a time.[9]

In the 1870s, however, bloomers reemerged as a topic of dispute in the discourse of a scientific dress-reform movement. This reform, bolstered by the claims of burgeoning fields in health science, eventuated in the far more acceptable version of the fabled emancipation drag. The new bloomers were designed as an aid to physical activity, specifically for cycling. But even this new version faded from view over time. No longer considered indecent, although still eroticized, trousers for women were considered sportswear or made only for children, and so became specialized and were stuffed back up under skirts whence pantaloons had once descended, returned by custom, fashion, and common sense to the realm of the private underthing, those unmentionables that girls were supposed to blush over.[10] Or as physical education pioneer Mabel Lee observes in her memoir *Memories of a Bloomer Girl (1894–1924)*, circa 1914:

> Bloomers had won their battle in the mid-nineteenth century as a garment for general wear by women and then had died out to be revived in an altogether different style in the 1890s for a garment to wear for bicycling. Now, with the bicycling fad over, this bloomer of the 1890s became a special garment for women pursuing physical education as a career and for their female pupils while engaged in gymnastics or sports. As I started upon my career, bloomers, however, were to be worn only indoors.[11]

And as Valerie Steele notes, in Paris "even feminine underpants were regarded as 'demi-masculine' apparel, and it was only gradually over the course of the century that they entered the respectable woman's wardrobe. At mid-century, they were still mostly worn by little girls, sportswomen, and *demi-mondaines*. Dances like the *can-can* and the *cahut* exploited the 'naughty' image of underpants, as dancers raised their legs to display knee-length *pantalons*" (*Paris* 164).

In fact, although middle-class women did wear trousers, until the late twentieth century all female trousers had particular uses or meanings and, when women wore them, what they wore had more than likely been made for a man or else tailor-made for a particular woman. For example, during World War I, the women who were recruited to work in the factories, particularly munitions factories, often wore what their husbands or brothers had worn, trousers or boilersuits, even if it was considered daring.[12] In World War II, many women, from Rose Will Monroe, better known as Rosie the Riveter, to Norma Jeane Dougherty, later known as Marilyn Monroe, donned workmen's jump-suits, overalls, and blue jeans, again to help the war effort. These pants signified the absence of laboring men, and when those men came home, women were expected to don the "New Look" and forget about those pants. Trousers for women did gain increasing acceptance as appropriate clothing, but it wasn't until the dust settled after the social upheavals of the 1960s that trousers truly became part of any middle-class woman's *public* wardrobe. Even so, questions about the propriety of when and how and why pants should be worn can, even today, still haunt job seekers, professionals (especially politicians), and the fashion pages.[13]

Meanwhile, by the 1940s, even if women could wear pants, the word *bloomers* had ceased to signify the politics of the women's move-ment. It was no longer a word that made a political statement about women's freedom. In fact, in colloquial use, the once-adult, once-political word *bloomers* now signified babyhood more than anything else. Children wore bloomers, even though the pantaloons that girls had worn as early as the 1820s had never been called bloomers and would not be called such until well after the heyday of Betty Bloomer's bicycle costume.[14] And the association between infancy and femi-ninity that had been foisted upon bloomers in the wake of what has since been called the first wave of feminist agitation in the United States was to reemerge during the 1960s, just as the second wave began to surge. As protests against the Vietnam War and racial inequality began to turn violent, as the sexual revolution heated up and bras were about to burn, at least by rumor, and as the parental complaint "you can't tell a boy from a girl anymore" grew into a howl of unrest, bloomers were introduced by the world of haute couture as a pert, sex-kittenish item for the hip young thing, particularly in England and France.[15]

Thus did this completely *American* English word lose its ability to index an intense and prolonged moment of nineteenth-century political conflict about gender in the United States (and elsewhere), as reflected in most American desktop dictionaries of the late twentieth century, which, when they list *bloomers* as something other than the plural of a flowering plant or, significantly, as slang for a blunder, list the word as "n. 1. bloomers, a. loose trousers gathered at the knee, formerly worn by women as part of a gymnasium, riding, or other sports outfit. b. a woman's undergarment of similar, but less bulky design. c. the trousers of a bloomer (costume)." Only rarely does the now-secondary meaning, "2. a costume for women, advocated about 1850 by Mrs. Amelia Jenks Bloomer (1818–94) of New York," appear, and without an explanation of what Mrs. Bloomer was advocating besides the costume itself.[16]

But, one might ask, why notice such a small matter as this single word's definition and common use? The fading political significance of *bloomers* seems trivial. In fact, common sense might tell those of us who avail themselves (in shrinking numbers) of these aforementioned dictionaries that any woman advocating the wearing of pants in the mid-nineteenth century was no doubt an agitator for other, presumably more substantive political and emancipatory projects. Historically, however, this assumption would be false, for, as Gayle Fischer has shown, the women of the Oneida Perfectionist Community in Oneida, New York, also adopted trousers for reasons rather different from those of the Bloomerites, reasons that had very little to do with emancipatory politics. "In contrast to mainstream critiques," writes Fischer, "Oneida Community criticism of clothing focused on the way dress made the 'distinction between the sexes vastly more prominent and obtrusive than nature [made] it'" (130). To these women, trousers signified both nature (after all, women, like men, have legs) and the virginity of youth—a submissive, girlish state. "The style unquestionably made Oneida women appear infantile or childlike," writes Fischer (132), which was encouraged in order that they appear virginal.

But historical accuracy and the Oneida Community aside, why should a dictionary be politically specific in addition to citing historical information—names, dates, and so forth? In this chapter, I wish to propose an answer to that question by using this entirely American neologism, *bloomers*, to show how common usage and the production of common sense are linked. By doing so, I will explore the ways in which common usage can help to alter the shape of what is generally recognized and understood as common sense. I do this in order to argue, in turn, that common sense orchestrates the tenor of everyday life, where feminism finds both the deepest resistance and yet, paradoxically, also a home, because it is primarily in the commonplaces of language—in the sayings and in the things we all just know—that common sense is both composed and torn asunder, both sustained and belied. I will also show that compressed within the history of this one word, *bloomers*, is the story of how our underlying common sense about such things as birth, breeding, and brawn was challenged by social, medical, and political changes during the latter half of the nineteenth century, which, in turn, affected our language and how we view the world.

To be more specific: if *bloomers* was once a commonplace watchword that signified women's emancipation, it did so by being caught between conflicting and changing versions of common sense; it was a term that could conjure up the commonsense belief that mobility meant practicality and that the physical health and well-being of wives, sisters, and daughters was important enough to warrant dress-reform movements in the 1850s and again in the 1870s. But it was also the watchword for commonsense assumptions about frailty and femininity that endured throughout the nineteenth and into the twentieth century, assumptions suggesting that masculinity and patriarchal authority were under siege the moment women wore pants. By 1854, however, despite the rational commonsense arguments in favor of trousers set forth by those women who proudly called themselves Bloomers or Bloomerites, the Bloomer Costume was judged indelicate, indecent, and overly masculine by the prevailing tide of another kind of common sense, the common sense of tradition and religion, as set forth by antisuffrage antireformists. And yet, by the 1890s, a new kind of common sense about gender had begun to take hold and to prevail. By 1895, bloomers were thought, by some, to be appropriate to the growing social mobility of the soon-to-be explosive phenomenon of the "New Woman." Certainly young women just coming into their own donned bloomers and went biking in numbers. Furthermore, although bloomers had become primarily children's underwear by the 1940s, they had reappeared as hip fashion by the 1960s and

'70s, adapted by designers such as Yves St. Laurent and Mary Quant, and as such signified a new sexual era. Such changes in the signification of one word can serve as an *index* not only to the shifts in commonly held cultural attitudes toward dress or hygiene but also to sociopolitical changes in the domain of sexuality. My point here is that if the word *bloomers* was once part of the everyday political language in the 1850s and tied, then, to what the Bloomerites saw as a rational logic of practical common sense about women's clothing and thus also women's place in the world, then prevailing modes of common sense would also turn the Bloomer Costume into bloomers as we now know them: a quaint, picturesque quirk or a brief, if politically curious, sartorial feature of the past linked to childhood, underwear, and fashion fads, with perhaps a sketchy relationship (and certainly an underreported one, if the dictionary is any indication) to serious political events.[17] And yet, along the historical and linguistic way, an American common sense about femininity was also radically altered. I should add here that I am not advocating the installation of a true or authentic meaning for this word or any other word in this book. As I've said previously, the romance of etymology is the lure of authenticity where none should be found. What I am interested in is how a word, such as *bloomers*, dances through history, changing its meanings and dimensions in concert with social and political alterations, showing us how language and knowledge—and common sense as a form of knowledge—cannot *but* go hand in hand.

A picture may very well be, as the common saying goes, worth a thousand words, but a word can also paint a thousand pictures. So loudly did the picture of a "panting" girl speak, in fact, that women who wished to tether the power of language to their own purposes finally gave up on pants. But although bloomers, as a costume, had a visual impact that spoke louder than words, I think it also worth seeing what other pictures can be painted by a look at the historical usage of the word. Women in antebellum America sought to forge new meanings and so to make a new home in the world for themselves. Indeed, reformists and abolitionists sought nothing less than to remake constitutional law. And while bloomers are only indirectly linked to the fight against legalized slavery, women such as Amelia Jenks Bloomer—who was also a writer, an editor, and a public speaker—did seek to change the meaning of another common word for which the United States stood and for which it would presently hurtle itself, sundered in two, into war: *freedom*. The larger public issues at hand for Amelia Jenks Bloomer in 1851 were temperance, abolition, and women's rights. But the underlying question, What is literally meant by freedom? was also, and more broadly, at stake.

To put this claim another way, if clothes are like words, words are like clothes: each speaks a cultural language; each has a gendered grammar; each is subject to interpretation, remotivation, and misunderstandings. The Bloomer, as both an American neologism and an American experiment in dress reform, offers up the site of a historical convergence of what we might call political language and material object, a site from which to examine the manner in which American women tried to alter the ways of their forefathers and, thus, a longstanding common sense about gender, particularly about femininity. They tried, but in the 1850s failed, to change the vocabulary of their everyday lives and the political life of the nation; they tried to make politics "mean" in a new fashion, one more suited to tell them of a future in which they and their children, especially their daughters, would have more mobility, more possibility. Or as Susan B. Anthony said, in a counter-Centennial address in Philadelphia on July 4, 1876, "Woman's wealth, thought and labor have cemented the stones of every monument man has reared to liberty.... We ask justice, we ask equality, we ask that all the civil and political rights that belong to citizens of the United States, be guaranteed to us and our daughters forever."[18]

Panting Girls

Common sense. As I stated in the introduction, most Americans are proud of it. Many will appeal to it in order to further a political goal. Certainly the women who were called Bloomerites used the logic of common sense when they spoke of their costume as the rational dress. How, they asked, could one properly care for children, bound by the frivolous dictates of French—*foreign*—fashion? Was it not easier to lift a child or perform other womanly tasks unburdened by whalebone? Following the same rationale expounded by Catharine

Beecher's continuing crusade on behalf of exercise for girls,[19] the Bloomerites asked, pragmatically speaking, why constrict the human body so cruelly that bruising, broken ribs, and intestinal injury result? Some doctors agreed. But health wasn't the only issue. The Bloomer soon had ardent adherents who saw the garment as a means to signify changes to both their physical well-being and their mental health, if not also their social condition. As Anne C. Coon notes, factory girls in Lowell, Massachusetts, organized the Bloomer Institute to help them achieve two stated objectives: "Mutual Improvement—in Literature, Science and Morals"; and "Emancipation" from the thralldom of fashion and other unnatural or unhelpful trappings (12). Women who were already in the labor force well knew the potential of pants.

On July 4, 1853, for the occasion of an address titled "Mothers of the Revolution" and given in Harford, New York, by Amelia Jenks Bloomer, a popular temperance speaker at the time and editor of an internationally known women's magazine called the *Lily*, this toast and poem were delivered by a contingent of young women who were "tastefully attired in the Bloomer Costume":

> The Bloomer Costume—The most appropriate as well as the most convenient dress for ladies—May it soon become their universal costume.

> Let sickly ladies talk and flirt
>   And tell their paper passion,
> Amid those trailing, draggling skirts
>   Because it is the fashion;
> But give *me* the gay and sprightly lass
>   Who "*pants*" for health so blooming,
> For her I'd fill the flowing glass
> And shout, "huzza! for bloomers!" (Coon 62)

Two years prior to this address, in 1851, Amelia Bloomer and Elizabeth Cady Stanton had designed their rational costume for women. Goaded by an opponent of women's rights, who had jestingly endorsed dress reform as a means to ridicule those agitating women of Seneca Falls who had stirred up such a fuss in 1848, Bloomer and Stanton responded by adapting a costume that Stanton's cousin, Elizabeth Smith Miller, or Libby Miller, the daughter of dress-reform abolitionist Gerrit Smith, had worn in European spas: a shortened skirt over large, so-called Turkish trowsers, gathered in at the ankle with a string or button.[20]

Such a costume was not wholly unfamiliar to many middle-class women, who might have worn pantalets or pantaloons as children. Certainly, many had heard of or perhaps had fantasized about the harem, or seraglio, where "Oriental" women wore voluminous pantaloons and veils—thus the epithet "Turkish." Dropping pounds of muslin while also obviating the need to corset tightly, the new costume was hailed by some women and their male supporters as more sane and sanitary than the fashions then current. Amelia Bloomer, who took up the dress with relish and dedication, soon found her name bowdlerized into a plural noun, *bloomers*, and bestowed on a garment that was also referred to in the popular press as the Camilla, the Tom-Boy, Turkish trowsers, the Oriental Costume or that indecent dress, "'an abomination unto the Lord'" (as quoted in Fischer 120). A British broadsheet in 1851 lampooned the attire thus:

> Listen, females all
> No matter what your trade is,
> Old Nick is in the girls,
> The Devil's in the ladies!
> Married men may weep,
> And tumble in the ditches
> Since women are resolved
> To wear the shirts and breeches.
>
> Ladies do declare
> A change should have been sooner,
> The women, one and all,
> Are going to join the Bloomers.
> Prince Albert and the Queen
> Had such a jolly row, sirs;
> She threw off stays and put
> On waistcoat, coat and trousers.
>
> The world's turned upside down,
> The ladies will be tailors
> And serve Old England's Queen
> As soldiers and as sailors
> Won't they look funny when

> The seas are getting lumpy,
> Or when they ride astride
> Upon an Irish donkey? (Gattey 75)

Some forty-four years later, on January 17, 1895, about two weeks after the seventy-six-year-old Amelia Jenks Bloomer had died in Council Bluffs, Iowa, the *New York Truth* ran a "suggested epitaph" for her:

> Here lies
> (Quite safe at last from reckless rumors)
> The erst well-known and
> Well-abused Miss Bloomer
> Living too long,
> She saw her once bold coup
> Rendered old-fashioned by the Woman New.
>
> By noisy imitators vexed and piqued,
> her fads outfadded and her freaks out-freaked
> She did not die till she had seen and heard
> All her absurdities made more absurd.
> In short,
> She found Dame Fortune but ill-humored,
> And passed away
> In every point out-Bloomered. (Coon 32)

And so it might have seemed to Amelia Bloomer herself, for although she had seen the causes of colleagues Frederick Douglass, Angelina and Sarah Grimké (related to Charlotte through marriage and slave-holding), and Lucretia Mott change the nation through Civil War and legislation, neither her own cause of temperance nor a woman's right to vote became law before she died.

Yet the dismissive mockery of the aforementioned epitaph serves also to indicate that the "bloomer craze" caused more disturbance than *Truth's* biting humor suggests. Not only does the epitaph nervously record the growing visibility of the New Woman, whose agitation would finally lead to women's suffrage in 1921, but in the heyday of the Bloomer Costume more than simply a *few* sprightly, scandalous, gay lasses, as the first poem coyly names them, panted in the public eye. Despite ridicule and censure, the Bloomer as a public day dress for middle-class women, rather than as an immodest private dress donned at spas, had spread quickly from Seneca Falls, where Bloomer lived and worked as an editor and speaker, to Scotland, England, Canada, and Australia—all across the fractured English empire. It spread by word of mouth, through correspondence, and through the *Lily*, where Bloomer offered free patterns for the costume in return for subscriptions (Coon 11). There was "Bloomerism in Picadilly," "Bloomerism at the Crystal Palace," and Madame Tussaud and Son's Exhibition offered the public the "Bloomer Costume: Five beautiful varieties by which the public may judge if this dress may ever become popular" (Gattey 67–72).

Moreover, as the rational dress craze spread, it carried with it implications that would soon erupt in other debates that, at the end of the twentieth century, were often considered more serious than either prohibition or dress reform. Advocates claimed that the costume freed the *natural* form of a woman's body from the unnatural constraints of fashion. Despite Amelia Jenks Bloomer's belief in temperance, Bloomerites were ready to "fill the flowing glass / And shout 'huzza! for bloomers!'" presumably with all the (masculine?) gusto of their newfound health. Aghast at such a picture, opponents cried that panting girls were unnatural, that only men were naturally suited to the suit. And so the nature of woman herself, a question that Sigmund Freud would soon spend his life attempting to answer, was up for debate. Bloomers became a referendum on nature itself and the nature of freedom. But what such an argument about the naturalness of trousers also suggests is that nature is not a transparent or immutable category, but one that might have to be shaped, written, or even theorized in order to be seen, or read, at all. What is natural—natural clothes, a natural sexuality? How should the natural be handled or determined if it is not, well, natural? If Charles Darwin set the term *natural selection* into motion in 1859 with the publication of *The Origin of Species*, the scientific, public, and legal debates that raged in the wake of Darwin's theories about nature and evolution set the stage for the Scopes "Monkey" Trial, in the 1920s. This conflict about the nature of the natural reerupted in the summer of 1999, when the Kansas State School Board ruled that Darwin should be stripped from public school curricula because evolution is not a fact but a theory; in 2004, Georgia attempted to remove the single word *evolution* from biology classes in which evolution was taught, because the word alone was regarded as too controversial. It seems that the nature of nature remains a site of conflict. And certainly any theory about nature—whether biological, religious, or psychological—will help to shape ruling commonsense ideas about sex, class, race, and gender.

In July 1851, *Harper's New Monthly Magazine* reported that "there appears to be a decided and growing tendency on the part of our countrywomen to wear the trowsers" (288). So *Harper's* kindly offered to the "practical reformers, bold as Joan d'Arc" a "sketch of Oriental Costume, as a model for our fair reformers," which they titled the "Turkish Costume." The next month, *Harper's* ran a page titled "Woman's Emancipation. Being a letter addressed to Mr. Punch, with a drawing, by a strong-minded American Woman" (424). A cruel if acute parody of American reformist tracts, whether antislavery, temperance, or suffragist, this letter, signed by Theodosia Eudoxia Bang, M.A., MCP Phi, Delta, Kappa, KLM &c.&c. (of Boston), reads:

> We are emancipating ourselves, among other badges of the slavery of feudalism, from the inconvenient dress of the European female. With man's functions, we have asserted our right to his garb, and especially to that part of it which invests the lower extremities. With this great symbol, we have adopted others—the hat, the cigar, the paletot or round jacket. And it is generally calculated that the dress of the Emancipated American female is quite pretty—as becoming in all points as it is manly and independent. I inclose a drawing made by my gifted fellow-citizen Increasen Tarbox of Boston US for the *Free Women's Banner*, a periodical under my conduct, aided by several gifted women of acknowledged progressive opinions. (424)

I quote *Harper's* at length because this paragraph and the sketch tell a tale of what was to be almost a century-long resistance to the politics of female suffrage. Independence was first and foremost a white man's prerogative and had been since the founding fathers signed the Constitution into law. Until 1921, the vote, as a sign of that independence and freedom, was a man's civil prerogative as a citizen. Progressive opinions about changing the vote, and about female suffrage in particular, were deemed silly, ugly, and indecent, as evident in the name Increasen Tarbox, perhaps an allusion to the supposed perils of racial intermingling or to the outrageous indelicacy of women smoking cigars, wearing hats, their ankles scandalously exposed.

Another month later, in the *Lily* of September 1851, Bloomer published an engraving of herself. Neither as dainty and fantastically orientalized as *Harper's* first version nor as short and as fantastically masculinized as the second version, Amelia Bloomer's costume was presented by her as serious, sober, and decidedly female, according to the gender norms of the day. Intriguingly, though, the engraving does not refuse to suggest that the Bloomer might speak of something else, for this fashion is still clearly not the fashion. Although, in one hand, Mrs. Bloomer held a fan, her other hand rested pointedly upon an uncorseted and generous (but not too!) waist. Demure *and* defiant, she counters the other versions. However, it should be noted that Bloomer herself seldom wrote or spoke about her clothes. She never gave a public lecture on dress reform, for example. She preferred to let the Bloomer Costume speak for itself, and evidently, for a few years, it spoke quite loudly. There were Bloomer polkas, waltzes, theatrical productions; there were songs with lyrics such as "I want to be a Bloomer." Staffordshire China figures were also made of Mrs. Bloomer, one showing her wearing a man's collar and holding a cigar (Gattey 73). In 1852 in Montreal, women reenacted a mild version of *Lysistrata*, using the Bloomer: they threatened en masse "to don the new outfit if the city did not immediately take measures to clean the streets" (Coon 13). And there were those Lowell factory girls working in the mills or in the garment industry, who were among the most poorly paid laborers in the United States, a circumstance that Amelia Bloomer, who did speak about women and labor, never forgot. In fact the garment industry and women as workers would continue to be a site of political and cultural turmoil and reform well into the twentieth century.

However, the ladies of Montreal did not, in fact, don the Bloomer en masse, and by 1854, few besides Amelia Bloomer herself still wore the costume in public. The sheer dailiness of wardrobe began to blast away at the women's resolve.[21] "We put the dress on for greater freedom," lamented Elizabeth Cady Stanton, "but what is physical freedom compared with mental bondage? . . . It is not wise . . . to use up so much energy and feeling that way" (Stanton et al. 890). In March 1856, Charlotte Forten (Grimké) reported that she was persuaded to go to a party dressed "in full Bloomer costume, which [she] since had good cause to regret" (Grimké 151). As Susan B. Anthony said, the Bloomer had become something of "an intellectual slavery; one never could get rid of thinking of herself, and the important thing is to forget self. The attention of my audiences was fixed on my clothes instead of my words."[22]

Anthony's and Stanton's sense that their words and their clothes were in competition for meaning, and that by adopting clothes— and then, finally, political positions—more in keeping with majority expectation, one could forget oneself, is a forcible reminder that appearances speak but don't always say what was intended, nor do they guarantee the meaning of the message. As Joan Brumberg notes, for women in the nineteenth century, appearance was linked to moral character: "Becoming a better person meant paying *less* attention to the self. . . . When girls in the nineteenth-century thought about ways to improve themselves, they almost always focused on their internal character and how it was reflected in outward behavior" (xxi). Appearance was supposed to be a matter of sober indifference; excessive frippery was seen as a moral failing in a woman. Thus, it mattered very much what Susan B. Anthony wore; her appearance played a large part in how an audience would respond to her, and she was perhaps the most public figure of the women's rights movement. Some of the reports she received about the Bloomer were not encouraging. Among the most virulent was the claim that the Bloomerites were "a hybrid species, half-man, half-woman, belonging to neither sex" (Gattey 85).

Such descriptions hounded those women who felt impelled to speak in the public sphere, no matter what clothing they wore, because, like it or not, appearance figured as part of the conflict. Dress was a persistent topic of concern for women in the nineteenth century, whether or not they were of the middle class, whether or not they advocated temperance, abolition, or women's rights. In 1845, the outspoken editor Margaret Fuller exclaimed with pride that the freedom of a woman's body was going to signify the dawn of a new era; woman in the nineteenth century was not to be either "the tool of servile labor, or the object of voluptuous indulgence," and she reports that a "woman of excellent sense told her that 'one of the most favorable signs of the times was that ladies had been persuaded to give up corsets'" (164). But Fuller, both in her work and in her life, was consid-

ered almost as immodest as the Bloomer itself. Yet, although she and
the other Bloomerites went too far in the direction of "masculinization," the increasingly seductive dictates of fashion, often seen, as I
mentioned earlier, as a foreign French import, threatened to enfeeble,
degrade, and imperil womanhood; or as Sara Parton (aka author Fanny
Fern) wrote in "To the Ladies: A Call to Be a Wife," a woman who
thinks "more of her silk dress than her children" is an abomination
(*Leaves* 307–8). "If there is one phrase more universally misapplied
than another it is the phrase 'well-dressed.' The first thing to be considered in this connection is *fitness*. . . . Bows of ribbon, jewelled combs
and head-pins at breakfast, either at a hotel table or at home, do not
convey to me an idea of *fitness*," fumes Fern in 1868 (*Folly* 80). Not
surprisingly, the kind of rhetoric used against the enfeebling effects of
Fashion mirrors that which was launched in the early nineteenth-
century against the supposedly enervating effects of "silly" novel reading. Indeed, as historian Mary Kelley notes, when novelist Caroline
Howard Gilman (aka Clarissa Packard) recounted the events surrounding her first publication, in 1810, she recalled that she had wept
bitterly about it because it seemed shameful to her at the time, as if
she "had been detected in man's apparel" (Kelley 180).

But despite the fear and the warnings, the novel gained a place in
the household, and as the nineteenth century progressed, more and
more women became literate and turned to writing—or as Fanny
Fern remarks by 1868, "Women can relieve their minds, now-a-days,
in one way that was formerly denied them: they can write! a woman
who wrote used to be considered a sort of monster—At this day it is
difficult to find one who does not write, or has not written, or who has
not, at least, a strong desire to do so" (*Folly* 60); meanwhile, more
and more magazines, such as *Godey's Ladies Book,* entered the home
carrying images of and patterns for the latest styles. Riotous fashion
was winning out over sober maternity, and although Amelia Jenks
Bloomer saw her invention as a "modest proposal" on behalf of sobri-
ety in dress, other women saw it as an even worse alternative to frippery—a coarsening of womanhood's true grace and beauty. Sadly, as
late as 1963, when Betty Friedan wrote *The Feminine Mystique,* part
of what she sought to correct was the notion, still prevalent at the
time, that the women of the suffragette movement had been coarse

and unfashionable: "These women," she felt compelled to write, "were not man-eaters" (86). Common knowledge, however, said otherwise: in the early 1960s, the feminism of the nineteenth century, as well as the soon-to-come second feminist movement, was generally thought to be a "dirty joke" (Friedan 78), perpetrated by hard-faced, humorless, embittered, unfashionable, sex-deprived or alien (i.e., lesbian), lower-class, foreign, hybrid shrews. Never mind that both Anthony and Stanton had been middle-class white "ladies" of their time. And never mind that both knew full well the impact of appearance, using it, when expedient, to further their own cause. Early supporters of the rational dress, they dropped it in 1854, when it began to become a source of such persistent abuse that it was a political liability.

However, in 1868, Stanton and Anthony undertook a rather more radical, conservative, and distressing campaign. With the Civil War over and the cause for women's equality no further along than it was in 1848, they found themselves faced with abolitionists such as Frederick Douglass turning their attention to winning the vote for freedmen. Outraged, Stanton and Anthony severed their ties with what was left of the abolitionist movement by forming the National Woman's Suffrage Association and later began to court southern politicians by claiming that a white woman's *racial* superiority outweighed the claims of freedmen. The proposed constitutional amendment that would grant "Manhood Suffrage" was, wrote Stanton, "an open, deliberate insult to the women of the nation." Universal male suffrage would allow men of the "lower orders, natives and foreigners, Dutch, Irish, Chinese and African,"[23] to legislate for white women, and this, she argued, was an abomination, much to the horror and dismay of many former abolitionist colleagues, such as the Grimké sisters, who stayed with the Woman's Suffrage Association because it continued to support the fight for African-American emancipation and equality (Lerner 333). Finally, by 1881, when Stanton and Anthony wrote the first volume of the *History of Women's Suffrage*, whose focus had yet to be achieved, certain alliances were downplayed or scripted out. As historian Anne C. Coon notes, "References to Bloomer and the *Lily* in the *History* were minimal, and Bloomer's chapter on Iowa was heavily edited" (30). Their association with Bloomer, it is true, had never been an easy one, given Bloomer's far more tentative and sometimes conservative approach to the issues that motivated Stanton and Anthony. But the Bloomer household had also moved. In 1853, the Bloomers moved to Ohio, where Amelia tried to keep the *Lily* alive. But later, after they moved again, on to Council Bluffs, Iowa— at that time still a frontier town—she was forced to give it up. In Iowa, although she continued to work on behalf of women and temperance, she was removed from "the geographical, emotional and political center of the woman's movement" (Coon 30). In addition, Amelia Bloomer had always been a somewhat difficult colleague, shy but outspoken, irritable, and well aware that she had neither the class privilege nor the education nor the social position of either Anthony or Stanton; she was not a "lady" of the same sort of standing (31). In fact, some commentators at the time blamed the failure of the Bloomer on class prejudice. "Mrs. Merrifield, whose *Dress as a Fine Art* (1854) is one of the most enlightening books on fashion at this time, says: 'We are content to adopt the greatest absurdities in dress when they are brought from Paris or recommended by a French name, but American fashion has no chance of success in aristocratic England'" (Barnes and Eicher 64).

Thus did the story of Amelia Jenks Bloomer and the costume to which she had given her name begin to shrink. As Anne C. Coon writes:

> In histories of the early feminist movement, Amelia Bloomer's con-tributions are often summarized in a brief reference to the garment that bears her name. While her support of dress reform did indeed focus national attention on the "Bloomerites," and did result in a sweeping, yet fleeting, national preoccupation with a new style of dress, Amelia Bloomer has left us with much more than a "costume." Still, the substance of her work has been eclipsed by the image of the "Bloomer" as a "shocking" and "immoral" costume in the nineteenth-century and, in later years of "bloomers" as frivolous or "unmention-able" undergarments. Thus, our memory of Amelia Bloomer has regrettably been reduced to caricature. (16)

Bloomers crept back into the closet in 1854 and vanished from the streets until the 1890s. In fact, their disappearance was helped along by the way in which the suffragettes themselves used the prejudice of appearance and responded to the pressures of everyday abuse and

ridicule. Although some, like Gerrit Smith, Libby Miller's activist fa-
ther, remained adamant that dress reform was a necessary and integral
part of any movement that would emancipate women, others—and
significantly, those politically prominent, white, middle-class women
who had attempted to wear the garments—found the daily grind of
being associated with children and the working class or of simply
sticking out like a sore (masculine) thumb among their peers too
dispiriting and physiologically taxing. As J. C. Flugel reports in his
curious, oft-cited study, *The Psychology of Clothes*:

> Of course there is such a thing as negative prestige. A fashion may
> be killed in its infancy by being adopted by persons whom it is con-
> sidered undesirable to imitate. The classical instance of this was the
> sudden disappearance of "bloomers" in 1851 when a London brewery
> dressed all their barmaids in nether garments of this type. Another
> (and in a sense more literal) method of killing fashions was by asso-
> ciating them with public executions—in the persons either of the
> executed or the executioner. In Queen Anne's reign there was con-
> siderable pother about women appearing in the street in their night-
> gowns. But this fashion speedily came to an end when a woman was
> executed in a garment of this description. In the terminology of the
> behaviourist, the habit was "deconditioned" by being thus brought
> into association with an event of such a painful character. (152 fn. 2)

It would seem, then, that until the latter half of the twentieth century,
middle-class women who panted in public found not freedom but,
rather, associations that were too painful and counterproductive to
endure.

Cycles

Thus appearance can speak louder than words. And yet, the word
bloomer itself remained in the vocabulary and in use. As Charles Nelson Gattey wrote in 1967, "Mrs. Bloomer has indeed had her revenge
and we should be grateful to this singular woman who gave the world
so useful a plural" (14). By 1873–74, dress reform once again became
an issue for widespread public debate, first in Boston and then in other
cities, when Abba Louisa Goold Woolson, a teacher, popular literary
essayist, and an officer of the New England Women's Club, sponsored
a series of lectures about dress.

This is not to say that the *issue* of dress reform had died out utterly in the intervening years, but these lectures were offered so frequently and became popular enough that Woolson collected and published them. The lecturers were four women doctors—Mary J. Safford-Blake, Caroline E. Hastings, Mercy B. Jackson, and Arvilla B. Haynes—and Woolson herself, and the lectures were designed to convince the general public that "the whole structure and the essential features of our present apparel are undeniably opposed to the plainest require-ments of health, beauty and convenience" (Stein and Baxter, vi). These women saw to it that an "accessible and attractive room, which is intended to serve for a bureau of information on all matters connected with dress reform," was set up at "25 Winter Street, over Chandler's dry-goods store, room 15" (Stein and Baxter 1). They also provided, at the lowest cost possible, garments and patterns for gar-ments designed on "strict hygienic principles" (1).

Overly heavy skirts, corseting, flimsy materials: these might all prove to be physically dangerous. Although she seldom said so in public, Woolson herself favored pants, but in 1874, bloomers were still seen as far too radical a move. The doctors who agreed to help Woolson still had to manage the tradition of the "American Costume" rhetori-cally by designating it as a brave, intelligent attempt but one that both delayed true dress reform and, in the end, gave too much credit to what Woolson termed "thoughtless women." Because the Bloomer

> sought to accomplish an immediate result by ill-considered and
> inadequate means . . . to the majority of thoughtless women it
> remained an object of indifference or of ridicule. . . . Men sneered
> at the costume without mercy, and branded it hideous. As made and
> worn by many of its followers, it was certainly not beautiful: but had
> it been perfection itself, it would have utterly perished; for arrayed
> against it were the force of ignorance and of habit. . . . [Even] had
> the costume succeeded in establishing itself as our permanent and
> recognized dress, it would not have rendered further reform un-
> necessary. . . . So long as the trunk of the body is girded in the middle
> by bands, with too little clothing above and an excess of it below, so
> long will the greatest evil of our present dress remain untouched.
> (Stein and Baxter, x–xi)

The doctors had changed tactics. Rather than cite the rational politics of emancipation, which had been the clarion call of the midcentury suffragettes, they chose to use moral patriotism and the science of hygiene to argue the same things their predecessors had argued: that fashion was a foreign import, thereby un-American; that women of the upper classes had a moral duty to dress with less ostentation; and that American women should begin a gradual shift toward a more healthful style befitting the natural shape of a woman's childbearing form. They had, they said, a far more *scientifically* sound version of *common sense* than that of either the radical Bloomerites or previous doctors, and they offered a series of talks that presented what they saw as up-to-date medical and historical evidence to prove that women's fashionable clothing was physiologically dangerous and morally repugnant, a threat to the life of the (white) woman, her child, and the future of the nation. As F. O. Matthiessen so astutely observed, in the latter half of the nineteenth century *scientia* had come increasingly to mean "science" rather than simply knowledge, and if common sense was to remain viable, it too had to sound scientific (247).

"In presenting to you some thoughts upon the subject of dress," says Mary J. Safford-Blake, MD, "I do not desire you to accept my *ipse dixit* of right or wrong; but I hope you will probe the facts presented, and, if they appeal to your common sense and reason as truths, that you will heed them, not alone for your own good, but that your influence may go forth as a help and guide to others" (Stein and Baxter 5). Mercy Jackson, MD, goes further:

> We are a republican nation, at least in form, and have no distinct classes where the lines are so tightly drawn that citizens cannot pass from one to the other.... We should therefore, as good citizens and as Christian women, do all we can to foster self-respect.... Is not society accountable in a great measure for... breaches of trust in private citizens and public servants? And who but women control the customs of society, and make them either prudent, wise, and moral, or extravagant, foolish and immoral? I appeal to the moral sense of the ladies present, and I ask them if they are willing, by their example and influence, longer to countenance a mode of dress which is so little fitted to answer the reasonable demands that should be made upon it, and so destructive of health and morals? (Stein and Baxter 91–95)

In other words, according to these female physicians, *their* mode of rational dress reform was more scientifically and medically rational than the previous rational dress; their garments would not speak so directly of anything like "emancipation," as the famous, nay poetic, failure had, but rather spoke of moral (eugenicist) strength and (pseudo)scientific fact. Significantly, almost none of the physicians use the term *bloomer* when describing the various costumes they urge their middle-class audiences to adopt, even when the item in question looked a lot like, well, bloomers. Yet a corset and hoops remained, to many, indispensable; a "lady" in 1874 was hooped, and the persistence of the corset and hoop shows that the women physicians ran into at least as much resistance as their supposedly misguided mothers. It should be noted, too, that many of the physiological, hygienic, and antifashion arguments would continue to be made over and over again, as in, for example, Miss Ada S. Ballin's *The Science of Dress in Theory and Practice,* published in 1885. Miss Ballin thought the Bloomer had failed because it was too violent a change from tradition. She promoted the demure divided skirt.[24]

Still, as I've noted, most middle-class women continued to tightlace and hoop. The general public resisted dress reform, and the idea of the Bloomer as a radical, unfeminine costume remained to haunt any type of so-called rational alteration, especially one that included pants. Very few middle-class women, even if persuaded that their health might be at risk, took heed of medical or scientific common sense, because a lady was not born, a lady was *made*, and middle-class women wanted to be seen as genteel, white ladies, not as something "Other." If that meant corsets and hoops, so be it. Otherwise, what you had was not a "natural" (white) lady. Fashions that signified gender, race, and class, through the material means of laces and stays, held sway, and so did the taint of past ridicule and caricature, which kept gay and panting lasses straitlaced and off the streets.

Then, fifty years or so after the initial failure of bloomers, the bicycle arrived and bloomers finally came into their own. "Women began riding bicycles and for this new sport, they wore bloomers. Soon after that bloomers became the name of a style of feminine drawers or knickers which had a great vogue in the early twentieth century, especially under sports clothes and schoolgirls' gym tunics" (Ewing, *Undress* 64). Sometimes called knickerbockers, but more often and more generally named bloomers, the cycling costume spread with the bicycling craze.[25] Like the bicycle itself, Betty Bloomer had arrived. And so had changes in the manufacture of clothing. Beginning as early as the 1830s but culminating in Isaac Merritt Singer's patent in February 1854, the sewing machine greatly aided in the mass production of men's clothing, but as the twentieth century came into view, more and more "ready-to-wear" clothes were also being made for women. As Nancy L. Green remarks, "The masculinization of certain feminine styles encouraged the transfer of ready-made techniques to women's wear" (27). Therefore, even if "Betty Bloomer was ahead of her time in pushing pants," her ubiquity and familiarity, along with changes in manufacturing, labor practices, and technology, paved the way for the public's acceptance of trousered women. This was particularly so in France. As Valerie Steele notes, "Bloomers indeed seem to have been far more commonly worn in Paris than in England or the United States ... and this was the case despite the fact that many fashion writers strongly disliked the costume, regarding it as ugly and unfeminine. But ... everyone wore bloomers. ... Very likely this was precisely *because* bloomers were presented in France as a fashionable item (rather than as a quasi-feminist statement)" (*Paris* 176). Thus, by 1895, many middle-class girls in the United States had not only adopted the bike and the Bloomer; they had also begun to adopt the epithet "the New Woman" and so ushered in the twentieth century.

This is not to say that the New Woman was launched without controversy; sharp battles were still being fought over woman's proper place. As Marta Banta remarks:

> Consider what it meant to be a feminist at the turn of the century in light of the problems of identification created by her ideological position. A woman who elected to advance a body of social and political principles was compelled to resolve the question of how to embody those abstract values pictorially. ... Somehow the feminist had to *dress* her ideas and her inner convictions in order to let them be expressed, however inadequately, by the surface she presented. Only then would society's perception of her image translate into collective conduct that would advance her principles and protect her from hostility and ridicule. (78)

And it should also be noted that although bloomers had gone public, they were increasingly understood as a *specialized* costume. So if bloomers no longer bore the same stamp of a colonialist seraglio erotic fantasy that the original spa clothing of Turkish trowsers might have borne, they did retain the eroticism of gender transgression that had made George Sand's trousers so infamous. Furthermore, as bloomers moved further and further into the realm of the narrowly particularized—as they became more of what we might think of as a true costume, for gymnastics, for bathing, for biking, or for titillation, rather than as an everyday habit donned socially in lieu of a dress or skirts—what they took with them was their history of female political resistance to patriarchal domination.

Common sense about women, however, had been changed. Although the athletic woman was undoubtedly still the subject of scoffing throughout the 1890s into the early part of the twentieth century (or as Willa Cather has Marian Forrester say to a young Niel Herbert in *A Lost Lady*, "Athletics and going to college and smoking after dinner—Do you like it? Don't men like women to be different from themselves? They used to" [95]), by the 1920s the athleticism of girls was generally considered natural and healthy. Marian Forrester is, after all, a lost lady, a woman whose generation is passing away, as Niel notes in this same scene. A story published in *McClure's* magazine in June 1922 illustrates such changes to a woman's common sense about herself, as well as the ambivalence with which those changes were received. The story is a satire titled "She Didn't Have Any Sense," by Scammon Lockwood, and it tells us that "the chief reason all the women had for saying that Allegra Bascom didn't have any sense was because she laced. This, to a strong-minded, sensible lady who believes in suffrage and the equality of the sexes is the very last word in female folly." But Allegra is still the heroine of this piece.

Nevertheless, the Gibson girl gave way to F. Scott Fitzgerald's Jazz Age flappers with their bobbed hair. Trousers for women were no longer a complete outrage and no longer viewed with as complete a popular disdain as they had been in 1851. A new common sense about femininity was burgeoning, helped along by the Bloomer girls, the New Woman, and by medical and scientific reforms regarding hygiene and gynecology. As Joan Brumberg notes, by 1913,

American middle-class women were developing a heightened sensibility about issues of feminine hygiene. They found the new disposable napkins extremely desirable because they promised less work, more comfort, greater mobility and a germ-free environment. The new hygiene also provided middle-class mothers with a safe script for their private conversations with their daughters. Instead of talking about the "curse of Eve" or "nerve stimulation" (which they could not see), they focused on the logistics of "sanitary protection." (40)

By the 1920s, too, the American middle-class woman had, after a long and bitter struggle, gained the vote. But she had not, nor has she yet, gained the equal rights amendment early suffragettes sought. Still, more and more girls, despite discouragement, took to the sports field; more changes to the commonsense understanding of femininity were introduced through new scientific fields such as psychology and gynecology. And if some of that new common sense looks questionable by the standards of the late twentieth and early twenty-first centuries, it nonetheless shifted the sphere of woman's influence.

At the same time, bloomers, as an item of clothing, were being thoroughly tamed, stripped, as it were, of their emancipatory meaning. Once the Bloomer was made into a semi-acceptable costume, the brashness and anger it represented seemed less brazen. With women's vote achieved, the point of bloomers was less sharp. Soon these pants would be relegated to childhood and to the past. The word *bloomers* would reflect such a change, because as the pants themselves were translated from the rude, the revolutionary, and the indecent to the practical, the pragmatic, and finally the childish, no longer was the word able to signify anything like a bold new (female) tongue.

Feminism and Fashion

By the 1940s and '50s, it was not unusual for women to wear trousers or slacks, as they were called, for a host of particular reasons. They did not, however, don anything like the suffragette bloomers. Meanwhile, generally speaking, men still wore the pants. As noted earlier, during both World Wars I and II, women who worked wore boiler-suits and blue jeans. Between 1915 and 1954, skirts lengthened and shortened according to the dictates of fashion and need, and the feminine profile went from the corseted hourglass to the pencil-thin flapper and back again to the hourglass, at least as that hourglass was constructed through those binding but flexible girdles and bras that had been made possible by the wartime inventions of nylon, rayon, and polyesters.

But all this time, only children were dressed in bloomers or knickers. And although actresses such as Marlene Dietrich and Katharine Hepburn or fashionable, infamous women such as Coco Chanel might wear trousers in public, in general the middle-class woman wore some variation of a dress: from the Chanel suit to the Dior "New Look," they wore skirts, house and cocktail dresses, or evening gowns. By the late 1950s, although certain types of pants had come into vogue, such as the tapered ski pant or stirrup pant, slacks, as the name implies, were still considered leisure wear. A working woman would seldom, if ever, wear slacks to the office. Indeed, when Capri pants became fashionable in the late 1950s, some fashion magazines once again lamented the sheer ugliness of trousers on women, a lament reminiscent of the fashionable disdain for bloomers that had helped to drive the garment off the streets nearly one hundred years earlier.[26]

But by the late 1950s and continuing into the early 1970s, significant social and political alterations were underway. These alterations of the social order began to be reflected in and, indeed, managed by the fashion pages. And in 1967, an old familiar word was dusted off and made its way back into use, at least briefly. As the Paris *Evening News* reported, "Bloomers peep boldly beneath the hemlines of short as ever smocks and shifts . . . beguiling bloomers in acid colors, aimed at the young and gay. . . . Miniskirts are dead, long live bloomers" (Gattey 177–78). Although the concept of Parisian haute couture had existed for years alongside the always-increasing mass production of ready-to-wear lines, the late 1960s and early 1970s saw resistance, subversion, and nostalgia inundate fashion. Widespread demand for the unique, for the ethnic, the hand-made, and the antiestablishment made a significant impact on what women wore and how they wore it. Thus the late '60s and early '70s, then, were a period in which "personal" or "individualistic" styling, as it was called, went hand-in-hand with more traditional modes (Ewing, *Twentieth-Century* 227–28). Both saw rapid change. But it was the "London Look" that took off and did so in more ways than one. After years and years of covering themselves head to toe, young women ditched the yardage for skin. This look was dominated by the miniskirt, introduced in 1966, and by Mary Quant's bell-bottoms covered by a tunic that sometimes doubled as a miniskirt. Such comparative nudity was followed by a rage for culottes, hot pants, microminis, and a bashful little pair of panties called bloomers. Even Turkish trowsers came back, as an "ethnic" item. Midi and maxi lengths also appeared, but from 1966 on, young, carefree, and childish held sway, and "the glossy magazines went overboard with the new fashion mood.... It began to mean that you could wear anything anywhere" (Ewing, *Twentieth-Century* 200). By insisting on fantasy and youth, by returning to the Oneida mode of seeing girlhood as sexy, fashion played down political revolution. *Young* and *individualistic*, these were the terms being marshaled both to describe and in effect to contain the "youth revolution" or "youth explosion." Of course, the "erotic child," the sex kitten, the "nymphet," as Humbert Humbert put it, has enjoyed a long history in the United States.[27] The Oneida Perfectionist Community knew full well that women adopting the fashions of girlhood took on an attractive, virginal glow (Fischer 134). But the contrast between the vision of femininity that appeared on the fashion pages of the 1960s and the images of the women who took part in various social or political rebellions is nevertheless a marked one. That is, despite wild oscillations in image and fashion, in 1972, as Elizabeth Ewing notes, most middle-class "women still derived their position mainly from their relationships with men, so fashion aimed to attract men and in its development the 'seduction principle' was closely bound up with the hierarchic or status one" (*Twentieth-Century* 229). The predominance of this pattern was no doubt under siege. Divorce rates spiked; second wave feminist activism took shape. Meanwhile, however, the fashion pages put women in pigtails and baby-dolls, kneesocks and bloomers. Thus, for example, although Motown might have been changing the face, race, and sound of popular music, the title of the Supremes' breakthrough hit single in 1964, "Baby Love," is suggestive. And yet, although the predominance of the Baby Doll over and against the Bra Burner may seem to belittle the angrier aspects of the youth revolution, at the same time a new common sense about sexuality was being forged, one in which it was no longer wholly unusual or "unnatural" for a woman to "wear the pants." Such a new common sense about femininity has not been achieved without pain, of course, or without struggles that look to continue into the twenty-first century.[28] It was, however, a new way of understanding one's place in the world and a far cry from the last turn of the century, when, even after fifty-two years of agitation, women were still unable to vote as full-fledged American citizens.

The word *bloomers*, however, after its brief fling as mod style for the hip flower child of the 1960s, and perhaps in part because of that fling, still refers to undergarments or children's clothes. If mentioned at all, the Bloomer Costume is most often deemed a failure that had politically bankrupt, or at least counterproductive, colonialist effects. Cultural critic Marjorie Garber's narrative about the ill-fated costume is a typical one:

> As an innovation, unfortunately, the Bloomer Costume ranks with the Susan B. Anthony silver dollar; only a few convinced individuals, and some utopian communities, adopted the style. The Turkish connotations attracted some unfavorable attention, despite the rage for artifacts *a la Turque*. . . . A writer to the *New York Tribune* pointed out the lack of freedom of Middle Eastern women compared to Americans, and suggested that the spectacle of female reformers in Turkish trousers was properly a cause for cultural irony. (314)

Not only has Garber reduced the number of people who wore the Bloomer to "a few convinced individuals"—a description that contradicts the historical record—but she also insists, here, upon the Oriental aspect of the dress.[29] However, while it is certainly true that critics of the costume at the time pointed out the Bloomer's association with things Oriental and Turkish, it is equally true that the Bloomer Costume was neither called nor conceived of as precisely Turkish or Eastern by many who adopted Amelia Jenks Bloomer's particular version. To these women, Bloomer had made panting, a male prerogative, female. The alterations made to the Turkish idea had Americanized it, had made the Bloomer as American as apple pie, and, as Gayle Fischer has persuasively demonstrated, the "complexities of cultural borrowing within fashion" are profound in the case of bloomers (123). She argues, "If the women's rights dress reformers chose Turkish trowsers in order to distance their costume from male dress and make it more palatable to the general public, then they

failed. Although many disliked the freedom dress because of its Eastern origins, they were far outnumbered by those who simply felt that
women dressed in 'Turkish' pantaloons looked like men" (129).

To a contemporary cultural critic, the seeming refusal on, say,
Amelia Bloomer's part to fully acknowledge or understand the irony
of bloomers may, of course, read like another indication of the imbal-
ances of colonialism, as Garber suggests. But again, the historical
record suggests otherwise, inasmuch as the abolitionist and suffragette
women in the nineteenth century knew full well that their so-called
rational garment had an erotic and exoticized irony. Debates about
"other" cultural practices of female oppression, from the so-called
slavery of Eastern women to the practice of Chinese foot binding,
raged in the pages of the *Lily* and in other emancipation or abolitionist
newspapers.[30] What the dress reformers believed they were seeking,
by adopting bloomers, was a commonsense dress, one that was based
on logical arguments regarding the natural shape of the female body,
just as the dress-reform physicians argued in the 1870s.

However, history, as surely every historian must know, is seldom
recounted or recalled with an accuracy that reflects archival records.
Similarly, rationality and common sense often have nothing to do
with each other. And clothes, as women from the Bloomerites to the
supposed bra burners knew only too well, often speak more loudly
and far less rationally than the person wearing them. Clothes will tell
tales—or have tales told of them—and there is no lack of idiomatic
or historical evidence to prove that they are made to tell particular,
commonsense (seldom rational) stories about politics and everyday
life. For as historian Kathy Peiss notes, it isn't just bloomers that speak
about politics:

> Women strikers in a thread-mill (1890s), for example, linked fashion—
> wearing bonnets—to their sense of American identity and class con-
> sciousness, contrasting their militancy to Scottish scabs who wore
> shawls on their heads. Believing in the labor movement's ideology
> of self-improvement, organization, worker's dignity, these women
> devoted their leisure to lectures, evening school, political meetings
> and union dances. (64)

Furthermore, at the end of the twentieth century, idiomatically one
could still be told that "clothes make the man" and that women "dress

to kill." Indeed, although the stricter *Man in the Gray Flannel Suit* dress codes for men and women did give way to the pressure of love beads, *Hair,* and the wilder extravagances of glam rock or disco, women are still often counseled to wear something "appropriate" to an interview; rape cases can be won or lost depending on the victim's choice of clothing, down to her underwear. Cross-dressing on the job, unless it *is* your job, can get you fired. As Roland Barthes reminds us in *The Fashion System,* clothes signify. Like words, they are subject to both vastly different interpretations and changing mores. In 1900, when Theodore Dreiser made clothes actually speak to Carrie in his novel *Sister Carrie* (as if to ratify Karl Marx's theory of commodity fetishism, first published in 1867), clothes spoke both with a "moral significance" to the wayward Carrie and with the pressure of a desire not to be withstood. As Carrie wanders through the newfound glories of an urban department store, she finds fine clothes "a vast persuasion; they spoke tenderly and Jesuitically for themselves," in a voice that a shoe fetishist might have longed to hear: "'Ah, such little feet,' said the leather of the soft new shoes, 'how effectively I cover them'" (98). Despite her sense that she ought to be married rather than living as a "kept" woman, Carrie's desire for nice clothes overwhelms all other considerations.

Indeed, clothes speak to us of ourselves as we exist in a dense cultural web of multiple class boundaries, ethnic or racial heritages, and sexual dimorphism, as well as changes made to those systems over time. Clothes and fashion can serve to code what is now called sexual orientation (as in, for example, the green suits and red ties of men seeking the company of men during the 1930s)[31] and sexual availability (as in the variety of statements the wearing of a ring can make, although jewelry is technically not clothing, and I could no doubt fill the pages of an entirely different chapter about it). My point here is that the politics of the everyday makes clothes speak and that clothes speak to us of the dailiness of our politics, as this brief history of "panting" girls demonstrates.

The social upheavals during the 1960s and 1970s ushered in distinct changes to the sociopolitical landscape for the average American woman, and fierce arguments, both private and public, about the significance of so-called traditional women's accoutrements still rage:

Should one wear lipstick? under what circumstances? Should one
shave one's legs? armpits? wear high heels? Is one oppressed if one
does so? What about tattoos? piercings? Or are we simply making a
choice? How do others respond to these choices? Any choice is politically inflected and received as such, whether one follows a conscious
feminist politics or not. According to Kath Weston, for example,
"many feminists regarded traditionally feminine dress as impractical,
uncomfortable attire that objectified women and rendered them vul-
nerable to sexual attack. Skirts, heels, long hair, and makeup were
the first to go. A woman who walked into a lesbian bar in a dress . . .
was likely to have her lesbian identity questioned and unlikely to have
anyone ask her to dance" (15). Impractical, uncomfortable, oppressive: are these not the same commonsense terms by which the mid-
nineteenth-century Bloomerites condemned corsets and the yardage
of crinoline they were supposed to wear? And those who donned the
more practical, less oppressive, more rational Bloomer Costume, as we
have seen, also had their femininity questioned—sometimes humor-
ously, sometimes vilely and violently. One thus might be tempted to
conclude, along with both Gayle V. Fischer and Marjorie Garber,
that what bloomers speak about is failure. The Bloomer may be merely
a demonstration of another commonsense adage—that everything
changes and everything stays the same. However well we know that
clothes speak a multitude of conflicting meanings, we also always
already know what they say.

   And yet, as the history of the word *bloomers* suggests, such stasis
hardly reflects the historical record because, over time, common
sense about femininity, repeatedly challenged by new social practices, new medical and political understandings, *was* and is changed.
The history of the word *bloomers*, then, can serve not only as an index
to a certain kind of failure but also as a testament to the changes
made in commonly held cultural attitudes and to the sociopolitical
domain in which we all live out our lives. Rather than lay blame for
the failure of bloomers at the feet of Amelia Jenks Bloomer herself,
or on the concept of frivolity, or at the doorstep of a misguided Western colonialism, I want to argue that what failed was not bloomers,
not really, because eventually, in changing, they helped to accomplish

change. What failed, rather, was the suffragettes' reliance on the idea that rationality is equal to common sense and that both would prove persuasive enough to produce the political changes they sought. Because common sense is not simple, or plain, or rational, or scientific. It is fickle, variable, crazy, and sometimes poetic. The problem with the Bloomer Costume is the problem of common sense. Logically, Amelia Jenks Bloomer, Libby Smith, Elizabeth Cady Stanton, and Susan B. Anthony were being rational. Everyone knew that trousers were more convenient and comfortable than a dress. To wear a garment that increased one's mobility was not a mere frivolity, and they designed one along the lines of women's garments with which they were already familiar. The problem with the Bloomer was that it interfered with a common sense about that most irrational of domains, sex and sexual desire. Until and unless common sense is altered, no amount of panting will change the general public's mind.

Furthermore, in hindsight, much of what these women wrote about their hopes and ideals not only seems movingly eloquent today but also sounds resoundingly like current common sense. Here is Amelia Jenks Bloomer, speaking in the 1870s:

> We are not content that the universities at Ithaca, Ann Arbor and Iowa City should open their doors to the equal admission of both sexes to the advantages of collegiate education, but we would have the same generous policy control all the colleges and universities in the country. The doors of Harvard, Yale, and Union, in this country, and of Oxford and Cambridge, in England, should be also open to woman and the contest will not be ended until this is accomplished. Everywhere, in every form, the just claims of woman to equal educational privileges must be ultimately acknowledged. And not only this, but we claim that she shall nowhere be debarred from any form of industry or any sphere of labor for which she has capacity, and when she accomplishes as much by her day's work as a man does by his, that she shall be paid the same price. (Coon 183)

In effect, then, if bloomers failed, Amelia Jenks Bloomer did not, not entirely, even if many are still waiting to be paid the same wage as a man. However, creating a new politics and a new political language, whether of dress or of words, is next to impossible if a common usage does not take hold. And as the activist women of antebellum

America also knew, one must repeat oneself ad nauseam to be heard over the din of common sense. Therefore, if the domain of the everyday, in language or in dress, remains one of the most resistant to political agitation, it is also the place wherein the politics of change eventually comes to reside. It should not be surprising, then, to find that voice and image have long been the staging ground from which American social activism such as the feminist movement—first, second, or third wave—has launched campaigns. Thus, it might be wise indeed to insist that the *entire* history of a word such as *bloomers* be noted, that is, to insist that the infantilization of this American *political* neologism not be forgotten. For visible in the historical process of such linguistic change is an ongoing struggle over the nature of nature. Women in the nineteenth century did make a bold bid indeed to tether the power of language to their own purposes; they sought to forge new meanings, in clear, eloquent, and rational arguments that were nevertheless received by many as gibberish. Still, through persistence and the repetition of such so-called female blather, everyday *common sense* about femininity did change, and if the Bloomer became bloomers, we would be wise to try at least to recall, from time to time, how and why.

Sucker. Courtesy of Arnold Mesches.

sucker

To Suck or Not to—

Suck, as in "you suck," and *sucker*, as in "sap" or "what a loser," are, like the neologism *bloomer*, peculiar to American English. In British slang, a sucker is a sweet, the lollipop. In the United States, to say that something sucks became a trademark insult during the 1990s ("it sucks!"), a protest ("meat sucks!"), a complaint ("life sucks!"), even a bumper sticker ("mean people suck"). *Sucker*, on the other hand, may have had its heyday during the 1920s and 1930s, as slang for "naïf" and "greenhorn" or "rube" and "dupe," although *sucker* both predates the mid-twentieth century and persisted through it. Perhaps it is known best through a statement attributed to nineteenth-century American impresario P. T. Barnum: "There's a sucker born every minute"; there is also W. C. Fields's "Never give a sucker an even break" and a host of other, less common aphorisms ("I'm a sucker for a pretty face"). As a synonym for the average Joe Blow who is routinely cheated or misled, *sucker* has appeared in any number of American narratives from Robert Penn Warren's *All the King's Men* to Ralph Ellison's *Invisible Man*.[1]

37

Of course, there are yet more, less familiar definitions of both *suck* and *sucker,* to which the *OED* attests: tobacco plants have suckers, which require suckering, or removal; insects, fish, octopi, and baby rabbits all have been called suckers at one time, as have the native inhabitants of southern Illinois. And if it's fair to say that no one cares to be on the receiving end of a sucker punch, then finding the perfect sucker to play can be considered a grifter's dream. By the same token, no one fancies being the one "sucked in" or "suckered." Seldom would anyone want to be caught "sucking up." Or sucking a thumb. Only infants or toddlers can suck their thumbs in public.

Favored by graffiti artists, *suck* and *sucker* are familiar, popular terms of derision. Yet innocent and lovely is the intimate sucking of a child at the breast, often featured as the hallmark posture of the holy mother and suckling child on Christmas cards; and the popular fashion during the early 1990s of wearing a fluorescent "adult" pacifier in order to get in touch with one's "inner child" also suggests that "to suck" is condoned when associated with infancy and innocence. Indeed, neither breast-feeding nor thumb-sucking has ever found its way into the domain of oral sex acts, despite the sensuality of sucking, which Freud underscored in a 1920 footnote in *The Three Essays* (181). Neither act has been categorized as criminal sodomy or pathologized as perverse by popular psychotherapy, although controversies over the desirability of breast-feeding have a long history in both the United States and Europe.[2] And no one would confuse a Hallmark Baby Jesus with actress Kirsten Dunst as Claudia the child-vampire who sucks blood in the 1994 film *Interview with the Vampire.* Common sense intervenes against identifying a suckling as vampiric or thumb-sucking as a sex act. Such common sense provides for a logical division of suckers, a calculus of difference on which judgment will rest, even in the face of Freud's famous assertion that "no one who has seen a baby sinking back satiated from the breast and falling asleep with flushed cheeks and a blissful smile can escape the reflection that this picture persists as a prototype of the expression of sexual satisfaction in later life" (182).

Curiously, though, both Hallmark and Freud assume that their interpretation of the image of a baby at the breast (i.e., innocence on the one hand, sexual satisfaction on the other) is a self-evident one.

Freud says no one who has seen this image can escape knowing it to be the prototype of later sexual satiation. In fact, both Hallmark and Freud might say that their reading of the baby at the breast is an "accessible" one. Surely everyone can see that the baby at the breast means innocence/sexual satiety, although I very much doubt that Hallmark's expectation of readerly interpretation is capacious enough to accommodate Freud. We may all be born suckers, but there are varieties to be avoided thereafter. All sucklings may be suckers, but all suckers are not sucklings. This is common knowledge.

But precisely how is this commonsense understanding achieved? And how is it made accessible, reproducible? Why are some interpretations so self-evident that they require little or no discussion? I ask this question and tie it to a consideration of a common Americanism, *sucker,* because in the latter half of the twentieth century, clarity and accessibility, often conflated, became key concepts in political and critical debates about writing (and other communication practices). They also became key terms in debates about democracy as a political form. From legal demands for equal access, to ongoing arguments about whether or not universal access to the Internet is good, accessibility has been both presented as and presumed to be a prerequisite for equality and community. Of course, to engage all such debate about either clarity or accessibility is beyond the scope of this chapter; however, through a meditation on the multiple registers and historical permutations of what most would understand as a common, familiar American slang word, *sucker,* I will argue that what is at issue in debates about accessibility is not whether meaning is perceived as accessible, but rather which meaning will be accessible to whom, how, and when, as well as what value will accrue to any given meaning—which meaning will we entertain as common sense, as a meaning understood by all?

To argue that meaning is contingent upon cultural value may itself sound like common sense, but in this chapter, I will show how the frequent demand (both popular and critical) for the "common sense" of unambiguous, unconflicted, and inescapable decipherability regenerated, during the late 1990s, a residual positivism bound to and by a violent, coercive phenomenal real. Rather than enabling knowledge production, or community, or even communication, as I said in my introduction, this real is instead the ravenous vampire of an impossible demand reimagined as a basic necessity. Like the bloodsuckers lurking at the edge of my chapter's title, this demand haunts the political economy of any democracy as indebted to humanism as the United States is, because the real should remain—indeed, is—unrecoverable. If not, that is, if the real should be frozen into legibility, then verity will vanish as if a vampire in glass.

"Even very intimate contact with a body leaves room for mistakes."

A sure locus of reality, or so it has seemed, is the actual of the inescapable, mortal body. During the late 1980s and early 1990s, a whole "body" of criticism about "the body" came into being, a locution that suggests there is but one body, the indubitable, real body. As Judith Butler says by way of introducing her book *Bodies That Matter,* one of the most frequent questions she was asked in the early 1990s was, "What about the materiality of the body, *Judy?*" as if she "needed to be brought to task, restored to that bodily being which is, after all, considered to be most real, most pressing, most undeniable" (ix). The question she cites here has a curious emphasis, too, on the familiarity of a nickname, as if "Judy" were somehow a more authentic, more accessible version of "Judith."

The words with which I began this chapter—*suck, sucker, suckling*—are words that refer to the "body," to the physical, even if they are still words. Since the physical is often presumed to be as close to the actual as one can get, one might imagine these words as being able to borrow a certain gravid authority from their "actuality," and yet it is also the very physicality to which these words refer that lends them a certain volatile vulgarity. The implied act of sucking imbues a colloquialism (such as *sucker*) or an obsolete usage (such as *suckering*), or an idiomatic phrase and simple noun, with anxiety. This anxious ambivalence makes all of these words ring with an echo of bodily insult. Consider the continued political bite of the word *bloodsucker.* Although your average mosquito is called a bloodsucker, making the word seem tame, the statement of the Nation of Islam's Khalid

Abdul Muhammad that "Jews are the bloodsuckers of the Black nation" fueled considerable outrage ("NAACP Will Invite"). Even in 2004, lawyers and litigants who might be engaged in "frivolous" lawsuits against, say, McDonald's for serving fast food that causes obesity are still derided on the floor of Congress as bloodsuckers.

In fact, abusiveness will abide in any form of sucking, as in the taunt "cocksucker," despite how this variation of a *sucker* can on occasion be used jokingly or to express desire.[3] The body, then, while used as a prop for claims about the absolute bedrock of reality, is also fraught with potential reversals, confusions, and anxieties, particularly regarding the surety of knowledge; or as Thomas Laqueur takes pains to demonstrate in *Making Sex,* "even very intimate contact with a body leaves room for mistakes" (2); in other words, what we perceive as our body is not a permanent given but, rather, a dense anatomical palimpsest of learned topographies that have shifted over time. Surely it is this instability, the tantalizing possibility that even the most intimate contact can mislead, that makes cross-dressing both a popular fascination on the stage and in film and a potentially fatal or violent act.[4]

Of course, it might be argued that a film and hate speech hail from different contexts. Political denunciation and popular novel, film, television, and theatrical performance are not seen as working in the same fashion or even speaking to the same audience. And yet, they do share an underlying logic that emerges when one considers how the use of a commonsense understanding embedded within a shared language determines interpretation — in the way in which the word *sucker* and its derivations convey meaning to us. Drama and politics both rely on the common sense that a sucker — any kind of sucker — is a loser. And a dangerous loser at that, even when the audience is supposed to find the loser alluring, as in the case of Tom Cruise as a bloodsucker in *Interview with the Vampire*. Lestat may be sexy, but the film reduces him to pathos. Indeed, what both this film and the statement of Nation of Islam's Khalid Abdul Muhammad imply is that to be in danger of losing one's communal identitarian strength — to lose one's evident membership, for example, in an identifiable community — is to be sucked dry.

A number of logics are inhabited by the assumption that losing one's identity is the equivalent, at least metaphorically, of being the vampire's victim. But in a search for, say, political clout or psychic wholeness, in the search for coherences posited as necessary to any successful political intervention or to the attainment of psychic health, such strategic logic indefinitely puts off addressing conflict perceived as interior to the group, to the self, to the community, or to the nation. As I said in my introduction, the United States persistently faces the paradox of being e pluribus unum: the identity of the nation lives on the diverse tongues of its separate households, all of which, nevertheless, try to be like a single family through a sharing of familiar household words. Or as Lora Romero put it in her analysis of the direction that ethnic studies took during the 1980s, there may be acknowledgment of, but there is seldom any sustained attention to, "the diversity within constituencies" (137). In addition, such logic generates a praxis and a politics bound both to and by the often violently coercive constitution of a stable, knowable, unambivalent, eminently accessible, and transparently "real" identity.

But if being the "sucked upon" is unhealthy, being a sucker isn't promising either, even if sucking is sexy. In American English, a sucker is, as I've said, a loser. Even if modified, the verb to suck signifies the act of bringing about a state of loss or lacking. If we extend this common sense and read back through the texts I've cited here, what becomes clear is that hiding, losing, or altering one's real identity is fatal. Whether that alteration is the result of individual denial or genocide, the result is the same. Survival, says this common sense, rests in the maintenance of, and the adherence to, your real identity! Otherwise you risk being sucked dry, deprived of a vital essence (blood), even if and when the alteration is desired, even if you occupy the supposed position of power, that of the bloodsucker. At root, sucker is tied to flesh and thus to a fear of flesh, a fear that hearkens back to the image of the helpless baby at the breast and to the vulnerability of thumb-sucking, and so to a culturally inscribed, ambivalent terror of/desire for the real of all realities, mortality. Indeed, to invoke the real forestalls it, like an exorcism; to claim to know what is real is, in effect, to ward it off. Thus the body is often presented as

a fetishized, material site of the "really" real without sustained consideration of the body itself as ambivalent, readable, multiply interpretable, and mortal.

Vampirology

Bloodsuckers, however (as everyone knows), lack both the body and blood. And if I am concerned, as I claim, with the real, then why insist on invoking this fantasy? Is it not true that the scary old bloodsucker, now a favorite of children's programming and Halloween getups, is *not* real, no matter how fancy a theorist can get? As numerous critics note, the bloodsucker has become now too familiar to induce fear, unless it be of a vampire killer (or cult) that kills or harms someone or some animal. These sorts of vampires are, of course, deemed insane rather than preternatural.[5] From the daily news to cultural critique, in television series and mass-market paperback, from the self-conscious art film to Hollywood, the bloodsucker is salable merchandise, a popular icon of neo-Gothicism or romanticism, of film noir, mock horror, comedy. Dracula can't really hurt you because "Dracula," as Judith Roof writes, "is just another household name" (146). Furthermore, while the bloodsucker is as common as a household word, vampirism also appears with a frequency and ubiquity that rivals (or perhaps confirms) the vigorous, if harmless, longevity of the undead. And by writing these lines, I, too, add to the phenomenon of which I speak: the sucker who sucks is a figurative predator, useful as a commonplace but not itself a real threat, since vampirism is just a gag or a metaphor.[6]

And yet, whenever such metaphors are used, they activate a vampirology, a logic that relies on a familiarity with vampirism, in order to locate the site of a mythically resonant, dreadful loss: a deadly hunger, a seductive fatality, a vortex of exploitation, cannibalism. Vampirism is a kind of common knowledge, shorthand to describe that which is calculated and powerful, or evil and attractive, or fatal yet eternal. I could multiply examples ad infinitum, but here let me cite merely two, one popular, one political. Popular: In Marilyn Monroe's (ghost-written) autobiography, she tells us that people responded to

her as if she were a "vampire with a rose in her teeth" (27).[7] Given
how ubiquitous and profitable Monroe remains in and outside America, her prescient statement becomes uncanny. After all, according to
Parade magazine, Marilyn Monroe had made eight million dollars as
of March 2004. That's quite a remarkable sum of money for someone
who has been dead over forty years. Political: In reviewing two book-
length accounts of the Serbo-Croatian conflict, Aleska Dijilas offers
that both Serbs and Croats have been haunted by the "vampirism of
nationalism" (7). To continue in a political vein (no pun intended),
perhaps one of the most famous uses of bloodsucking as metaphor is
Karl Marx's oft-cited Gothic analogy between vampirism and economic
relations under capitalism: "Capital is dead labor, that vampire-like,
only lives by sucking living labor, and lives the more, the more labor
it sucks" (257). Mark Seltzer, in his "Serial Killers (I)," echoes this
Marxian analogy by making vampirism a sign of the "quantitative
equivalencies and compulsive seriality in the culture of consumption" (99–100), while Laura Kipnis reads *Capital* as a "marriage manual," making marriage between the vampire and the adulterer an
everyday utopia and then bewailing love's labor lost (309). In 1995,
Donna Haraway made the whole of the twentieth-century United
States a "vampire culture" ("Modest" 213) as if in echo and response
to Eve Kosofsky Sedgwick's 1993 characterization of all American
public culture as "sumptuously" vampiric (*Tendencies* 222). In psychoanalytic criticism, the vampire literally abounds, as Ken Gelder
has noted in his 1994 *Reading the Vampire*. Indeed, when Lacanian
theorist Slavoj Žižek writes, "The usual Marxist vampire metaphor is
that of capital sucking the blood of the workforce, embodiment of the
rule of the dead over the living; perhaps the time has come to reverse
it: the real 'living dead' are we, common mortals" (220–21), he has
called for that which both Seltzer and, in a sense, Kipnis imply has
already occurred at the level of the middle class: that is, the metaphor
has been reversed. It was in the process of reversal even as Marx wrote.
Harassed about the future, about your children's welfare, about your
retirement funds, harangued about maintaining your weight, health,
longevity, youth, and hammering away in the deadening (re)produc-
tive stalag of marriage, most working (for which read lower- to upper-
middle-class) Americans work very, very hard to consume.

That we perceive the vampire as the ultimate consumer and so a version of ourselves shouldn't surprise us. Nina Auerbach's *Our Vampires, Ourselves* performs the self-proclaimed diagnostic role to which its title points. Everywhere you look, there goeth the vampire. Surely the observation that "vampires are us" (Roof 148) is not late-breaking news! As Chris Craft wrote of *Dracula,* "The monster indeed is 'no one except myself'" (236), although I prefer Paul Scofield's remark in Robert Redfield's film *Quiz Show,* which offers a more pungently American version of the "our bodies, ourselves" logic by suggesting that "if you look around the table and you can't tell who the sucker is—it's you." Such identifications serve to confirm Freud's contention that we are all suckers when it comes to the demands of desire. So I find it quite tempting, if perhaps unpopular, to say that Freud was onto something after all, especially given that recent critical treatments of the vampire repeat, gloss, and embroider the tiresome observation that "we are all of us (blood)suckers, everyone," echoing Dickens's Tiny Tim. Because once you start talking about vampires, you become enmeshed in a ubiquity that rivals the ubiquity of, well, say, Charles Dickens. You are "forced to inhabit the swirling semantic field of vampire stories" (Haraway, "Modest" 215), because, like Dickens, the bloodsucker can show up everywhere and anywhere. Particularly and paradoxically a figurative effect of a modernist, rational, capital economy, the vampire is both the child of colonial Britain and an adopted child of America. A "seductive, fascinating creature of the night, tied to reproductive technologies of the modern age and to the accumulation of capital" (Gelder 88), the vampire is a meet emblem of technologies of reproduction: of cinema, video, and the Internet.[8]

This is not to say, of course, that a figure is the same as a technology. But as Luise White demonstrates in "Cars Out of Place: Vampires, Technology, and Labor in East and Central Africa," the relationship between bloodsuckers and industrial capitalism is not a distant one.[9] Since the 1910s and '20s, says White, African stories about bloodsucking firemen, or *wazimamoto,* arose; indeed, African working men often represented "the conflicts and problematics of the new economic order in stories about public employees who sucked blood.... Vampires were new symbols for new times... uniquely well-suited to represent the conflicts and ambiguities of labor" (33). "Ghosts," writes Mladen Dolar, "vampires, monsters, the undead flourish in an era when you might expect them to be dead and buried.... They are something brought about by modernity itself" (7).

As many critics are quick to point out, the vampire's ubiquity stems from its ability to serve simultaneously as both cultural conservator and diagnostic symptom. The vampire is insider and outsider, perverse and familiar, a figure for the potent conceptual hinge of the either/or, neither/nor, as Hortense Spillers names it in her 1989 essay, "Notes on an Alternative Model—Neither/Nor." The term *vampire* is akin to (but, again, not the same as) nouns that work at the hinge of a binary opposition: *mulatto, hybrid, half-breed, mestizo, cyborg*. It is the lure of this hinge that leads Donna Haraway to say she's been "instructed by the vampire" as a "figure that both promises and threatens racial and sexual mixing" ("Modest" 214). And Haraway is hardly alone; many critics have worked away at the hinge of the promise/threat of the neither/nor, either/or, in an impressive sustained attempt to break the logic of binary opposition. Those engaged in this collective intellectual effort often seek, as Haraway does, to construct "models of solidarity and human unity and difference rooted in friendship, work, partly shared purposes, intractable collective pain, inescapable mortality, and persistent hope" rather than in rigidly polarized categorical oppositions (265). Terms such as *cyborg, vampire*, and *morph* serve as indices of the partial, fragmentary, multiple, rhizomatic, diverse. They both locate and critique binarism, for "defined by their categorical ambiguity and troubling mobility, vampires do not rest easy (or easily) in the boxes labeled good and bad" (214).

In addition to pursuing those figures that appear both to identify and to unlock rigid polarizations, many critics have adopted a rhetorical gesture that would seem to take instruction from the vampire. Acknowledging sociopolitical binaries, Haraway characterizes herself through "a list of personal, qualifying adjectives—white, Christian, apostate, professional, childless, middle-class, middle-aged, biologist, cultural theorist, historian, U.S. citizen, late-twentieth-century, female," in order to identify the habitus from which her voice rises ("Promises" 322). Indeed, many feminist critics have performed similar enumerations, in part as a response to the frequent charge that femi-

nism is a white, middle-class phenomenon, complicit with the perpetuation of racial inequity, class boundaries, and heterosexism. Such
self-nominations serve as gestures of self-reflexivity. They locate "the"
voice at an acknowledged site of privilege in the sociopolitical nexus
of race, class, and gender. However, more often than not, this enumerative particularity has been, as Michel Foucault might have argued,
more a confession than a fulcrum for debate—what Gayatri Spivak
once called "confessional attitudinizing" ("Response" 208). Still, I
take note that this by-now tedious gesture of self-nominative confession has been expanded by Haraway. The list, as she says, is "neurotic" in that it "makes a false promise," because what drives it is her
desire to "write about the universal; that is, about 'the human,'" because "the human is the category that makes a luminous promise to
transcend the rending trauma of the particular, especially that particular non-thing and haunt called race" ("Promises" 322).

So as we are being launched forward in the twenty-first century,
that once-dead conceptual haunt called the human has been returned
to the critical terrain, undead. Driven back into articulation through
a variety of conversations about "the body" of "the human" and the
supposed reality of material historical circumstance, the universal
Human, like his analog the bloodsucker, rises again. This human,
however, has been shriven; he no longer believes in his former pre-
tension that difference does not exist, at least in Haraway's version of
him. Hopeful because made aware of diversity, perhaps this time "he"
can transcend the divisions of particularity, because when it gets right
down to the nitty-gritty, every single one of us must bear the stigmata
of a rending, mortal historicity, which is also, because a historical
product according to Haraway, a nonthing, as in the "haunt," as she
calls it, of race. Again, Haraway is not alone in turning back to what
she calls a tentative but luminous promise of the universal Human,
or in a return, more generally, to universalism as a logic, which has
been a critical trend for some time now. Indeed criticism of "the body"
during the 1980s is a predecessor of this revamped universalism, laying
down the intellectual pavement for such a return. The question as to
whether the multiple conceptual vectors of difference are useful or
divisive as a means to interpret or understand the relationship between

American culture and politics informs both those who imagine themselves on the left and those on the right. Whether you celebrate or deride diversity, the term *diversity* itself remains a common denominator in both discussions.

However, such debates about diversity often remind us in the course of pursuing their argument, as Haraway does, that representative democracy, as a form of governance in the United States, was never premised on that imagined, wholly phantasmic level playing field of the universal Human; moreover, given that the history of what Nancy Fraser terms "actually existing democracy" (1)—from ancient Greek city-states to the United States—sprang from the muck of constitutive inequities, questions about multiculturalism go hand-in-hand with the query, Can democracy, premised on the equality of, well, men, and the fraternity of our shared humanity be reradicalized as a pragmatic politics? Can democracy be revivified to serve the idealistic ends envisioned by the rhetoric, if not the policies, of the Enlightenment-influenced revolutions? As Haraway notes when she contemplates the category race, the differences that mark a body as other than the white, propertied, heterosexual male have long served as "fracturing trauma[s] in the body politic of the nation—and in the mortal bodies of its people" ("Promises" 321), a recurring violence that has characterized the history of the United States from the Civil War to civil rights to civil liberty.

Yet to identify identity as immaterial has done little to help untangle how such nonthings have had potent historical effects. And as the long aftermath of the civil rights upheavals of the late 1950s and 1960s continues to play itself out slowly in the wake of the Cold War and 9/11; as the acrimonious snarl of the identity-affirmative politics that rose out of those upheavals is tied to the now risible specter of so-called political correctness; as affirmative action is repealed, returned, debated, reviled, upheld; as reverse discrimination suits abound; and as sexual harassment suits become pervasive, more and more commonsense appeals to the "true" goodness of human community are made as correctives to the divisive particularities of history and identity. This "imagined community"[10] of the universal Human, sustained by positive identities that, despite superficial (or disposable?)

differences, all share a Nature (Human, Vampire, or Cyborg) and the Body, seems to offer the utopian promise that a return to universalism can win out over the evident losses and fears inflicted by difference.

Lip Service

So it should not be surprising that in this age of renewed utopian possibility, bloodsucking itself came to be seen, for a while, as identity forming and community building. Those who engaged in "blood sports," such as piercing, blood drinking, cutting, and scarification, claimed that being cut or sucked constituted the truest intimacy, because only in doing so can one give oneself over in a complete act of trust. "Cutting is a psychic orgasm," said one participant in blood play; "it creates intimacy" (Eurydice 66). From Salt Lake City, where the Camarilla Domain of Utah described itself as a Gothic movement in which blood sport was a "character-building thing," to the Internet, self-proclaimed vampires work the streets or ride the information superhighway (Fulton 10). Buffy was cool. Vampires rule.

But vampires aren't real! Aren't these people who cut themselves deluded? Benighted? In need of therapy?

Such questions sustain a myriad of cultural productions devoted to the answer. Much is at stake (as it were) in determining an answer to what might seem frivolous questions, inasmuch as the answer often serves to sustain various political positions. Which is to say, if the vampire is not precisely an "identity," it is nevertheless a figure for other identities that claim political status. For example, in his essay "Undead," Ellis Hanson finds the bloodsucker to be, far too often, a monster; that is, he finds a monstrous homophobia coiled within the semiotics of vampirism that makes of "every cocksucker a kind of bloodsucker" (325). But, like those who practice blood sports, Sue-Ellen Case, in "Tracking the Vampire," argues that the vampire is not a monster but a lover. To Case, "the vampire is the queer in the lesbian mode," whose power enables a fantastically empowered lesbian identity (9). In other words, even if identifying yourself as a bloodsucker can be called self-destructive or fantastic, the bloodsucker can also inhabit, as a figure, the logic of "identity politics."

Condemnation, or dismissal, may attend my claim. Identity politics should refer to those groups indebted to what Cindy Patton has called "the liberationist identity-based movements" of U.S. civil rights activism in the '60s and '70s ("Tremble" 145). So to claim that vampires have civil rights can be called irresponsible, trendy, frivolous, even if a logic of vampirism does sustain identitarian projects, since, in order to redress the loss of a group identity or the disruption of a coherent self, the identitarian subject, whether of politics, poetics, or popular psychotherapy, is enjoined to empower a "positive" and "life-affirming" identity by consolidating a self-esteem, but a self-esteem always gained at the expense of another. Even the fabled postmodern fragmented subject can be valorized, so long as it is an "empowering" fragmentation that allows for multiple positions to be inhabited without breakdown. So, while we confess our diversity, the goal remains unification. Hanson and Case give the sucker different evaluative status in their respective essays, but the logic they use to make those evaluations is the same. In each essay, what must be conquered is the loss incurred as the result of another's predation. This loss must be repaired, repaid, confessed, or revenged. And so it would seem that the production of a successful identitarian subject must siphon off loss—and the confusion of internal division or of inauthentic or inaccessible strategies of representation—and at the same time nurse, and thus reproduce, the outrage targeted for elimination.

In other words, the critical outrage against predation so evident in arguments such as Hanson's ends up being hyperbolic and painfully flawed because it pays only lip service to its own professed political allegiances. Hanson wants, after all, to disable the deadly cultural linking of homosexuality with vampirism. This is, he says, a task made urgent by HIV/AIDS activism. Certainly the logic of a 1993 CDC poster, in which a Gothic-revival casement features fog, a full moon, and an incoming bat juxtaposed with the legend BEWARE FLY BY NIGHT RELATIONSHIPS AIDS and, in smaller type, the words *see the light*, activates the bloodsucker as a figure of lethal violence: a vampire's victims always die, even if they die into a new life. The CDC poster was *supposed* to do a public service for the common good of U.S. citizens. It was designed to provide a widely accessible, prophylactic message against disease; everybody can "read" the vampire bat, can't they?

Yet, knowing with what virulence gay men have been attacked for an imagined promiscuity, one also knows how this representation amplifies homophobia. To combat such unconfessed homophobia, Hanson insists that trope and reality must not be confused. His argument discriminates between a real friendship with someone who has AIDS and his readerly relationship to the vampire by distinguishing between what he sees as living phenomenal history and mere trope. Using that distinction, Hanson writes that his friend "Richard simply does not have what I was led to believe was the 'Face of AIDS.' Richard's face looks the same to me as it always had and always will. Rather charming" (338). Angry at the mid- to late '80s representations of PWAs and the way in which a semiotics of monstrosity laced these portrayals, Hanson's essay locates the "real" of his experience outside the falsity of trope.

But to stay always charmingly the same is one of the curses of the undead, as the film *Interview with the Vampire* reminds us when the child-vampire, Claudia, cries out, "Which of you made of me this thing that cannot change?" If her state of perpetual childhood is presented as horrible, it is also her charm. To assault or despair of monstrosity, it would seem, also asserts a longing for the seductive potency of the monster's promising, unchanging, presumably ahistorical charm. Because he assumes that language and living are somehow distinct from one another, Hanson repeats and preserves the trope he wishes to disable. The living history of his friend Richard's face bears a permanent charm—an attribute of the undead—through the agency of Hanson's prose. And while charm may be an excellent quality, is it really so pure or innocent as to be devoid of ambivalence?

That is, although both Prince Charming and Count Dracula may seem childish, both are figures for (nominally) heterosexual seduction fantasies rooted in a history of blooded and bloody aristocratic privilege and the politics of colonial imperialism. There is nothing ahistorical or harmless about them—or about any figure or figure of speech, no matter how innocent or productive or positive the intended use might be. A language bears a history of use, and no matter how familiarized, commodified, or domesticated that history, it also bears the supposedly superseded violences of the past that have been compacted into it. The violence of the past may be forgotten—or, as is more often the case in political registers, denied—but it can also be rearticulated and reproduced through the agency of those same figures. As Haraway says, although she wants to be on the side of the vampire, "Since when does one get to choose which vampire will trouble one's dreams?" ("Modest" 264).

And yet treating experience and trope as polar opposites became a common—and, I would argue, quite dangerous—critical move in the 1990s. Discursive theory is inattentive to material reality, we were told. Aligning the experiential with an intimate knowledge other than that being peddled by so-called elitist academic or philosophical abstraction became a proliferative claim, and these claims echoed Hanson's insistence that history lives while trope is dead. An unquestionable reality had been distorted by the formal, fatal, and politically suspect operations of metaphor and abstraction. In short, complexity, ambiguity, ambivalence (theory) sucks.

Admittedly, Ellis Hanson's essay does not take aim at any of these things, particularly not at that vaguely defined baggy-monster theory. Yet the underlying logic of "Undead" depends on an appeal to a phantasmic coherence of meaning when it imagines that the ambivalence of a word not only can be but will be halted by a reality so completely evident as to lie beyond the darkness of semiosis and the suspect intrigues of that abstract interpretative practice some have called "difference criticism," or the politics of difference.[11] But if poststructuralist difference criticism (theory) is only dead abstractionism or reanimated New Critical formalism, would something called "sameness criticism" give us an alternative rhetoric? And what would that alternative be? Is it to be found in the universal Human? How would we all just *know*, as if by common sense, the inherent goodness of this sameness, this humanness?[12] Let us suppose, for a moment, that sameness—as in the Human with a capital *H*—should be revived. Haven't we been uselessly bickering about difference for over three decades now? Can we all just glow together, like the luminous humans we are?

Of course not. To claim to be merely human, as Haraway's enumerative particularities are meant to signify, can be and has been a racist, homophobic, and misogynist claim. Few would argue that the concept of the Human does not carry a history of past violences along with it. But do we believe, then, after all is said and done, that white people just aren't the same as black people and girls are just different from boys? Polls, essays, books, even comic strips tell us so. In other words, how is it that the concept of diversity has been neatly disengaged from any complex consideration of how *difference* comes to be at all? How is it that *diversity* now appears to denote nothing more than acceptable stylistic or cultural variations on the theme Human? Why do we celebrate this sameness without much argument? Or if we do argue, we are called querulous, elitist, post-structuralist. So while sameness may be contingent upon a recognition of difference (as in the lip service offered by a self-reflexive confession), any conceptual density that one might find in difference has been effaced. And it is this flattening effect that produces an utter clarity of meaning. Hanson's essay offers us a partial recognition that clarity is achieved only through commonsense, popular use, inasmuch as his argument depends on an audience whose common sense tells them that vampires *are* monsters. Yet if this is so, if vampires are clearly readable as monsters, then it should also stand to reason that to be this accessible, clear, and unambiguous about meaning is precisely to deny the pertinence of multiple readings or to accord very little value to ambiguity or, in effect, to eradicate the conflict of interpretation and thus, perhaps, to court an absolutism regarding interpretation that may be worthy of the slur *fascistic*, if one stops to consider the dictatorial nature of demanding that all readers understand a story, or a picture, in the exactly same manner. To demand that all writers write "clearly," without stopping to consider the question, What is clear?—is this not policing? In other words, if vampirism is unarguably as monstrous as Hanson claims, then Sue-Ellen Case must be crazy, unless all lesbians are monsters. It stands to reason, given the nature of his argument, that Hanson would not want to say such a thing. But when the baby of ambiguity, made redolent with the stench of bourgeois elitism, has been thrown out with the bathwater of post-structuralism, there isn't going to be much room for an argument that engages *both* Hanson and Case. One of them will simply have to be right and the other wrong.

I hasten to add that I am not arguing with the idea that language and power go hand in hand or that complex, complicated terminology can be alienating. But by downsizing our language and calling that diminishment a gain in "accessibility," poverty is made a virtue. Language surely consolidates power, but to move from that statement to a wholesale condemnation of linguistic complexity is a mistake. If an alternate rhetoric offers a ringing clarity in the stead of ambiguity, and if that clarity also brooks no interpretative leeway, no hint of double entendre or the simple potential for confusion, what have we gained except a new (old) orthodoxy?

The Jargon of Authenticity

It is painfully easy to see how the complex history and political goals of the civil rights movement have been reduced to political correctness, if complexity itself has been made a monster. Although a synonym for *complexity* is *heterogeneity*, during the late 1980s and early 1990s *complexity* became a synonym for *theory*, and theory, we are told, is jargon, and jargon sucks because it is the professional babble of experts who use big complicated words such as *heinous* instead of simple meaningful ones such as *suck*. Many bytes have been consumed by the argument that accessible language rather than jargon should be the proper mode for authentic communication. Given just how often calls for some pure form of emotional or historical verity are driven by the assumption that verbal complexity is synonymous with obscurity, this assumption represents one of the most outrageous problems for both critical and political engagement, because a politics premised on the authenticity of an identity that is demonstrable primarily through the voicing of an authentic "voice" often and ironically provides the means to sustain a modernist, industrial logic of scarcity, inasmuch as the commonsense version of identity politics often provides the very means by which the logic of capitalism continues its devastating economic operations. That is, if the logic of capitalism (to return to Marx's metaphoric ground) is vampiric, then it depends on an inexhaustible source of "new" victims who will, no matter what differences can be made visible among them, remain structured into the economic system as victims until and unless that economic system is razed. The victim-laborer can raise an authentic voice to shout back at capital, as collective labor does when it says to the capitalist, "I demand . . . a working day of normal length, and I demand it without any appeal to your heart, for in money matters sentiment is out of place. You may be a model citizen, perhaps a member of the Society for the Prevention of Cruelty to Animals, and in the odor of sanctity to boot; but the thing that you represent face to face with me has no heart in its breast. That which seems to throb there is my own heart-beating," but, as Marx notes in this verbal exchange, "force decides" (259) where force resides in the continued ability of capital to act vampiric, sucking collective labor dry. In other words, industrial capitalist (vampire) logic allows for "an" other only as structural victim, despite the seeming multiplicity of othernesses that have been generated since at least (if not before) the 1970s. And, like it or not, the by-now traditional political and cultural rhetoric of "minority" identity is the spawn of a capitalist system.

Cultural viability for such identities is presented in public discourse as dependent on the capital resources with which to make a (clear) authentic voice heard, which in turn is imagined as a power, in and of itself. For example, the Uncommon Clout MasterCard's plea entreated me to support my community by contributing to causes the market imagined *should* be mine: feminist, environmentalist, or gay and lesbian organizations. Never mind that to say lesbians and gays form "a" community, or that this is "my" community, or that these organizations have political goals in common remains cause for dissent, especially if one act confers the entirety of an identity before the law— say, for example, the act of fellatio. Or is this Latinate term jargon? Is "sucking dick" more accessible? And often it is one single mode or act that confers a legal identity. For despite Haraway's neurotic listing of the many sociocultural placements she inhabits, the logic of race on a birth certificate still offers only limited and limiting legal choices to what some call the multiracial. And the logic of gender on that same document offers little to the ambiguously sexed, who are routinely submitted to "corrective" surgery at birth so that they might better fit the M or the F box. Indeed, these limitations have been vociferously upheld by those who fear that offering the category multiracial will reduce the political clout of a minority population. And then there are sodomy laws, which depend on criminalizing an act— say, technically, cunnilingus—that in turn defines both the accused and the accuser, as Janet Halley has argued in "The Construction of Heterosexuality" (87). Such singularity is the why, wrote Michael Warner, of the anti-essentialist, anti-assimilationist term *Queer*. Queer opposes a state apparatus that has room only for the Other. Still, as Warner says, "people worry that the political experience of lesbians and gays is being trivialized. Through the rhetoric of queer, they say, straight people score coolness points without suffering" ("Something Queer" 16). The urgent political demands for gay and lesbian equality have been diluted, some have said, by this use of an empty term that has no real identitarian referent. Everybody and nobody is or can be queer.[13]

Meanwhile, in the public academy, programs tied to identitarian logic are pitted unsentimentally against one another for pieces of shrinking budgets. A comment about these laughable education budgets appeared in June 1996 when New York State's Republican governor George Pataki's Division of the Budget (better known as DOB) passed a $63.7 billion dollar budget that provided only a starvation sustenance to SUNY's already strapped higher education system; curiously, under the "State University of New York" entry in the budget, a $30,000 fake appropriation read: "Department of Biology—Student Using Corroborated Knowledge Satisfactorily," or DOB SUCKS ("Hidden Message"). Nothing more than a prank, according to newspapers and the governor's office, the joking message is canny. It points out the fundable worth of already corroborated, already accessible knowledge, and it may be no accident that the discipline named here is biology (the body? blood?), a discipline that is often characterized, in popular discourse, as being about "reality" and therefore regarded as more relevant to everyday life than other disciplines, as in, for example, how the supposed biological necessity of reproduction is offered as proof of the naturalness of heterosexuality or how genitalia supposedly secure the reality of gender, despite historical physical evidence and argument to the contrary.

In fact, identitarian rhetoric has had to pump up the supposed unnatural violence of loss in order to support claims that a more acute representation of the real, the intimate, the accessible, or the authentic is available, somewhere. An always more real authentic is waiting round the corner to be discovered. Enabled by the shaping force of a desire either to embody, or to own, or to represent the pragmatic potency of a knowledge designated as relevant—while simultaneously refusing to recognize that violence is necessary to the project of distinguishing between the relevant and immaterial, between belief and make-believe—the concept of an "authentic identity" still organized most coalition politics of the late twentieth century and continues to in the early twenty-first. How often is an audience told "Until you've walked a mile in my shoes, don't pretend to know what this is like for me?"[14] My point here is not to invalidate the painful fact that nobody can walk that last long mile for you whether that mile leads to a nursing home, to the gas chamber, or head-first into a tree. My point is that no matter what the specific content of an "it" might be, knowing what "it" is like and being able to claim "it" as a particular experience have been a canny political strategy, a useful strategy, but one that has also served to shore up the idea that information is capital. If we are indeed living in a post-everything-but-information techno-economy, it would stand to reason that generating information particular to you and indeed more or less inaccessible to others except through you (for a fee) appears to be a secure investment. It could mean that you have a corner on the market, and, as the fairy tale of the free market tells us, competition for that corner provides an expansion of the already rich mixture of cultural wealth in this society. More voice. More choice.

The problem is that some rather historically predictable choices and voices are being muffled or snuffed out. I could enumerate several, but let me consider just one here: a U.S. military service person's medical choice of an intact D and E as a late-term abortion procedure.[15] The procedure was proscribed by a Senate judiciary committee in 1996 amid virulent (and ongoing) debate, in which the procedure was tagged as "brain-sucking," and one woman who had undergone the procedure was called an "exterminator" and "part of some perverted cult" (Alterman 39). Such rhetoric has already proved useful in other bans of this procedure, particularly in light of the AMA's approval of such bans,[16] although the AMA has also found its membership still riven over the issue, with some physicians going to court to challenge the federal Partial Birth Abortion Ban Act in 2003.

Indeed, as the life blood of our civil liberties (including medical care and privacy) is drained away, much blood continues to be spilled over the question, Who sucks? in order to provide some with aid (middle-class tax exemptions, capital gains increases) and others (read the lazy, poor, incarcerated, unwed, or populations otherwise deemed unproductive) with meet discipline. Or, in order to legitimate certain "serious" causes that have real consequences for real people and to hasten those loony, ludic post-structuralist decadents to their just demise. The painful irony here is in how easily the political logic of individual rights, once used to combat invidious or unjust discrimination, is now often also used as the logic by which certain forms of social injustice are reinstituted or maintained.

"Take care of him. He bites."

This painful irony has not gone unnoticed, of course, particularly in the wake of 9/11. Politicians and critics alike continue to search for a way around or through the logical binaries of identity politics and yet argue for its continued necessity. Essentialism was offered as one provisional political strategy, often associated with Gayatri Spivak and Stephen Heath, who have argued that the "risk of essence" is necessary, the unavoidable use of something dangerous. Spivak insists that essentialism and identity are not the same and that essentialism should be regarded as a provisional strategy, "something one cannot not use," akin, perhaps, to using a live virus as a vaccination. It can backfire. Indeed, Spivak warns that often "it's the idea of a *strategy* that has been forgotten" and a "strategy is not a theory" (*Outside* 4–5). Unfortunately, however, strategic essentialism is sometimes used as if it were a theory rather than a strategy, familiar to the point of being too comfortable.[17]

"How shall I put you at your ease?" asks Brad Pitt's Louis de Pointe du Lac of his interviewer, played by Christian Slater. "Shall we begin like David Copperfield, 'When I was born'? Or when I was reborn, into the dark life?" Seeking narrative ease for a twentieth-century American audience, Louis finds Charles Dickens. Indeed, Dickens was never far away from *Interview with the Vampire*, either as a film or as a novel. Anne Rice has been called by her editor at Knopf a cross between "Charles Dickens and a rock-star" (Ginsberg 24), and *Rolling Stone's* Peter Travers notes what Kirsten Dunst says, as the vampire-child Claudia, at her first taste of blood: "I want some more."[18] These bald Dickensian echoes rely on a cultural currency, a reassuring familiarity: if everyone, as I've noted earlier, knows Dracula, isn't Dickens, too, a household name?

But then again, how easy, after all, is Dickens to read? How accessible? In one sense, the answer to that question is simple: Dickens has been everywhere in American popular culture. By the time most of us graduate high school, we have been acquainted with Mr. Dickens in some fashion. But might not these Dickensian echoes function equally as warning signs, the ambivalent effects of which are similar to those of the placard Mr. Murdstone affixes to David Copperfield's back, the placard that reads: "Take care of him. He bites" (94). To "take care" is a cautionary statement; and in the American slang of the 1930s, to which *sucker* belongs, to take care of someone was synonymous with "rub out." And yet the injunction of the placard invites one to be a heroic rescuer, a role as seductively familiar as the vampire's own exterminating one.

Such commonly understood, accessible inscriptions can produce both communal anxiety and community, as a Hallmark card of a baby at the breast might, if its multiple resonances were not blocked by common sense. Copperfield, as Daniel Cottom writes in *Text and Culture*, "has been marked a deviant—even questioned as to his species [and] tormented . . . by the fact of other readings, by the fact that different readings create a cacophony of stresses on a text, all of which seem directed against him"; moreover, according to Cottom, these stresses situate him as if he had become an object "weighed, bought, delivered and paid for" (144–45). D. A. Miller argues that the placard "imposes on him the forfeiture of even linguistic subjectivity, its reduction to the pronoun of the nonperson," giving Copperfield "more grounds for panic than he knows" (192–220). Eve Kosofsky Sedgwick writes in *Tendencies* that Copperfield's position demonstrates "the aptitude of the child's body to represent the fears, furies, appetites and losses of the people around it" (199). Sedgwick's recourse to the pronominal *it* would seem to further underscore the "thingness" that both Cottom and Miller stress.

And yet, doesn't this cacophony of stresses also speak about David Copperfield, both the novel and the character? In other words, as inhuman or nonperson, the *he* of the placard may reside in what Judith Butler has described as a "domain of abject beings," in which "the abject designates here precisely those 'unlivable' and 'uninhabitable' zones of social life which are nevertheless densely populated by those who do not enjoy the status of the subject" (Butler, *Bodies* 3); however, what if the dreaded general acclamation Copperfield fancies in this scene should make of him not only an abject being but also a cynosure, the object of fascination? Why does this acclamation not name him as the "he" who is at the center of the school's attention, those five-and-forty all speaking of him, taking care of him? Both Cottom and Miller stress the potential for loss in this moment. Indeed, Miller's argument suggests that only a noun can provide personhood, despite the way in which the English pronoun *he* does indicate a grammatically gendered subject position. That is, despite the anxiety of expulsion that Miller sees here, is there not, also, an urgency of interpretation? Here is the passage in question:

> There was an old door in the playground, on which the boys had a custom of carving their names. It was completely covered with such inscriptions. In my dread at the end of the vacation and their coming back, I could not read a boy's name without inquiry in what tone and with what emphasis *he* would read "Take care of him. He bites." There was one boy—a certain J. Steerforth—who cut his name very deep and very often, who, I conceived, would read it in a rather strong voice, and afterwards pull my hair. There was another boy, one Tommy Traddles, who I dreaded would make a game of it, and pretend to be dreadfully frightened of me. There was a third, George Demple, who I fancied would sing it. I have looked, a little shrinking creature, at that door, until the owners of all the names—there were five and forty of them in the school then, Mr. Mell said—seemed to send me to Coventry by general acclamation, and to cry out, each in his own way, "Take care of him. He bites." (94)

If the names on this door do threaten Copperfield with expulsion and deviancy, don't these names also cry out a general acclamation directed at Copperfield? As a result of his own sign of expulsion, Copperfield is urged to creativity and inquiry. You might say he becomes dreadfully curious. Because of his own painfully exposed position, he is moved to conceive of Steerforth as strong, Traddles as a tease, and Demple as a songbird. Read in this way, dread and punishment are anticipatory, even productive. And as Sedgwick writes, such a scenario denotes "the learned misrecognition of injury as nurture," a misrecognition that can serve to "propel the maturing child toward a position of sadism and cultural authority" (*Tendencies* 199). As such, "Take care of him. He bites" becomes a crib for reading the oh-so-familiar vampire. That is, the bloodsucker is a consummate figure for both sadism and cultural authority.

Logically then, both categories with which I began this chapter, childhood and vampirism, are dreadful and common, familiar and sadistic, or, to put this another way, no matter how common or comforting we find the domestic, the familiar, the accessible, and the clear, they aren't safe. Clarity won't remove the semiotic dangers of slippage or the ambiguity of language. The domestic doesn't exorcise excitation; it is the *venue* of excitation. Reading is as potentially violent as sucking. And, in a political community envisaged as a democracy wherein the late nineteenth-century drive to establish free public schools took on the ability to read as one of their primary missions, reading is, like sucking, something we are all supposed to have in common. The bloodsucker, as a figure of common violence, is, like the suckling child, a violence-marked legible body, endlessly readable despite persistent and sometimes well-meaning attempts to forestall the multiplicity of interpretation. In fact, when Hanson concludes "Undead," he does so with the proviso that he thinks "there is much more to be said about homophobia and AIDS hysteria. . . . I might have addressed issues of race, class, female sexuality, AIDS in Africa and *children who bite in public schools*" (325, my emphasis). This list's length and breadth seem almost as eager to be comprehensive as Haraway's self-nomination; moreover, the list both returns us to the public school and suggests that if to be seen as legible is to be as open as a book, exposed to public violence—to be a sucker?—it is, as well, to be widely and wildly available, to be an incitement or a lure. It is this wide and wild availability that is discernible in Hanson's eagerness to prove that his argument could "take care" of an endlessly expanding list of political issues. Bluntly: a suckling child is not innocent; charm is vampiric, wishes to the contrary notwithstanding.

Who Sucks?

Many will insist, perhaps, that there must be *some* verifiable means by which to discriminate, some clear sign that what you have before you is, without a shade of doubt, an *evil* bloodsucker. Knowing who has actually done whom the dirtiest is to be able to blast a homophobe or singe a cocksucker with the exhilarating fire of denunciation, pungent even when polite. Politicians and priests, activists and academics, all call for the blood of their enemy while also denying that they themselves are out for blood. Indeed, as Cindy Patton writes in "Tremble Hetero Swine," radical political conservatism availed itself of identitarian logic, arming itself with "a new-right identity" that carefully "occup[ies] the hazardous space of being able to 'know it when you see it' while evading the charge that 'it takes one to know one'" (144–49). So Patton moves that we should recognize how "the referents of identities are now less important than the capacity to look like an identity" (161). Patton's insistence that ontology is no longer relevant puts the emphasis on "looking like," which would seem, once again, to raise the specter of Haraway's hopeful vampire (or universal Human), that arch-chameleon, everywhere and nowhere, infiltrating and polluting any pure category. Indeed, according to transgender Internet enthusiast Alluquere Rosanne (Sandy) Stone, the vampire sees "identity as performance, as play, as wrench in the smooth gears of the social apparatus of vision . . . sees the play of identity from the metalevel, sees the fragrant possibilities of multiple voice and subject position, the endless refraction of desire. . . . Ultimately the gaze of the vampire is our own transfigured and transfiguring vision. Claiming that vision is our task and our celebration" (183). Except to look like an identity can work only if "to look like" and "to be" remain secure in their opposition. No matter how fine the capacity for acting, "to be" is still imagined as the locus of reality, while "to look like" is fakery; one is natural, the other unnatural, even if you flip the equation and claim that vampirism, masquerade, play, and multiplicity are, in the era of the computer, arenas of the natural, as Stone knows only too well when she/he reiterates the worn-out commonplace that we live in "a moment which simultaneously holds immense threat and immense promise" (183). Impostors who look like an identity can be routed (or outed) for threatening, damaging, or insulting those who "are really," especially when the law condones, even seeks, such (r)outings. Identity theft is a crime, period.

Indeed, the discourses that have refused to address the brutal internal conflicts of identity, the disquietude of ambiguity, and, in the end, the sometimes violent and contradictory nature of democracy are not only those that require the "reality" of psychic wholeness or political coherence or the verity of historical materialism, but also those critical discourses that have sought to "celebrate" partiality, play, and multiplicity. If, as I remarked earlier, Sedgwick uses vampirism to damn "our culture," she does so because

> its epistemological economy depends, not on a reserve force of labor, but on a reserve force of information always maintained in readiness to be presumed upon—through jokey allusion, through the semiotic paraphernalia of "sophistication"—and yet poised also in equal readiness to be disappeared at any moment. . . . The "knowingness" most at the heart of this system is the reserve force of information about gay lives, histories, oppressions, cultures, and sexual acts—a copia of lore that our public culture sucks sumptuously at but steadfastly refuses any responsibility to acknowledge. (*Tendencies* 222)

This elegant condemnation sets a singular, homogeneous, and vampiric culture apart from the scrumptious plurality of lives, histories, oppressions, cultures, and sexual acts in order both to condemn our public culture and to argue that acknowledgment of this feeding is a responsibility that the dynamic of sucker and sucked lacks. But how would acknowledgment assuage or even excuse the hunger? For if, as Jacques Derrida has argued, "One eats [the other] regardless and lets oneself be eaten by him. . . . One never eats entirely on one's own . . . and in all differences, ruptures and wars (one might even say wars of religion) 'eating well' is at stake" ("Eating Well" 282), then sucking can't be condemned because it is constitutive. When we engage in condemnation, what often isn't confessed is the frisson one can get from the act of condemning another or the safety that some imagine comes from naming names and thus absolving yourself, for example, if you had answered the question, Are you now or have you ever been a member of the Communist Party? in the 1950s by turning over the friends of your youth to HUAC (the House Un-American

Committee) in order to purchase your own immunity. Or you have the nasty pleasure of sinking your teeth into a scandal, even given the pain it can cause. There is a comforting social illusion of safety in owning the proper ID papers when the police show up at the door; that driver's license and social security number pinpoint a socially identifiable "you," even when those papers can exact, by their very certitude about you, that which might be called a socially constituted, sometimes unconscious, self-loathing or, in certain political circumstances, that which allows the authorities to haul you off to an internment camp. Better to be a bloodsucker than a nobody.[19]

So, instead of grappling with the constitutive perversity of identification and desire, many opt either for revenge or for the cushioning illusion of a cure. Self-Mutilators Anonymous offers one such cure, designed for those who are "living with SIV (Self-Inflicted Violence)" (Eurydice 111), a '90s syndrome that bears a linguistic proximity to HIV and, in that proximity, illuminates how discourses that insist on a rationality of plenitude can entertain the vicious notion that HIV/AIDS is a matter of choice, thus self-inflicted. Indeed, the idea that SIV is located only among those who would wound themselves with needles and knives overlooks how any form of bodily alteration or disease, such as cancer, is open to blame. Almost any disease or condition can now be described as self-inflicted; the *Boston Globe,* for example, characterized Mickey Mantle's death as the result of "self-inflicted liver disease and cancer." Is this not malicious, to blame the dead for their own mortality? Does it not imply, as well, that to be alive at all is self-abuse, since living results in bodily alteration, from routine dental care to invasive surgery? By living, "the" body consumes itself. Extending this logic, then, and coupling it with the economic fact that postindustrial capital continues to depend on a denied abstraction (the concept of "the" other), we needn't wonder that critical and political discourse would have every "body" be Human (and/or Vampiric).

Such universalism signals the return of a unified and manifest "reality," out from under pressures begun by structuralist inquiries and then debated within and amplified by post-structuralism. And this renewed universalist logic indicates how a purged version of identity, one indebted to a form of residual structuralist thought, is abroad in popular and even, at times, critical discourse. Freud provided a spatial model of the psyche, a nonunified psyche structured by the fracturing and destabilizing function of the unconscious. Today, concepts from this model often are taken for granted, sometimes in the guise of simple common sense, and yet, at the same time, the model itself has been stabilized, flattened out, with the unconscious "forgotten" as necessary or important. Thus the structuralist concept of a universal Human subject, a most useful concept for capitalism that has been historically bound to the binary logic of Christian humanist philosophy and to the principles undergirding post-Enlightenment politics, remains alive and at large but shorn now of even its originary haunting inadequacies and stripped of any messy post-structuralist interventions that might complicate the picture. For despite a rhetoric of pluralism—of feminisms, ethnicities, or orientations—identitarian logic depends on the violent, differentiating concept of "an" other, "the" Other with a capital O, a phantasmic, homogeneous Other. Given this situation, I would argue that it is an ever more pressing task to reexamine once again the sustained attacks on post-structuralist "theory." Indeed, I would argue that the survival of "the" other, unnuanced, even when studiously ignored or denied, is one reason why monsters have made such a spectacular appearance in both critical discourse and popular culture. Monsters must exist, not in order to remind us of our own alterity, or of the necessary mortifying alienation in language—of being in the symbolic—but because we have come to believe we need an enemy in order to survive.

If the vampire and the child are figures for the real in the symbolic, figures for that which is both in us and not us, what Lacan called the "extimate," they should remind us that while we might indeed share the same structure of social and phantasmic identity (as child or vampire), that structure is itself defined by alterity. It is the extimate, writes Jacques-Alain Miller, that "makes the other Other, i.e. what makes it particular, different, and in this dimension of alterity of the Other, we find war...and it does not seem to me that any of the generous and universal discourses on the theme of 'we are all fellow beings,' have any effectiveness concerning the question" (125). It is, in other words, precisely to these unfathomable yet necessary reaches of alienating alterity that sympathy, empathy, and the concept of the universal Human simply cannot, and should not, go. Because without the constitutive psychic alienation to which the Lacanian concept of the Other points, we would be able to achieve an intimacy so intimate that it lacked nothing. We would lack lack and so become, at last, complete—as in dead. Not, indeed, as in the undead. If the semiotics of vampirism have been used against the deadly lure of intimacies with the hated Other, those semiotics also serve to indicate the necessary fatality of sameness; or, as Chris Craft notes, in *Dracula* "a dangerous sameness waits behind difference; tooth, stake, and hypodermic needle, it would seem, all share a point" (236). The point shared is lack, that which is both in us and not us.

We may prefer to forget that language is a sharp, uncertain, and communal tool. We may prefer to ignore its discriminatory, painful, cutting ability. We may hope to avoid knowing that it is through language that we become at once ourselves and alien to ourselves. We may try to blunt the point, to render language clear, as invisible as the vampire in the mirror. But if we refuse ambiguity in the name of accessibility, if we make complexity into jargon, what have we achieved? I think the answer is impoverishment. For if we are all common mortal humans and, as such, are all suckers, this pointed resemblance among us, whether defined as dangerous or as a cause for celebration, remains a linguistic necessity in order for us to constitute the parameters of difference and the parameters of any democratically conceived community as we currently understand it. Sameness is/is not difference. Ought that sameness be so reduced as to admit of no *différance*?

Bombshell: Marilyn Monroe. Courtesy AP/Worldwide Photos.

bombshell

Va-Va-Boom!

Shocking, stunning, shattering: so a literal bombshell might be described. Low, vulgar, silly: these words, on the other hand, characterize a rather different sort of bombshell, that of the 1950s burlesque, va-va-voom! variety. American tabloid news reminded readers of these differences in December 1998 with headlines such as the *New York Post's* "BOMBS AND BOMBSHELLS."[1] Such headlines linked the bombing of Iraq to William Clinton's presidential slouch toward impeachment; they also made former White House intern Monica Lewinsky's name a household word, at least for a time.

A bombshell, however, like a bomb, can explode. Curiously, the bombshell-as-woman seldom explodes with what many might call any serious effect. That is, although the word *bombshell* indicates potential violence, it also serves to sediment a common sense about sex and violence in which the former is life-affirming (the innocent child at the breast, the legitimate outcome of heterosexual congress) and the latter is deadly (a vampire). Connections between sex and violence continue to be understood popularly as criminal or aberrant—indeed, vampiric—rather than as prevalent or constitutive. So

69

although popular discourse continues to produce the idea of a cultural "war between the sexes," this war is usually treated as more of a joke than a problem, even if the conflict is frequently refracted through furious debates about domestic battery, rape, abortion, equal rights, gay/lesbian/transgender activism, and discrimination.[2] In the face of dispute, common sense maintains that sex, however potentially dangerous, is an insignificant "affair," unless, of course, undertaken as the labor of reproducing the race. When compared with the serious business of running America, sex is seen as a frivolous distraction.[3]

Therefore, although the 1998 visual joke of Moni-lyn—Monica Lewinsky's face superimposed on the famous *Seven Year Itch* costume Marilyn Monroe wore on the New York subway grate—was designed to inflame "serious" political opinion by pointing out how President Clinton tried to cast himself in the role of another infamous john/ John,[4] neither President Clinton nor President Kennedy is easily associated with the belittling frivolity that a Moni-lyn suggests. This is not to say that Clinton escaped from his rather too public affair untouched; unlike the press in the 1960s, which shielded JFK's so-called personal peccadilloes from public scrutiny, newspapers in the 1990s did not hesitate to call Clinton a bimbo. Yet regardless of such invective, in the end, the bombshell is the one who remained the fool. In fact, common knowledge tells us the meaning inherent in the epithet "Moni-lyn" or "Monroe" and, by extension, "bombshell": "hussy," "kewpie doll," "a slatternly mother in a trailer camp," "zombie," "dingbat," "troublesome bitch."[5] The bombshell may be as volatile as "the bouquet of a fireworks display," even a gold mine of monetary profit or political currency, but she's also just a joke.[6] We all know that a bombshell is just a "fat cheesy slut" because that's just plain old common sense.[7]

Bomb and *bombshell*: these words are linked. They are also disarticulated from one another, so that the *bomb* in the *bombshell* betokens an explosive potentiality that lies dormant. The bombshell may locate a culturally designated site of violence—she knocks your socks off, she knocks you off your feet, she knocks you for a loop, she can even knock you senseless. But a bombshell also, simultaneously, induces an enabling amnesia about that violence—she's not likely, all references to bombs aside, to take you out permanently (or to knock you up, even if recent reproductive technologies make such a statement at least theoretically possible).[8]

Indeed, while I will argue that the bombshell, as a word and as a figure, is troubled by an underlying traumatic knowledge of what Lacan calls the Real, a knowledge that leaves its trace in language, I also propose that at the same time *bombshell* activates an amnesiac common sense that substitutes *for* that traumatic knowledge. Using this description, one could also argue that the bombshell functions as a cultural fetish. Surely the seemingly endless commodity fetishization of Marilyn Monroe™ might provide evidence for such a claim: once you've entered "Marilyn Country" (Baty 4) you'll find her on your lips and in your hair, on your tie or in your underwear. Like the figure of the vampire to which she compared herself (Monroe 27), as noted in the chapter "sucker," she is everywhere and nowhere, "a figurative effect of a modernist, rational, capital economy" and "a meet emblem of technologies of reproduction: of cinema, video and the Internet." And certainly a discussion of how the name "Marilyn Monroe" functions—as a cultural reference for the bombshell and as a site for both the creation and continuation of commonsense American narratives about sexuality, frivolity, and fatality—is of central importance to my argument. However, I am ultimately more interested in the word *bombshell* itself, because the continued circulation of this arguably outdated American word both reveals and reveils an ongoing common sense about sex, race, and violence, a common sense that remains necessary to the continuing composition of the United States as a democratic nation-state, a late-capitalist economy, and an "imagined community," the so-called promised land of the American dream.

Indeed, a word such as *bombshell* helps to create the impression that common sense itself is natural and universal. And in the early twenty-first century, this impression is perpetuated by both activist and reactionary discourse, inasmuch as demands for clarity treat language as so "common" as to be universally understood or so "intimate" as to be transparent. Such demands appeal to a most disabling and yet familiar form of humanist universalism, as I discussed in the chapter "sucker": one that has the power to deny and forget the sociopolitical history of conflict in America and the key role that language plays in the split structure of the psyche. The common sense that common sense is natural, universal, and does not need to be learned or reinforced grants a recalcitrant endurance to long-standing modes of injustice and inequity, economic, legal, and social.

Furthermore, by constituting what will be considered commonly understood or useful as opposed to recondite or frivolous knowledge,[9] common sense also secures what can be understood in general as recognizable knowledge, through which a primarily conservative balance of sociopolitical power in the capitalist democracy of the United States has been maintained, at least since the mid-1970s. This does not mean that common sense is immutable. One can sketch out historical mutations. And yet, common sense aids in the endurance of ideological "truths" that discourage the production of new knowledge and retard significant political change.

One can see the recalcitrant effects of common sense in how most recent versions of historicism increasingly seem unable to address— at least in any politically meaningful way—the endurance of basic inequities that common sense so effectively sustains. Critical debates about cultural studies, or about history, or about the role of politics in the academy over the last three decades have produced, among other effects, a new positivism: a strenuously renewed faith in hard, reproducible, scientific or material fact. I do not mean to quarrel about the value of researching, recounting, and interpreting historical change. Such historicism remains immensely valuable, and in this argument I rely on the important archival work of others. But more often than not, "historical" arguments fail to grapple with the persistence of ideological vision that enduring modes of common sense can achieve. For example, history suggests that *bombshell* is really only a silly relic of the past, meant simply as a joking insult. But why does the bombshell remain at all and as a commonsense joke? Why, despite the feminist activism of the late 1960s and the 1970s, despite the so-called sexual revolution of those years, and despite later ongoing attempts to alter or intervene in the repeated fetishization of "the" body as a biological site of indisputable verity—the contestation of the (supposedly) Freudian dictum of anatomy as destiny—does a commonplace such as *bombshell* survive?

What the bombshell indicates, I will argue, is how "the" body remains a taken-for-granted source of inevitable and irreversible fact and therefore fate, not only through the modality of commonsense adage or fashion, but also through the tried-and-true wisdom of an ongoing Cartesian duality that attempts to situate the body as a mere "object" that bears little or no relation to the "mind." For example, we all know, don't we, that (well-endowed) blondes are just dumb? And that they have more fun because gentlemen, often to their own fatal demise, prefer them? Once called a bombshell, any woman can be immediately associated with sex, stupidity, and, finally, with at least the potential for criminal or negligent behavior.

One needs, of course, to remember that since at least the nineteenth century in the United States, anyone publicly associated with sex—or with a disciplinary practice of the body not linked to a sport traditionally understood as masculine and competitive—is swiftly characterized as empty-headed, loose, or dumb and as potentially dangerous (although this has been changing with the increased popularity of weight lifting for both men and women).[10] Yet, this association between sex and stupidity, too, is just history, is it not? Surely we've come "a long way, baby" since the nineteenth century? Such an observation, however, still doesn't offer an answer for why *bombshell* can circulate as shorthand for a plausible common sense about the narcissistic frivolity and deadly fatality of (female) sexuality.

So: how can I make the bomb in the bombshell explode, as it were? And might such a detonation effect "a shift in the criteria of plausibility" (Sinfield 822) and so begin to change what can be seen or understood as feasible, either in politics or in everyday exchanges? Can a critical practice ever truly alter that which is too often taken for granted, that which "goes without saying"?

Words such as *bombshell* both store and carry forward common sense, and such words continue to have social and political effects. Even though a word such as *bombshell* might explode the very common sense to which it is attached (i.e., this particular word could reveal how violence is inherent to the formation of gendered, raced subjectivity in a capitalist democracy), it does not. But armed with such an understanding, are we not better able to oblige ourselves to think anew about the old?

Frivolity and Fatality: A Brief History of the Bombshell

In the seventeenth century, the word *bombshell* was coined to name a new weaponry for a kind of warfare in which incendiary vessels fell from the sky. It quickly became idiomatic for any unexpected, upsetting event that befell one, most often news associated with a letter. During the Depression in the United States, *bombshell* also became slang for a dangerous woman, generally a blonde, as in one of its first recorded usages, according to the *OED:* "Bonnie Parker was a rootin', tootin', whiskey-drinking blonde bombshell." Hollywood soon took up the blonde bombshell, and then, during the late 1940s through the early 1960s, brunette, exotic, and ethnic versions (e.g., Jane Russell, Dorothy Dandridge, and Sophia Loren) were also cultivated as complements to or satellites of the white standard of the blonde.[11] Thus while the "bombshell" is part of a racist dynamic,[12] it also signifies another, more literal sort of female "figure": the full-bosomed, narrow-waisted, full-hipped, 36–24–36 hourglass, which became a dominant standard for the fashionable female figure into the early 1960s.[13]

As Susan Bordo has argued, this figure can be read as both a relic of late-Victorian standards of maternal femininity and a reaction against the social and economic extravagances that came to be signified by and associated with the flatter profile of the flapper figure (208). However, upon Marilyn Monroe's death in 1962 a historically significant and rather abrupt interlude occurred in the popularity of the bombshell, blonde or otherwise. Although Hugh Hefner's Playboy bunnies kept large breasts-as-sexual-fetish visible during the 1960s, Hollywood film roles and televisual vehicles already on the wane for actresses who had either been deliberate parodies of Monroe (such as Jayne Mansfield) or had been groomed by the studio to take Monroe's place (e.g., Sheree North, Lee Remick, and Kim Novak) now dried up entirely. Burlesque as a particular circuit of bombshell striptease stage performance began to vanish,[14] while models such as Twiggy and actresses such as Audrey Hepburn and Mia Farrow brought back into prominence the gamine, the waifish, and a kind of slim elegance not seen prevalently since the 1920s (Brumberg 119–21). Thus, although blondeness as a sign of racial purity did not disappear during the 1960s (one thinks, for example, of Kim Novak), the popular fetishization of the ample hourglass figure that Monroe said would probably be her epitaph—"here lies Marilyn Monroe—38–23–36" (McCann 171)—went into remission.

Such waxing and waning of the fashionable female form, from hourglass amplitude to anorectic slimness, have often been read as a text for the economic cycles of boom and bust that marked the United States throughout the twentieth century. Much has been written about the breast as sexual fetish or as maternal signifier—even if, as I showed in the chapter "sucker," the fetish and the maternal are rarely allowed to occupy the same space. Breasts were particularly important to the boom of post–World War II culture, when Momism was blamed for every social ill under the sun, and no doubt much more could be said about the relation between economic cycles and bodily fixations. But again, what concerns me here is the curious endurance of the bombshell as a sign for both the excessive frivolity and the excessive fatality of (female) sexuality—witness the infamously "late" Marilyn Monroe's wry comments on her cultural status as "the Body," such as: "'Everyone's just laughing at me. I hate it. Big breasts, big ass, big deal. Can't I be anything else?'" (McCann 173); or her observation that her hourglass "numbers" would serve as a most "fitting" obituary.[15] Such statements have served as anecdotal evidence for the circulation of commonsense narratives about the plain dumb idiocy and yet the real, if alien, fatality of flesh, to the point where Monroe's name is shorthand not only for sex but also for both frivolity and flesh, as evidenced by the following quotations taken from two quite different political contexts—the first from conservative critic Barry Sanders, the second from queer theorist Eve Kosofsky Sedgwick:

> The highly literate writer knows how to deconstruct real space and time and reconstruct an imaginary universe through casting counterfactuals: "If Marilyn Monroe were president of the United States." Counter-factuals speak of a supreme, human arrogance, a profane IF set against the intolerable IS of God's creation. But an IF has sufficient power to negate even the fact of Kennedy's presidency with the *delightfully frivolous* notion of Marilyn's. For a moment, Kennedy is placed in doubt, or vanishes altogether. History turns tail and hides; the writer has something better up his sleeve. In our mind's eye we see Marilyn occupying the Oval Office. At this level,

language carries all the dynamic charge of good fiction. (Sanders
55–56, my emphasis)

The Sonnets present fair youth-as-ingenue, as the *prerational, pre-
moral, essentially prehuman creature* that it is not possible to resist,
to understand, or to blame. *Like Marilyn Monroe, the youth makes
the man viewing him feel old*, vitiated, responsible, even as the man
luxuriates in the presence (the almost promise) of youth and self-
possession. (Sedgwick, *Between Men* 43, my emphasis)

Frivolity on the one hand, an alien, prehuman, irresistible fatality on
the other, Monroe is a delightful "doll" who came from "outer space"
(Mills 44), who was also cited for the genius of her flesh impact on
film, an impact that was likened to light itself, to the radiance and
sublime luminosity echoed by descriptions of the first Trinity site tests.

Marilyn Monroe was, of course, deliberately groomed to play (and
helped to produce herself as) the quintessential comic-yet-dangerous
blonde bombshell, even if she did ask Richard Meryman, in her last
interview, not to be made into a thing or a joke. Rendered a commodity, and remembered within that form, the "new blonde bombshell" of 1951 (Mills 25) was the "it girl" of her time; she restaged
Harlow, Dietrich, and Clara Bow; she was "Mae West, Theda Bara and
Bo Peep" (Story 90), a sexual rocket-bomb for the Cold War, atomic-
bomb generation.[16] As photographer Cecil Beaton once enthused,
Monroe was

the wonder of the age. . . . As spectacular as the silvery shower of a
Vesuvius fountain . . . she had rocketed from obscurity to become our
post-war sex symbol—the pin-up girl of an age. And whatever press
agency or manufactured illusion may have lit the fuse, it is her own
weird genius that sustained her flight. . . . She's American and it's very
clear that she is—she's very good that way; one has to be local to be
universal. (quoted in Arnold 32, 71)

Beaton's description pinpoints how Monroe was, as Richard Dyer
notes, not only something like "a household word for sex" (23) but
also an ambiguous, sometimes adored, and often maligned emblem
of a 1950s America, that "blatant decade: cars grew fins; neon signs
became an art form; pop music discovered the electric guitar and turned
into rock and roll; the Yankees won the pennant year after year after
year; and the Russians exploded record mega-tonnage of nuclear

weapons" (Mills 11). She was an American "Saint Marilyn," and yet a "cruel child tearing off butterfly wings...gay, mean, proud and inscrutable" (Rollyson 66); she kept whole film ensembles waiting, or as Billy Wilder once quipped, "You can always figure a Monroe picture runs an extra few hundred thousand because she's coming later. It demoralizes the whole company. It's like trench warfare. You sit and sit, waiting for something to happen. When are the shells going to explode?" (Mills 84).

Thus was Monroe positioned like the atomic bomb itself—"her very body was a white beam of truth" (A. Miller, *Timebends* 370)—as the spectacular best and the spectacular worst the nation had to offer. Indeed, such descriptions of Monroe obsessively situate her, ironically, as if she were yet another American female icon, like Hester Prynne, attached to Art(hur) and wearing the A on her chest: Monroe was seen as absurd, atomic, and American. Absurd as a "frightened waitress in a diner" (Jack Paar), a "baby doll" (Jane Russell), all foam. Yet also dangerously Vesuvian, "a shimmering, molten wraith" (Eve Arnold) with an "electric something...she seemed to shine like the sun" (June Haver); "a flash of white" (Lena Pepitone) with "the face of a beautiful ghost" (Dame Edith Sitwell). Famously, Monroe gave her attention to any information on how to improve one's body. Long before jogging and weight lifting became regular activities for the healthy American woman, Monroe practiced both; she read whatever she could get her hands on about the body, from the Renaissance anatomist Vesalius to Mabel Elsworth Todd's idiosyncratic book, *The Thinking Body* (recommended to her by one of her early drama coaches, Michael Chekhov) (Spoto 190). She was also an all-American, linked, as she was, to baseball through her marriage to Joltin' Joe DiMaggio in 1954 and then to American "high art" when the Bombshell married the Brain, playwright Arthur Miller, in 1956.[17] Photographer Eve Arnold's comments sum up such observations. Monroe, she claims, was regarded as an ordinary girl who became the "icon enshrined in the workman's toolbox" (20), a symbol of democracy. There was

> a glow about her: skin, fingernails, toenails are all translucently silvery.
> Everything about her becomes exaggerated. Finding that her nose
> photographs a bit long, she learns to drop her lip so that the shadow

cast by her nose seems shorter. This gives her a slight tremor, a look
of expectancy that adds to the sexiness. Later she will add the pursed
lips, the open mouth. This so affected her imitators that, going
through fashion pictures of the '50s, you find yourself looking at so
many open-mouthed models who seem to be gasping for breath that
you wonder whether you've wandered into an aquarium. (17)

As American, and as dangerous, as the atom bomb, yet seen as absurd,
mindless, and alien as a fish—or a mermaid[18]—Monroe's treatment
as the bombshell of her time demonstrates that while the very stuff
of reality itself is presumed to preside in "the" body (i.e., a reality so
real that it "goes without saying,"[19] a reality often represented by that
most absolute of realities, death; the body is also the site from which
laughter is launched, a laughter that is the symptom of the knowing-
ness of flesh, the "carnal knowledge" that film captures so well).
because the "body" is not mindless; consciousness and flesh are inter-
dependent, and flesh does "know," it is articulate, it has impact, as
jokes about men who think so much with the head below the belt indicate. *Bombshell* is a signifier of such knowledge, and it participates in
an anxious logic: it points to a commonsense script about sex in
which anyone identified with flesh or sex will be located at the Cartesian ground-zero of the supposedly mindless body, a fatal site at which,
nevertheless, knowledge sits and from which hilarity—or joy—often
erupts.

"She had no common sense."

As an emblem of both hilarity and fatality, then, Monroe exemplified
the joyous, excessive plenty and the deadly price to be paid for the
so-called American dream in the 1950s—or as Arthur Miller writes,
"She knew she could roll into a party like a grenade and wreck com-
placent couples with a smile, and she enjoyed this power, but it also
brought back the old sinister news that nothing whatsoever could
last" (*Timebends* 359). His statement remarks on how Marilyn Monroe
came to define—indeed, inhabit—the word *bombshell* for the post-
war, postatomic generation. At the same time, the statement situates
her as part of a historically older commonsense narrative about "the
beautiful and the damned,"[20] a story of the inevitable demise of

the beautiful or famous, which is, of course, a story about fate, always the fate of Edgar Allan Poe's beautiful woman. The doom-of-fatal-beauty story has well served countless American novelists, dramatists, and filmmakers, from the culturally "serious" domain of Hawthorne and Henry James to mass cultural versions endlessly repeated for a whole range of figures who have died, as the common saying goes, before their time, from Sylvia Plath, whom Jacqueline Rose calls the "Marilyn Monroe of the literati" (Rose 26), to actor River Phoenix.[21] And Monroe's demise did call forth a slew of popular elegies about "the beautiful and the tormented," as *Vogue* described her in Bert Stern's fashion-shoot-turned-memorial, although up to that point, the press had been increasingly hostile to her own attempts to remake herself as something other than the dumb blonde whom gentlemen preferred.[22] Suddenly dead, however, she became the essence of a lost joy.[23] Once no more than a conniving idiot, she was made over into a "lively, intelligent woman" (McCann 1) whose buoyancy about sex had had a "bracing candor" (A. Miller, *Timebends* 381). In death she became the lovely child who had never had the chance to grow up, a psychiatric mess who had needed help and hadn't gotten it.

Indeed, her death at the age of thirty-six from an overdose of barbiturates has been associated with dark conspiracy theories linking Hollywood, Kennedy, the CIA, the FBI, and the Mob. Repeated accusations that the LAPD's original investigation "had not been a marvel of thoroughness" (Weatherby 225) prompted a reinvestigation in the 1980s and have provoked a morass of narratives about "what really happened" the night of August 4, 1962, a night recounted, discussed, and dissected in popular texts such as Anthony Summers's 1985 *Goddess: The Secret Lives of Marilyn Monroe* and Donald H. Wolfe's 1998 *The Last Days of Marilyn Monroe*. Still, the coroner's original legal decision of "probable suicide" stands. None of the nonfictional accounts constructed over the last thirty years—neither those that have quarreled with the story of Monroe's death as preordained nor those that attempt to correct the image of "Little Miss Bubblehead" (Mills 56)—have put much of a dent in the endurance of such commonsense stories about her, even if and when those stories are contradictory. No factual account has set the record straight once and for all, although gradually the various accounts have shifted the ground of common sense about her, from the elegiac version of beauty lost to the more sinister version of beauty murdered.

But whether monster or angel, victim or vamp, Monroe remains also a "candle in the wind" who might have had "a mind out of the ordinary" but didn't have the good sense to come in out of the rain, a basically intelligent woman who lacked that most basic American form of knowledge, common sense: "Many people commented on her quick wit and native intelligence, but no one ever accused her of having any common sense."[24] Arthur Miller also described his wife as having no common sense, as in the quotation that serves as a heading for this section (*Timebends* 359). Yet, for someone who lacked common sense, not only has Monroe-as-bombshell produced *a* common sense, but her life's "story" has also given rise to—and continues to sustain—a lot of common sense. You can try, as Gloria Steinem did, to rescue the supposedly "real" Norma Jeane from the objectification of the Body; you can reprint forensic evidence about official discrepancies extant in the LAPD's investigation, FBI files, and coroner's reports, as *Crypt 33* and *The Last Days of Marilyn Monroe* do;[25] or you can ransack archives; yet despite, or perhaps *because* of, these counternarratives, both the script of fated, narcissistic doom and the force of Monroe-as-floozy—that giggling bombshell whose performances define the meaning of nonsense—remain stubbornly intact.

Makeup

So while we might eventually learn to take some blondes seriously, this particular blonde is not a likely candidate,[26] which doesn't mean, however, that Monroe wasn't and isn't "taken," and quite seriously, if one means by this colloquialism that she's been, like David Copperfield, "taken care of": exploited, dead and alive, for every ounce of flesh and every last dime and nickel. At the same time, it would seem that establishing a truth—whether it be an economic truth about the exploitation of her labor, buried in her bank statements, or a historical truth about her relations with the Kennedy family, buried in an archive, or even the so-called biological truth, or what is left of it, buried in a Westwood, California, cemetery crypt— isn't a particularly effective means to nail down "the" truth. True-life, supposedly real narratives about "Norma Jeane" don't impair the ability of the "Marilyn Monroe" bombshell to signify a common sense that says sex is just naturally frivolous.

As Richard Dyer persuasively demonstrates, Monroe's specific popularity resided in her ability to combine "naturalness *and* overt sexuality, notably in a series of gags that became known as Monroeisms" (133). The ground for this naturalization of sex as frivolous was laid down much earlier than the 1950s, of course, and has had a long half-life since. Significantly, Miller calls his ex-wife a sheer force of nature, "the astonishing signal of liberation and its joys. Out of the muck, the flower"—an observation that is at once couched in the terms of a yet-to-come 1960s sexual revolution but is also lifted almost verbatim from Stephen Crane's first, late nineteenth-century novel, *Maggie: Girl of the Streets* (curious, too, that Miller would choose Maggie for the name of the character who enacts Marilyn in his play *After the Fall*).[27] In fact, Monroe's endurance as a kind of cultural shorthand for the frivolity and fatality encoded in the word *bombshell* should be likened to the endurance of "sex as a political issue," to quote Foucault. Sex, like Monroe as a visual icon, remains too much with us, and if "we as a culture cannot forget Marilyn Monroe, so we make her up again and again" (Baty 4), it seems that what matters is *not* the truth. What matters is the making up.

Now, Monroe may be a rather obvious symbol of "makeup"—by which I mean to indicate both the process of production and a commodity product. But I think it is worth remembering that as cosmetic ad and studio-system product, Monroe was on, and of, the assembly line. Curiously, too, it is worth noting how Antonio Gramsci once argued that the assembly line, a Fordist mode of labor, would require a "new type of man" in whom "the sexual instinct has been suitably regulated and rationalized" (297). He also cautioned that "until women can attain not only a genuine independence in relation to men but also a new way of conceiving themselves and their role in sexual relations, the sexual question will remain" (296). Back in 1931, Gramsci was quite leery of any sexual regulation, because, he said, it could "make way for unhealthy 'feministic' deviations of the worst sense of the word" (298). Despite this statement, however, contemporary feminism might still find his observations about genuine independence rather bracing, given the ongoing global "traffic in women" as reflected by statistics on the rise in sex work, particularly in impoverished countries such as Thailand, or even given the ongoing traffic in Monroe as lucrative commodity.[28]

Yet I would caution, as Karen Newman has argued, that the feminist "reiteration and critique of the exchange paradigm is a disavowal of the object position and at the same time an over-valuing of subjectivity" ("Directing" 50). Using work by both Leo Bersani and Theodor Adorno, Newman demonstrates how feminist arguments that continue to decry the "objectification" of women, of which Monroe is often cited as an example, cannot see how the object position might be made to exert a seductive lure that could potentially shatter the sovereignty assumed to inhere to the subject position. Indeed, Newman's argument not only continues the work begun by Gayle Rubin's influential "Traffic in Women"; it also attempts to break the impasse of the once-fruitful "traffic" paradigm. What is crucial for feminism in Newman's argument, however, is more than simply a paradigm shift. What is at stake is veracity itself.

Why? To begin to explain this claim, I will start with a very bald example. In the legal game of "he said, she said," historically the "she" has had a harder time proving her case, no matter how much she is legally granted the position of enunciating, sovereign subject. This is especially true when both sides of the conversation exert the force of a truth.[29] Such a case might be described, using Lyotard's term, as a *differend*, "a case of conflict between (at least) two parties, that *cannot be equitably resolved* for lack of a rule of judgment applicable to both arguments. One side's legitimacy does not imply the other's lack of legitimacy" (xi); or, as Lyotard argues, a *differend* marks the site of a conflict wherein something true cannot, as yet, be put into words. "What is at stake," he continues, "in a literature, in a philosophy, in a politics perhaps, is to bear witness to differends by finding idioms for them" (xi). What the concept of the *differend* allows for here, in my argument, is the conceptualization of radical alteration whereby a different idiom for "new" truths might be forged and, in turn, disrupt the sediment of inequitable common sense in which a rule of judgment is mired. Or to recur to Michèle Barrett, if it is "better, perhaps, that we oblige ourselves to think with new and more precise concepts, rather than mobilizing the dubious resonances of the old" (*Politics* 168), then the *differend* as a concept, along with Newman's argument, may offer us a means to actually do so, to think new, more precise concepts.

Indeed, one might even pause here to consider if second wave feminism wasn't a site of conflict from which a new idiom about sexual inequality arose in the face of what might have seemed a political *differend*. Although women won the vote in 1921 (after at least a *century* of bitter conflict) and thus gained, in the language of constitutional law, the legal status of full and equal citizens, by the mid-1960s it became more than simply clear to many women that they did not, in fact, enjoy anything like "equal rights" in domains other than that of the Constitution. One might, then, see the conflicts enacted between activists at the time and those who opposed them as conflicts "between (at least) two parties" that could not "*be equitably resolved* for lack of a rule of judgment applicable to both arguments." Feminism might be described, then, as a collection of oppositional idioms, all of which attempted to speak to existing states of inequality (economic, social, and cultural) to find an idiom in which to talk about ongoing sexual exploitations and injustices, an idiom through which increasing voice could be given to previously unvoiced or indeed unvoiceable grievances that could find no means of equitable address under the existing rule of constitutional judgment. Could it not be argued that the public feminism of the mid-1960s to the late 1970s functioned as an aggregate of idioms wherein a prevailing common sense about sex—say, questions about economics or the common sense spelled out by bombshell-as-embodied by Monroe—was once disputed? At least for a time.

At the present moment, however, common sense tells many of us that feminist discourses—third wave or no—are *not* viable as idioms in which to voice oppositional politics in the first decade of the twenty-first century, unless forcing Iraq to include a quota of 25 percent female representation in its provisional constitution can be regarded as feminist. Much feminist terminology, of course, has been incorporated into existing rules of judgment to the extent that an understanding about sexual equality has been woven into the fabric of common sense. Title IX and the resulting rise in women's sports might be construed as a legal result of a new commonsense under-standing about women. And yet, we are told, feminism, *tout court*, is old hat, too narrow, irredeemably classist and racist; oh, and by the way, Marxism, too, is moribund, especially "after the fall" of the Berlin Wall in 1988; and psychoanalysis, well, that's just as dead as poor old Sigmund himself. We don't need any of these "extreme" conceptual idioms anymore. Plain old common sense about such matters now prevails.

Yet take note: in the historical context of these multiple invalida-tions, it is interesting just how often any claim to validity has had to dress itself up as a clearly identifiable "*body* of knowledge" or to offer hard, incontrovertible, scientific, and material evidence, as if in a liti-gation, as in the controversies over whether Nobel Laureate Rigo-berta Menchú and Binjimin Wilkomirski have lied in their widely acclaimed and prize-winning memoirs;[30] has had to appear unified, unambiguous, and objective, to pronounce itself the "real and only truth" as opposed to memory, illusion, or fantasy, even as there is an ever-increasing economic demand for the proliferation and dissemi-nation of information-as-capital, one that requires endless amounts of novelty, of making up.

But again and again, demands are made for the real, the true, the authentic (his)story (Marilyn was a bitch, wasn't she? She was abused, wasn't she? She said as much, didn't she?). Authority and security appear to reside in making these kinds of final judgments, particu-larly through the truth-claims of actual experience. But as critic Patricia Hill Collins notes, authenticity is a "hot commodity," and so "break-ing silence by claiming the authority of experience has less opposi-tional impact than in the past," particularly in the context of a capi-talist political economy, wherein a "synergistic relationship" exists between people and knowledge as commodities, so that "knowledge becomes inseparable from the container in which it is packaged, namely, Black and White bodies" (51). Further, if "reality" as Lyotard has claimed, "is not about what is 'given' to this or that 'subject,' it is a state of the referent (that about which one speaks) which results from the effectuation of establishment procedures defined by a unani-mously agreed-upon protocol" (*Differend* 4), then it would seem imper-ative to change the agreed-upon protocol in a sustained, collective fashion, rather than to continue to produce ever more individual authenticity to fill the needs of the market.

In other words, when reality becomes so utterly transparent as to be rendered only as an unquestionable given, or truth an object subject to no serious dispute, then it is confused with the referent and, as Lyotard notes, "so speaks positivism" (*Differend* 28), a positivism that relies on the essential universality of a commonsense truth—as if the violent breach opened up at the site of the formation of the subject through language might be defused by a utopic fusion whereby the referent is collapsed with the real. And one of the most significant problems posed by such a collapse of referent and reality—or, if you will, a problem posed by the substitution of a universalized common sense for new forms of knowledge—is how the status of "truth" will be determined. For example, the Holocaust, as Jacqueline Rose points out, has often been used as "the historical event which puts under greatest pressure—or is most readily available to put under such pressure—the concept of linguistic figuration." When "faced with the reality of the Holocaust, the idea that there is an irreducibly figurative dimension to all language is an evasion, or denial, of the reality of history itself" (207). But paradoxically, as Lyotard observes, such a positivistic refusal to know the power of language has been used to make the Holocaust itself seem illusory. For example, in 1981, Faurisson claimed:

"I have tried in vain to find a single former deportee capable of proving to me that he had really seen, with his own eyes, a gas chamber." . . . To have "really seen with his own eyes" a gas chamber would be the condition which gives one the authority to say that it exists and to persuade the unbeliever. Yet it is still necessary to prove that the gas chamber was used to kill at the time it was seen. The only acceptable proof that a gas chamber was used to kill is that one died from it. But if one is dead, one cannot testify that it is on account of the gas chamber—The plaintiff complains that he has been fooled about the existence of gas chambers, fooled that is, about the so-called Final Solution. His argument is: in order for a place to be identified as a gas chamber, the only eyewitness I will accept would be a victim of this gas chamber; now, according to my opponent, there is no victim that is not dead; otherwise this gas chamber would not be what he or she claims it to be. There is, therefore, no gas chamber. (*Differend* 3–4)

Part of Lyotard's point is, of course, that Faurisson's demand for authenticity along the most positivistic lines—to really see with one's own eyes a gas chamber from the inside!—nevertheless provides evidence for the frightening power of language. History still is, after all, narrated—as conservative Barry Sanders clearly understands when he writes that one rousing good "if" and "history turns tail and hides; the writer has something better up his sleeve. In our mind's eye we see Marilyn occupying the Oval Office. At this level, language carries all the dynamic charge of good fiction" (56). In this light, fact is *always* a matter of idiom, despite those who devoutly wish otherwise, and so veracity, which depends on what is or will become a matter of fact, remains also a matter of whose history can fit established protocols of adjudication. Marilyn, by all legal rights accorded to her by the Constitution, *could have* occupied the Oval Office; in some stories about her, she virtually did, if she spent time with either RFK or JFK. But she was born a citizen of the United States, and like any other born citizen, she could have grown up to be the president. But that was not her history, and so the picture is mere foolishness—isn't it? But perhaps the more pertinent question here is: Can our daughters ever hope to become president, or is First Lady as far as we'll get with respect to equality?

After the Fall: The Drama

Positivist logic is, after all, a stubborn logic. And history—or experience or autobiography—is judged, especially in the popular press, by positivistic standards. The autobiographical "I," for example, must present an absolute historical veracity, which often depends on the positivist logic of the true, authentic eyewitness, the victim of a proven trauma. Memory and illusion, fantasy and amnesia, these hold no legitimate place. As a result of such logic, however, history, in fiction or poetry, is viewed as "either dearth or surplus, either something missing... or something which shouldn't be there" (Rose 206), and while Jacqueline Rose may refer here specifically to those critiques of Sylvia Plath's poetry that have claimed the poet had no business speaking of Nazism, the same can be said about critiques of Arthur Miller's autobiographical play that isn't supposed to be autobiographical, *After the Fall.* In this play, Miller is said not only to have abused the real Marilyn Monroe by making her over into the likeness of sexpot-songbird Maggie (a version of history as surplus) but also to have trivialized both the atom bomb and the Holocaust by putting sex onstage against the backdrop of Hiroshima and the concentration camps (a version of history as dearth).

Almost more than anyone else who was either associated with or wrote about Monroe, Arthur Miller has been condemned for telling both too, too much and too, too little. Any number of Monroe narratives—from the academic to the pornographic—exist, but Miller's 1962 stage play, *After the Fall,* is still often presumed to be the most tasteless display. So shameless was it considered at the time of its first performance that it was said James Baldwin "was seen stalking up the aisle and out of the theater before the end" (Weatherby 221). Attacked repeatedly as "an exploitative exposé of Miller's relationship with Marilyn Monroe" (Savran 56) in face of the playwright's protest that the play was not autobiographical,[31] *After the Fall* set off a firestorm of press in January 1964, in part because it cannot *not* be read as autobiography, even if it is also clearly a negotiation of "the distinction between autobiography and fiction" (Savran 56).

To be reductive here: common sense insists that nonfiction *must* tell *the* truth, while fiction, instead, must ring true. Even in a publishing era that has seen the rise (and some say fall) of a lucrative genre called creative nonfiction—a form that is, in part, the result of two writers, Truman Capote and Norman Mailer, who also took up Monroe as a subject[32]—*After the Fall,* as a drama, still runs aground on the distinction between fact and fiction. I hasten to add here that I am not arguing for a complete breakdown of that distinction, particularly given the troubling ethics of historical truth. There remains a difference between fact and fiction; gas chambers did exist, Kosovar Albanians have been executed, *Apollo 12* did land on the moon; and autobiography is a genre that presumes to present a historical truth. Drama is presumed to be a performance only. And yet, performance must also have truth, must it not, if it is to be respected or revered? But the autobiographical demands that have been made on *After the Fall* as a *drama* are very curious demands to make about a drama that, from the outset, "takes place in the mind, thought, and memory" of a

retired lawyer, Quentin. Staged as an internal, psychic "trial" of memory that shares its scene of interrogation with that of the "talking
cure," the subject who speaks, Quentin, is split into multiple positions
of enunciation; he investigates himself in an attempt to assimilate
what he finds to be the unassimilable betrayals of history. He wants
to understand his own political and personal history as well as that of
the Holocaust; he wishes to come to terms with traumatic events
through which he has lived and after which, he believes, any prior
concept of personal, sociopolitical, or cultural innocence has been
rendered irrelevant. For Quentin, the fact of the Holocaust and the
fact of America's creation and deployment of the atomic bomb (it is
significant that Miller regards both as central to this play's genesis
[*Timebends* 516]) divide a then from a now. Before Hiroshima and
Nagasaki, before Auschwitz and Dachau, there were the illusions of
progress, innocence, honor; afterward, nothing. The Fordism that saw
a functional apogee in the Nazi concentration camps has left a blank
for Quentin where there was once a meaningful (his)story.[33] As a
lawyer, a proponent of rational discourse, Quentin treats Auschwitz as
if ventriloquizing Adorno, who, as Lyotard remarks, "pointed out that
'Auschwitz' is an abyss in which the philosophical genre of Hegelian
speculative discourse seems to disappear, because the name 'Auschwitz'
invalidates the presupposition of that genre, namely that all that is
real is rational, and all that is rational is real" ("Sign" 162).

Such devastation challenges any rational, universalist narrative
of progress and so challenges all narratives of causation. But while
Quentin appears to know this, he also resists it. He can look "back at
when there seemed to be a kind of plan," when everything seemed so
simple, right and wrong, no confusions, as if it were "some kind of
paradise," and simultaneously seek a cure for the nothingness he knows
is there. As he says, on the day we "stop becoming, . . . the word 'Now'
is like a bomb through the window, and it ticks" (A. Miller, *Fall* 47).
Quentin is referring, here, to his view of his dead wife, Maggie, as the
"Now" of being; she lacked common sense about causality, she lived
"where nothing whatsoever is ordained" (48). But his leap into her
Now reveals to him how the immanence of being is as deadly as a
bomb, because the Now denies the truth that humans are all separate,
murderous beings "after the fall" and all guilty. Desire, or what Quentin

calls the "truth" of "symmetrical, lovely skin, undeniable" (48) as represented by Maggie—"'Cause all I am," she says "... is love. And sex" (124)—becomes as lethal as a nuclear blast if untempered by an acknowledgment of universal guilt. As Quentin says to his terrified, suicidal wife, "If you could only say... I have been hurt by a long line of men but I have cooperated with my persecutors.... Do the hardest thing of all," he exhorts her, "—see your own hatred, and live!" (120).

In Miller's view, then, Maggie lacks a narrative of universal guilt after the fall, and this is, finally, intolerable. Such fatalism is familiarly biblical: Maggie is Eve, and Quentin has fallen into a temptation to forget history—"to violate the past, and the past is holy and its horrors are holiest of all!" (*Fall* 97). But as David Savran notes, when Quentin demands that Maggie understand herself as both the victim and the oppressor, he's created a problem, because "by demanding that oppressor and victim be telescoped into a single figure, *After the Fall* denies historical difference," so that "the concentration camp is simply a grotesque extension of the nuclear family" (70) and historical time becomes the forever Now of sacred time. The play reasserts the necessity of a universalist narrative of (masculinized) wholeness (Savran 71) and thus forecloses the possibility of other stories and different, perhaps as yet unarticulated, idioms. The play would rather reassert a humanist, bourgeois subject, suitably chastened by his guilty contact with the abyss of Now, than face the possibility of the "nothingness" (as Quentin sees it) of being—or "the Real"—that is.

Suicide, in this context, is an outrage and immoral, not because Maggie has died, but because Quentin has made Maggie (Marilyn) solely, sanely, individually *responsible* for her own death and so guilty of both suicide and murder. As Quentin claims, "A suicide kills two people, Maggie.... You've been setting me up for a murder" (*Fall* 116–18). But if, as Michel Foucault has argued, "We ... are ... a society 'with a sexuality'" that has an "insidious presence ... everywhere an object of excitement and fear at the same time" (*History* 148), and therefore a society in which the deployment of sexuality makes suicide both "strange and yet so persistent and constant in its manifestations, and consequently so difficult to explain as being due to particular circumstances or individual accidents" (139), then suicide must be something other than an individual act—as Maggie herself knows when she says, drunkenly, "Takes two to tango, kid" (*Fall* 116). Indeed, as Foucault puts it, suicide is "one of the first astonishments of a society in which political power had assigned itself the task of administering life" (*History* 139). It *must* have as collective a dimension as genocide. Perhaps, then, Maggie/Marilyn's fatality should be read as a symptom of *collective* trauma in a society where sex, unless undertaken as a serious job of reproductive labor, has been naturalized as a mere frivolity.

After the Fall: The Bomb

Indeed, despite the ways in which *After the Fall* bombed as a drama, the "blur [of] the distinction between the political and the domestic" (Savran 61) that it accomplishes by working through the link between society and sexuality, between the Bomb and the Bombshell, might seem strategic: for one thing, the "personal is political" as a radical statement about the frequently occluded relation between the domestic and the political had yet to be a rallying cry in 1964. Forcing a visible, dramatic, even spectacular relation between the effects of the nuclear family and nuclear holocaust, long before Greenham Common, could be read, at this distance, as a necessary move. Given that the possibility of planetary annihilation is part of the narrative of nuclear holocaust and the atomic bomb has been represented as all of humanity's drive toward mass suicide, the connections become harder to disavow. And, as previously noted, Monroe has been obsessively represented in descriptive terms that associate platinum with plutonium; her "whiter than white" radiance is the sublime beauty of an atomic blast. *After the Fall's* attempt to force this association between the bomb and the bombshell to mean something "serious" as opposed to "silly" should therefore not go unremarked. In his psychic fusion of Bombshell with Bomb, Quentin wants to reveal, not only to himself, but also to those with whom he has lived and has internalized as parts of himself, that the presumption of a white-clad innocence in a murderous world is finally more lethal than history itself.

Miller found, however, that this revelation could not unveil America's obsession with the blinding flash of its own treasured fantasy of

political and cultural "pure" innocence and so prove it deadly. Audience and critic alike in 1964 did not accept Miller's truth that innocence is—as Lyotard also notes—a nothing: "It is impossible to establish one's innocence, in and of itself. It is a nothingness" (Lyotard,
Differend 9). But Lyotard's use of the word *nothingness* and Miller's use
of the concept are strikingly different, and this difference, I think, is
crucial. To Miller, like Quentin, nothingness is a complete blank, a
fake, the terrible absence of the Now; to Lyotard innocence is in and
of itself nothing, *not* because it is a fatal blank, but because innocence
must take meaning within a symbolic system. It does not exist as a
universal given outside a system of representation.

Now, according to Miller, his play's reception showed him that "it
was impossible to seriously consider innocence lethal" (*Timebends*
534). Instead, many asserted a "true" Marilyn Monroe over and against
the character Maggie, both because and even though Elia Kazan and
Arthur Miller's staging of Barbara Loden as Maggie—they insisted,
for example, she wear a teased, platinum wig—had made it, in fact,
impossible to disassociate the historical blonde bombshell of 1951
from the lethal, fictional siren of the fatal Now. In this fusion of bomb
with bombshell, *After the Fall* does attempt to reveal that the *jouissance* of sex is a serious matter. But the play also reveils that knowledge in a cloak of common sense. It installs a universal truth about
being and "original sin" as a reality and invokes the seriousness of
death in the form of a suicide in order to dispel the effect of the
bombshell's frivolity. According to Quentin, then, a universal admis-
sion of human hatred must take the place of the innocence—in this
case Maggie's—that is a fatal delusion, a none, a nothing. And surely
Marilyn Monroe had hated to be "taken" as a nothing, "a kind of
joke taking herself seriously" (*Timebends* 532); she wanted to be "taken"
seriously. But, Miller says, "coming out of the forties and the fifties, she
was proof that sexuality and seriousness could not coexist in America's psyche, were hostile, mutually rejecting opposites in fact. At the
end, she had had to give way and go back to swimming naked in a
pool in order to make a picture" (532). Even when "her life would be
taken up by a writer whose stock-in-trade was the joining of sexuality
and the serious...he could only describe what was fundamentally a
merry young whore given to surprising bursts of classy wit" (532).

The professional jealousies and personal aspersions evident in Miller's remarks aside (he is alluding above to Norman Mailer's writing), let us pause here a moment to ask some potentially frivolous questions. Why must one assume that swimming naked in a pool means that Monroe gave way to her status as a joke? What's wrong with being merry about sex? Why isn't laughter a serious matter—why must nothing be, well, *just* nothing, rather than an indication of that which has been socially, politically, and culturally designated as that which is silly and does not matter? We might do well to remember that "philosophical style," as Derrida writes,

> congenitally leads to frivolity. But the reason for this is logical, epistemological, ontological. If philosophical writing is frivolous, that is because the philosopher cannot fulfill his statements. He knows nothing, he has nothing to say, and he complicates, subtilizes, refines stylistic efforts to mask his ignorance. (*Archeology* 125)

Nothing—a space, a gap, a silence, a lack, a blank page, or the force of laughter: surely all, as many feminists have repeatedly claimed, are something?

In *The Four Fundamental Concepts of Psycho-analysis*, Lacan reports a curious anecdote that he insists is "a true story" about himself as a young intellectual who wanted "desperately to get away, see something different, throw [himself] into something practical, something physical, in the country say, or at the sea" (95)—the philosopher throwing himself at nature (or the brain throwing himself at the bombshell?).[34] About one of the fishermen with whom he sets sail, Lacan says:

> Petit-Jean pointed out to me something floating on the surface of the waves. It was a small can, a sardine can. It floated there in the sun, a witness to the canning industry, which we, in fact, were supposed to supply. It glittered in the sun. And Petit-Jean said to me—*"You see that can? Do you see it? Well, it doesn't see you!"* (95)

Petit-Jean finds the winking can's indifference funny, because, as an intellectual, Lacan "appeared to those fellows who were earning their livings with great difficulty, in the struggle with what for them was a pitiless nature ... like nothing on earth" (96). Lacan proceeds, however, to show how the "nothing" of the "I" (eye) illustrates the "relation of the subject with the domain of vision," or as he says, "The picture, certainly, is in my eye. But I am not in the picture" (96). Indeed, the winking can *does* see:

> That which is light looks at me, and by means of that light in the depths of my eye, something is painted. . . . Something that introduces was elided in the geometrical relation—the depth of field, with all its ambiguity and variability, which is in no way mastered by me. It is rather it that grasps me, solicits me at every moment, makes the landscape something other than a landscape, something other than what I have called the picture.
>
> The correlative of the picture, to be situated in the same place as it, that is, outside, is the point of the gaze, while that which forms the mediation from the one to the other, that which is between the two, is something of another nature than geometrical, optical space, something that plays an exactly reverse role, which operates, not because it can be traversed, but on the contrary because it is opaque—I mean the screen. (96)

I cite Lacan at length here because both the anecdotal citation and his psychoanalytic exposition seem peculiarly apt when one recalls that Monroe's "weird genius" was essentially filmic: as a (screen) spectacle of pure light, like the diamond that became her trademark or like the silver nitrate, later platinum, atomic whiteness of her presentation, she is luminosity itself, a necessary and indifferent light that winks, that "space of light . . . that gleam of light" that lay at the heart of Lacan's story—"in short, the point of gaze always participates in the ambiguity of the jewel." And if the point of gaze is in the picture, says Lacan, it is always in the form of the screen—that which is opaque and cannot be traversed (95–97).

If we follow Lacan's logic, Monroe-as-atomic bomb(shell) reads as a filter for how the object (as Karen Newman wishes to insist), and indeed objectification as a process, is central to desire and thus to the formation of the "I." The winking sardine can, that gleam of light— a "witness to the canning industry"—like the bombshell as a word and as a trope, both insists on and studiously blinds us to the knowledge of the necessary flash point of objectification. It does so not only because of the various pertinent historical implications for Americans (for example, any true acknowledgment that people *are* also things raises the specter of slavery) but also because such an acknowledgment, howsoever an understanding of the lack at the heart of signification, strikes at the unifying labor of the Ego and so also at the myth of American individualism. It points to how the sovereign subject, who is supposedly that "unique individual" of universal humanism, like the shining star or the serious artist, is always also, and must be, "taken" as an object. But in a relentless capitalist economy, where the object is always a commodity conceived as a product of exploited labor, it is difficult to know that you are always more a (no)thing than not.

Finally, then, I would argue that the vernacular usage of the bombshell to signify sex naturalized as frivolity both marks and deflects the trauma of the subject's entry into the Symbolic precisely because the common usage and continued circulation of the word *bombshell* serve to deflect an understanding of the bursting violence of *jouissance* at the heart of subjectivity: the necessary trauma that is the violent coming-into-signification formed around the kernel of the Real, in which (sexual) desire is shaped and from which it erupts, like laughter. In the bombshell, and in any attempt to come to terms with it, particularly as exemplified by my discussion of Marilyn Monroe, one finds condensed common sense about the mind and the body, the serious and the frivolous, the factual and the fictional, the lively and the fatal—and how the distinctions among these pairings are at once constructed through reference to (female) sexuality and, in fact, constitute, in no small degree, what is taken *as* that (female) sexuality. Thus the word *bombshell* both conserves and carries forward the common sense that can produce a Moni-lyn in 1998, even as it might also explode that common sense.

But the word will not perform this explosive labor *precisely* because common usage requires us to forget the violence that inheres in it and so, indeed, to forget the shattering, structuring violence of language itself. Instead, the bombshell persists, to haunt the collective imagination: as Sammy Davis Jr. once said, Monroe "hung like a bat in men's minds" (Mills 37); or as S. Paige Baty claims, "Icon, American dream, dangerous passageway, corpse, goddess—she appears in all these forms and more. She radiates the stuff of history in our time, mass-mediated memory" (179). Oddly, however, Baty's concluding claim—and my own, if I should rest here—also seems to go without saying; it bears a curious and wearying intellectual stasis, as if in witness once again to how the radiant bombshell both gives evidence to and yet also carries forward a strenuous historical amnesia of the sort that American common sense now requires. And common sense will try to say that sex without (reproductive) "labor" is mere frivolity, that laughter is nothing, and history, although revered, is dead, while language must always be clear and useful; otherwise it is frivolous, in which case it is recondite. Such commonsense amnesia about the fact that common sense itself is a matter of history and language not only helps to produce universalist illusions but is also necessary for a perpetuation of effects tied to the founding inequities—particularly but not exclusively economic—that subtend the ongoing trauma of the American dream. Might it not be high time, then, to pay much closer attention to what the rocket's red glare says to the world and to hear why the bombs are bursting in air?

THE MOB CHARGING ON A "SCAB."

THE NEW YORK AND BROOKLYN STREET RAILROAD STRIKE.

The Mob Charging on a "Scab." From the Picture Collection, The Branch Libraries, The New York Public Library, Astor, Lenox and Tilden Foundations.

scab

There is no word in the English language so irritating as the word scab.

—*New York Evening Journal*, November 26, 1909

When, in *The Diary of a Shirtwaist Striker*, twentieth-century writer–labor activist Theresa S. Malkiel has her fictional diarist ask, "I wonder who was the first to use the name scab?" her character muses, "By Jove, it's the right one at that; nobody clean could be mean enough to step into somebody else's shoes" (84). In fact, according to the *OED*, the first recorded use of the word *scab* occurred around AD 1250, and it meant then what it still means, as Malkiel's diarist well knew: a blemish or crust on the skin, associated with diseases such as leprosy, scabies, eczema, and mange, which is why the diarist exclaims that nobody clean could become a strikebreaker. In the nineteenth and the early twentieth centuries, a diseased body betokened an impure or scandalous character, often associated with sin, sexual perversion, or sexually transmitted diseases such as syphilis.[1] By 1529, *scab* had begun to acquire this secondary meaning in England, where it became slang for a rascal or scoundrel: "Love is such a proud scab,

97

that he will never meddle with foules or children," showing, of course, that the tie between sex/"love" and disease/"scoundrel" continued to play across the meaning of *scab*. The first recorded use of *scab* for a strikebreaker did not officially make its appearance in the United States until 1806, at a trial of striking boot and shoemakers: to behave as a "scab" or "blackleg" was to step into the boots of the bootmakers. It also had a verbal form: *to scab* a job, that is, to perform, or employ another to perform, the job of a striking worker. As *The Lexicon of Labor* tidily reports:

> Scab was used in England by 1590 for a "despicable person in the Colonies." It has meant a shirker since 1690 and by 1806 acquired its current labor connotation. The phrase "to scab on" has been used since 1917. The term originally is from the Scandinavian scab and is "akin to the Latin scabies/scabere, mange." (Murray 160)

"The laborer who gives more time or strength or skill for the same wage than another, or equal time or strength or skill for a less wage, is a scab," said Jack London, to the Oakland Socialist Party Local on April 5, 1903. "It is not nice to be a scab. Not only is it not in good social taste and comradeship, but, from the standpoint of food and shelter, it is bad business policy. Nobody desires to scab, to give most for least." London, a socialist, had his eye on more than simply the individual scab; he also commented on the political effects of capitalism as an economic system, that is, the economic competition among nations that impeded the formation of international socialism, when he extended his description of a scab to argue that

> the role of scab passes beyond the individual. Just as individuals scab on other individuals, so do groups scab on other groups. And the principle involved is precisely the same as in the case of the simple labor scab. A group, in the nature of its organization, is often compelled to give most for least, and, so doing, to strike at the life of another group. At the present moment all Europe is appalled by that colossal scab, the United States.

From blemish (scabies) to heartbreaker (love's such a proud scab) to strikebreaker, the history of the word *scab*, like the word *sucker*, shows a displacement of meaning from the visceral or physical to the moral register; and yet the physical register, as metaphor, still inhabits the word, as it does *sucker*. Just as a scab is a physical lesion, the strike-breaking scab disfigures the social body of labor—both the solidarity of workers and the dignity of work. As Malkiel's diarist writes of the scab Mame, "The scab on the body, as a rule, comes from hunger and privation, but with Mame it is nothing but a case of sheer cussedness. She's just a mean, vile, paltry scab from scabby land!" (108).

Moreover, if, as classic Marxism insists, labor under capitalism is that which is most one's own yet most taken away, scabbed labor is a site of trauma. Prison labor is essentially scab labor; prisoners are routinely exploited as a "scab" workforce. Such a practice sprang up directly after the Civil War, when unpaid slave labor was no longer legally available. The criminal justice system stepped in to provide, so that any person found to be a vagrant (i.e., landless) could be arrested and sentenced to hard labor—thus assuring the South a new if old population of African-American laborers. Today, prison chain gangs, which had virtually vanished during the late 1960s and the '70s, have been revived by a number of states, and although equal opportunity may elude women in other spheres, the all-female chain gang was instituted in Alabama in 1996 as an equal-opportunity punishment.[2] Such prison labor, as unpaid labor, indeed hearkens back to the way in which slave labor and indentured servitude, modes of labor with which the United States was first built, were lifelong and wounding punishments to those enslaved or virtually enslaved, as well as a serious blemish on the political experiment of representative democracy; or as Herman Melville wrote during the Civil War, the American experiment from the outset seemed "the world's fairest hope / linked with man's foulest crime" ("Misgivings" 13).

Today, however, scab labor is an all-too-common feature of work: both labor and management expect an available scab force to materialize, either during a strike, in the form of workers who refuse unionization, or under the institutionalized rubric of "outsourcing." Indeed, although the political voice of the union can and does still speak and speak loudly against the scab, to scab barely causes anything like a social murmur. As Paul Le Blanc points out, the U.S. federal government's policy over the last four years has increased the vulnerability of many workers, especially undocumented immigrants who fear deportation and those forced into welfare reform programs such as "workfare" (124). In 1996, according to Jacqueline Jones, "public and private employers alike prepared to reduce their unionized labor forces through attrition in order to make way for 'workfare' employees. For the most part, an apparently indifferent public, composed of all kinds of workers fearful of losing their own jobs, shrugged off predictions of the impending immiseration of hundreds of thousands of mothers and their children" (381). So, Le Blanc writes, "it remains to be seen to what extent the promise of democracy—rule by the people—will become a living reality in the new century" (133), given that "the devolution of federal responsibility for the poor to states was matched by an expanding power among individual corporations to seek out and hire the most tractable workforces possible, and to extract from those workers the highest rates of productivity at the lowest possible wages" (Jones 382). However, as Jones notes, most workers in the United States today are content either to perform or to endure scab labor, so long as they continue working. Thus, unlike the words *sucker* and *nigger*, which can still be flung into everyday conversation like bombshells (depending on who uses the words and how they are used), and unlike the 1990s political reactivation of the term *bombshell*, *scab* doesn't perform at the same level of rhetorical labor as it did at the dawn of the twentieth century, when it was considered a term so vile as to cause shame, so politically and emotionally charged that it could be called the most irritating word in the English language. Although its political power has not vanished, unlike that of the word *bloomer*, the political and social significance of *scab* seems to have been softened, despite the term's continued use by labor unions and labor activists, who frequently cite Jack London's fiercely visceral definition of a scab, such as in the following:

> Scabs have been called many things by many people during the course of labor history but Jack London's description of the scab, "written with barbed wire on sandpaper," easily dwarfs all others. "After God finished the rattlesnake, the toad, the vampire, He had some awful substance left with which He made a scab. A scab is a two-legged animal with a cork-screw soul, a water-logged brain, a combination backbone of jelly and glue. Where others have hearts, he carries a tumor of rotten principles. When a scab comes down the street, men turn their backs and angels weep in heaven, and the Devil shuts the gates of Hell to keep him out. No man has a right to scab so long as there is a pool of water to drown his carcass in, or a rope long enough

to hang his body with. Judas Iscariot was a gentleman compared with a scab. For betraying his master, he had character enough to hang himself. A scab has not. Esau sold his birthright for a mess of pottage. Judas Iscariot sold his Savior for thirty pieces of silver. Benedict Arnold sold his country for a promise of a commission in the British Army. The modern strikebreaker sells his birthright, his country, his wife, his children and his fellow men for an unfulfilled promise from his employer, trust or corporation. Esau was a traitor to himself: Judas Iscariot was a traitor to his God: Benedict Arnold was a traitor to his country: a strikebreaker is a traitor to his God, his country, his wife, his family and his class."[3]

I quote London at length to demonstrate the level of fight this fighting word once put up. London, the socialist, seeking to make an impact on his audience, invokes both a Christian, moral register and a patriotic register: rattlesnake, vampire, toad, traitor, but scab exceeds all: a scab is a tumorous traitor whom even the devil scorns. Labor's epithets for the scab in the early twentieth century strove to reach the lowest, filthiest depths imaginable in order to underscore just how unclean the scab must be to do what the scab would do.

In this chapter, I will explore (primarily through a reexamination of Theodore Dreiser's *Sister Carrie*) how a new common sense about gender and labor arose in the United States in the early twentieth century; the next chapter, "nigger," then, will explore the concomitant "new" common sense about race and labor. This new common sense would eventuate in an ongoing junction and disjunction between work and words. In this chapter, I will argue that the word *scab* once served not only to mark the site of social and political conflict about labor but also to mark out how the gender of labor was changing as the workforce expanded to meet the needs of industrialization, mass marketing, and mass consumption. Such rapid expansion required the alteration of an earlier, nineteenth-century common sense about the "working man," as women, immigrants, and African-American laborers joined the paid labor pool. In order to manage the tensions brought about by such change, an ideological suturing of the past to the future had to take place, a suturing that altered older and increasingly destabilized beliefs about absolute gender (and in the next chapter racial) differences, yet left certain aspects of these beliefs in place. Therefore, as I noted in my introduction, rather than allowing for the possibility of radical social change, this ideological suturing reconstituted gender and race boundaries in a new common sense about labor. For if older beliefs based on nineteenth-century concepts of physiology, propriety, and "blood" became unsustainable, they were also necessary to the maintenance of a white, capitalist middle class that understood itself as superior. Thus, prior ideological certainties or common sense knowledge(s) about emotionally charged aspects of social and political life (such as the proper gender division of labor, the idea of raced capabilities, and the so-called natural tendencies of various ethnic groups) changed in order to allow for a rapid expansion of both an industrialized labor pool and commodity consumption. However, the new common sense would see to it that some certainties would not change *too much*.

Indeed, Jack London knew that capitalism, precisely because it relies on exploitation, would secure a common sense that would restrict significant social change when he wrote in "The Scab":

> In the social jungle, everybody is preying upon everybody else. . . .
> The woman stenographer or bookkeeper who receives forty dollars
> per month where a man was receiving seventy-five is a scab. So is
> the woman who does a man's work at a weaving-machine, and the
> child who goes into the mill or factory. . . . *The scab is everywhere.*
> The professional strike-breakers, who as a class receive large wages,
> will scab on one another, while scab unions are even formed to pre-
> vent scabbing upon scabs. (my emphasis)

Under the logic of late-industrial, global capitalism, at the turn of the twentieth to the twenty-first century, *everyone* is a scab. And once the scab is everywhere, the word must, perforce, lose its ability to locate and name the "other" as a dangerous creature, a vampire, or a villain—although I hasten to note, as I argued in the chapter "sucker," vampirism remains with us as a kind of common knowledge, short-hand to describe that which is calculated and powerful, or evil and attractive, or fatal yet eternal. The scab, on the other hand, is the fading linguistic scar left by the vampire of capital: a once viable, visceral sign, now drained of its most bloody meanings, which attests to Slavoj Žižek's insistence that "the real 'living dead' are we, common mortals" (220–21). There is, as Jack London already knew in 1903, no one left in late-industrial, twenty-first-century capital who has not been bitten—as the relative weakness of a once-powerful fighting word such as *scab* shows. It isn't as if a scab has been rehabilitated. No. But the puss and guts of a scab have been tidied up, at least in the United States, by the global expansion of capital.

Word Work and the Wages of Sin

A scab is someone caught at the flash point of contestation, the embodied agent and target of labor disputes. Significantly, the word implies no particularity of personhood besides that of work: a scab can be male or female and of any ethnicity or race. A scab can be anyone who would step into a striking worker's shoes. Of course, during the latter half of the nineteenth and the early part of the twentieth centuries, after the Civil War and before the outbreak of World War I, working conditions were poor and wages for any average laborer in the United States, male or female, were appallingly low; by the dawn of the twentieth century, labor activism, as well as international pressure with respect to what are now termed human rights, had brought about a public, sometimes violent, debate about labor, working conditions, and the rights of workers. Moreover, as both Michael Perelman in *The Invention of Capitalism* and Alan Trachtenberg, along different lines, in *The Incorporation of America* note, to work for a wage was a means of remuneration slow to be regarded as natural in either the United States or Britain. Indeed, before and during the Civil War, slavocrats, who in addition to being opposed to abolition were opposed to Northern-style industrial labor, called working for a daily or hourly wage "wage slave labor" or "industrial slavery."[4] And while capitalism was the economic system of the United States, it was by no means taken for granted as the best or most appropriate system. Even Abraham Lincoln—sounding curiously like Karl Marx—once argued that "labor is prior to, and independent of, capital; in fact, capital is the fruit of labor and could never have existed if labor had not first existed; labor can exist without capital, but capital could never have existed without labor. Hence . . . labor is the superior, greatly superior, to capital" (156).

Of course, by the end of the nineteenth century, most laborers in the United States did work for an hourly wage, particularly those employed in the industrial sector. As urban populations surged and as women in particular (white, immigrant, and African-American) entered the workforce in record numbers, they slowly began to join forces in order to better their circumstances. Between 1900 and 1919, the National Labor Union and the National Colored Labor Union gained membership; the IWW (sometimes vilified as the I Won't Work party) was formed; the Uprising of the 20,000 as well as the subsequent, infamous New York Triangle Shirtwaist Company disaster riveted the public's attention; and across the globe, in Russia, Japan, Germany, and Mexico, newly formed women's groups, such as the Japanese Seitoscha (Blue Stockings), were springing up.

But "working girls" had been working for the wages of sin on city and country streets in the United States long before the twentieth century dawned. Indeed, one of the social dilemmas young working women faced when entering the workforce during these decades was how to be able to distinguish themselves socially, publicly, and politically from a different sort of "working girl." As Nan Enstad remarks, "Shirtwaist picketers regularly encountered accusations or insinuations that they were prostitutes; their public activity called into question their sexual respectability" (91–92). Indeed, as Enstad reports, women strikers were often represented by the police and the popular press as "public women," and public women were vilified as impure or unnatural, which women abolitionists and Bloomerites and those involved in the women's rights movement during the second half of the nineteenth century already knew. In the early twentieth century, streetwalkers and strikers had become, according to Enstad, synonymous, just as bloomers had come to signify a certain kind of indecency some sixty years prior to the Uprising of the 20,000 in New York City. Of course in 1910, when anarchist Emma Goldman's essay "The Traffic in Women" first appeared, published by her own press, the Mother Earth Publishing Association, the suffrage for which women such as Elizabeth Cady Stanton and Amelia Bloomer had fought had not yet been achieved, nor did all women concerned with achieving the right to be "public" understand suffrage as key to their aim. Goldman, opposed as she was to all forms of organized government, certainly did not.[5]

But one of the most challenging claims for the middle class that Goldman set forth in the course of "The Traffic in Women" is that "the economic and social inferiority of woman" (177) was responsible for prostitution. Loudly decried in the press as the new "white slave traffic" by Christian reform workers and politicians, the "problem" of prostitution often served as a convenient screen for other middle-class "respectable" concerns about sexuality, labor, and the law. Not only did Goldman's argument raise the stakes of the debate, but she also tore away the polite screen of middle-class decency, particularly when she quoted sexologist Havelock Ellis:

> The wife who married for money, compared with the prostitute... is the true scab. She is paid less, gives more in return in labor and care, and is absolutely bound to her master. The prostitute never signs away the right over her own person, she retains her freedom and personal rights, nor is she always compelled to submit to man's embrace. (183)

Ellis's use of the word *scab* in this context compels attention, since it might seem that a scab would have little to do with a wife who married for money. And yet, given the sexual politics subtending the division of labor under capitalism in the early twentieth century, the economic system that shaped the industrial era in the United States, *scab* seems only too appropriate to describe a person who has no rights independent of her master, not to mention the term's ongoing implication of prostitution via the association of *scab* with disease. Thus did Ellis and Goldman pursue the links between gender and labor, not only in the domain of economics, but also in the social and moral registers by noting that any marriage contracted under circumstances of financial need or gain is the moral equivalent of prostitution, because a prostitute "properly defined is any person for whom sexual relationships are subordinated to gain" (Goldman 182). The practices of providing a dowry and marrying "up" were used as evidence. Goldman also argued, "Marriage is the goal of every girl... [but] thousands of girls cannot marry... [and] our stupid social customs condemn them either to a life of celibacy or prostitution" (182). Thus for Goldman,

all women, no matter what their race or social position, were func-
tionally prostitutes (unless they remained celibate, as perforce Carrie
is at the end of Dreiser's novel). As Goldman asked:

> What is really the cause of the trade in women? Not merely white
> women, but yellow and black as well. Exploitation, of course; the
> merciless Moloch of capitalism that fattens on underpaid labor, thus
> driving thousands of women and girls into prostitution. . . . Nowhere
> is woman treated according to the merit of her work, but rather as a
> sex. (176)

The only means of eradicating the "oldest profession," she claimed,
was "a complete transvaluation of all accepted values—especially
the moral ones—coupled with the abolition of industrial slavery"
(189). But such a complete transvaluation of accepted values and abolition of industrial slavery have not yet, a century later, taken place;
from the 1950s Marilyn Monroe vehicle *How to Marry a Millionaire* to
one of the television events of 2000, *Who Wants to Marry a Millionaire?* American popular culture suggests that marriage and prostitution
remain two sides of the same coin, although the rate of inflation has
so grown since 1956 that anyone marrying for a million these days
could be said to be selling himself or herself short.[6]

Therefore, by stigmatizing the middle-class wife with the vile name
of scab in 1910, Goldman not only brought street conflict into the
middle-class household, as newspaper reports could or as narratives
such as *Sister Carrie* and *The Diary of a Shirtwaist Striker* might have;[7]
she also inserted the scab into the ideological heart of the household,
as if to force the middle class to confront the social and political
trauma that the scab represented. As if, in fact, to keep open the
wound the scab might have been perceived, from the perspective of
management, to heal: like a physiological scab, scab labor might have
seemed, to the middle class, to stem a resource drain (capital/blood).
Scabs would, like Hurstwood in *Sister Carrie*, keep the trains running
or, like Mame in the *Shirtwaist Striker*, keep the sewing machines
humming, so that the husband could get to his office and the wife to
her clothes shopping. But the conflicts sparked by scab labor, as Goldman would have insisted, only deepened the wounds, particularly
during a strike—another word, as Alan Trachtenberg writes, that

ran deep in the history of work, naming a variety of simple, basic acts in the crafts of carpentry, surveying, bricklaying, tanning, farming, shipbuilding, fishing and sailing. Directly from the nautical meaning of lowering sails or taking down, and more generally unfixing and putting out of use, the term began to appear early in the industrial era in its familiar sense of work stoppage. To strike work or tools was to assert the power of workers over the process of production: to strike was, in short, an act of work, albeit negative. (89)

Of course, one of the other circumstances to which Emma Goldman speaks indirectly in her 1910 screed against marriage is that more and more women of the time—white, black, multiracial, ethnic, immigrant—were entering the workforce. Indeed, during the early part of the twentieth century, not only was the so-called laboring class expanding to meet the needs of the new corporate industrialism, but also the "face" of labor was in the process of changing its racial and gendered makeup. Such expansion soon required an alteration of a ruling common sense with respect to race, gender, and ethnicity. If not, the economy threatened to grind to a halt—or explode. As Alan Trachtenberg points out:

> By the late 1880s... the industrial working class took on a distinctly "foreign" cast with heavy immigration from Catholic and Slavic nations... and increasing ethnic diversity and the making of a new industrial working class constituted a single process, introducing cultural difference into American life on an unprecedented scale.... Work was often dirty, backbreaking, and frustrating. Working women and children seemed at odds with middle-class ideals of home and school. In the popular press, workers found themselves stereotyped as the unwashed, unenlightened masses, swayed by disreputable-looking bomb throwers and associated with brutish caricatures of Irish potato-eaters, slow-witted Slovaks, fun-loving Italians. On every count, labor seemed to represent a foreign culture, alien to American values epitomized by successful representatives of capital. (88)

Such introduction of cultural, ethnic, and racial difference obviously caused increasing amounts of tension and conflict as workers struggled to achieve what America had seemed to promise them: self-sufficiency, self-respect, and a living wage. Such conflict increasingly sparked resistance and civil unrest. As Jacqueline Jones writes, "Between 1870 and 1930, transformations in the 'racial' division of labor resulted from the initiative of black men and women themselves," since white employers frequently resisted hiring the "1.5 million black southerners who migrated from the South into northern cities between 1916 and 1930 to take jobs in steel mills and meatpacking plants, on auto assembly lines and in garment factories." Thus, according to Jones, "industrial expansion followed an uneven and bloody course, characterized not only by technological innovation but also by traditional, and coercive means of labor deployment" (302–3). African-Americans, sore pressed to achieve better lives than what sharecropping or domestic servitude could provide, frequently sought out new opportunities, even if that involved scabbing in order to get a foot in a door.

What kind of social change would emerge from this struggle and how the social and political fabric of the United States might be altered, however, remained a source of tension, debate, and violence, one that late nineteenth- and early twentieth-century narratives, especially those that understood themselves as naturalist or realist, treated or managed, as Amy Kaplan argues in *The Social Construction of American Realism*. Realism, as a narrative form, functions very much as common sense does, as "a strategy for imagining and managing the threats of social change—not just to assert a dominant power but often to assuage fears of powerlessness" (10). Writers such as Wharton and Dreiser came into a market in which the novel, particularly the realist/naturalist novel, had to compete in an industrialized, expanded mass market of magazines, dime novels, newspapers, and the like.[8] Although these conditions had existed since the mid-nineteenth century, mass production in the early part of the twentieth century grew at a much faster rate than in earlier years. Indeed, as industrialization changed production and consumption patterns with respect to clothing (see the chapter "bloomers") and other newly mass-produced items, produced in the home as late as the end of the nineteenth century, so too did the publishing industry change. Cheaper means of reproduction coupled with a growing literacy rate provided a changing marketplace for novels, which diversified the nature of the novel altogether.[9] A narrative that would sell big to a mass audience became as necessary to the marketplace as the cultural maintenance of a "tasteful" distance between the masses and the moneyed, the low and the high.

But how to retain the author as a cultural arbiter, a unique "genius," while demanding that the author have a professional writing "career" that involved the masses? Subject to the mass market, the author increasingly became a figure cognate with the industrial laborer, even as authors such as Dreiser sought to maintain the cultural status of authorship as something above the fray. Anxious that writing, like other forms of manual labor, might become mere drudgery, authors sought both to expose the devastating effects of industrialized labor and at the same time to hold out the possibility that there would be some form of labor that would not eat the self alive, such as the labor of knowledge production or the labor of art. However, the artist in a capitalist economy does work for a wage, even if the work might appear to serve as an escape hatch from the grinding demands of industrial capitalism. As Jack London said,

> When a publisher offers an author better royalties than other publishers have been paying him, he is scabbing on those other publishers. The reporter on a newspaper, who feels he should be receiving a larger salary for his work, says so, and is shown the door, is replaced by a reporter who is a scab; whereupon, when the belly-need presses, the displaced reporter goes to another paper and scabs himself.

Thus while I agree that realist/naturalist texts such as *Sister Carrie* both display and contain the potential for social change, I would also argue that such stabilizing narratives did help to neutralize images of more radical social, political, and psychic transformation, for example, of the sort imagined by other narratives of this time, such as *The Diary of a Shirtwaist Striker*. Realists may have assuaged fears of (middle-class) powerlessness, but in so doing they downplayed, and eventually helped to foreclose, more radical images of social and psychic change, which were available in fictions of the time. As editor Françoise Basch notes, avowedly socialist fiction such as Malkiel's was created and circulated in the early 1900s but has been critically dismissed as bad writing, "or at best regarded as 'a piece of socialist propaganda'" (Malkiel 62), thus assuring the narrative's virtual absence from the rolls of American realism/naturalism. *Sister Carrie*, on the other hand, is often said to represent American realism/naturalism, even if the novel was not received in its own time as literary but rather as crude and unpleasant materialistic truth. Of this novel, critic Stanley Corkin writes:

> When *Sister Carrie* appeared in 1900, it was into a nation in the midst of a fundamental economic and social upheaval, as the complementary processes of industrialization and urbanization were altering the way in which individuals worked, lived, and, ultimately, the way in which they conceived of themselves and the world. (606)

Corkin put his finger on the historical pulse of why this text remains important. But just what kind of society would this fundamental economic and social upheaval create? What new world would be conceived? Why, for example, did such wholesale change in the way individuals worked and lived produce a consumer society and not "'a work-centered way of seeing the world' moving decisively beyond a consumption-oriented 'what's in it for me' outlook that pits various workers, factories, unions, and communities against each other"? (Le Blanc 132). After all, capital expansion did spawn social change: populations were displaced, women entered the workforce in record numbers, and once again commonsense narratives about charged aspects of social and political life were thrown into conflict. However, the potential for a collective, labor-oriented self, embodied by the kind of working, pro-union real(ist) girl did not become the dominant vision. This union girl did not assuage the (capitalist) middle class. Sister Carrie, on the other hand, no matter how morally scandalous to that same middle class in 1900,[10] was the kind of real(ist) consumer girl who, in the end, did become a dominant vision, by offering a picture of the working girl who didn't really "work," which allowed for an ideological reconstitution of gender boundaries in a new common sense about femininity wherein a woman could enter the labor pool without being presumed a prostitute, thus maintaining an older idea: that a proper middle-class woman was and would always be a lady, not a vamp.

Whose Reality?

In *Sister Carrie,* Dreiser created one of the more poignant and conflicted fictional portraits of a scab in the character of Hurstwood, Sister Carrie's would-be but never quite (by law) husband. G. W. Hurstwood scabs during one of the more critically debated chapters of this novel, "The Strike," which recounts an infamous motorman work stoppage in Brooklyn. At this point in the novel, Hurstwood's downward trajectory toward suicide is well underway, as is Caroline Meeber's (Madenda's) rise to fame. But "Carrie's ascent on the stage," notes Amy Kaplan, "has long struck critics as unconvincing and unreal, while Hurstwood's decline has been singled out as the apogee of Dreiser's realism" (151). Indeed this desire for "a more hard-boiled, dirty reality" marks the critical history of Dreiser's novel, but the desire, as Kaplan argues, is misguided, because it fails to understand that both sentimentality and realism are narrative strategies that shape what can be understood by the reader as real. Indeed, both Kaplan and critic Richard Shulman demonstrate that Hurstwood's reading of his beloved newspapers after the strike (if not also before, indeed all throughout the novel) is analogous to Carrie's consumption of melodrama; when he returns home from one day of being a scab, he sits down to read about what he himself has just experienced. Reading gives Hurstwood a cushion, a distance from experience. Thus writes Shulman, "The novel's rendering of Hurstwood's experience illuminates the newspaper headlines and stories as precisely that—'stories'" (575). Readers are, after all, consumers, consuming stories that allow them to express sympathy or feel empathy for the other while believing themselves untouched. According to Kaplan, when Hurstwood is in the midst of the strike, "he must either be seen and attacked as a scab, join the strikers or leave. There is no neutral position" (10), whereas a (middle-class) reader in his or her comfortable (domestic) rocking chair can have the sense of being the "outside observer." But since both Carrie's melodrama and Hurstwood's newspapers tell stories, they function the same way, precisely because Dreiser cannily understood the fundamental sentimentalism that bespeaks desire, which subtends the emergent consumer culture of the early twentieth century. Therefore, as Kaplan argues, those readers and critics who would now, in the early twenty-first century, privilege a supposedly stripped down, hard-edged (traditionally masculine) journalistic real-text of the strike chapter over the gussied up (traditionally feminine) emotionalism that pervades the rest of the novel have missed the point: narrative determines how the real is apprehended. Documentary is no less and no more a story than melodrama: it frames, contains, and in effect cleans up and orders experience.

However, while I agree with Kaplan that the desire for a gritty real in narrative "works to sanitize and flatten realism by either ignoring or taking one side of the dialectic that informs realistic novels" (160), I would also point out that this desire depends on another, less visible assumption: that to read is not to work. Reading and thinking—or as Dreiser sees it, "the disease of brooding" (244)[11]—once associated with the rocking-chair comfort of middle-class leisure, which is in turn depicted as a passive, middle-class, feminine activity, become nonwork. When Kaplan argues that the reader-Hurstwood can occupy a neutral and invisible position, she also suggests that he becomes a passive and therefore "female" middle-class consumer, in sharp contrast to the all-too-visible, politically charged activity of the working-class, masculinized scab. Even as the novel might attempt to posit dreaming of a truly alternate reality (as Kaplan puts it) as conception or creative labor (after all, the first verbal meaning of *brood* is "to sit upon or to hatch an egg," according to the *American Heritage Dictionary*), it is labor already lost to the gender division of labor. Brooding has already been so thoroughly mystified as "natural" (i.e., feminine) as to be rendered invisible as actual work, even if to read and to think are work.

Sister Carrie cannot, in fact, picture reading or thinking as work, a constitutive failure, which in turn colludes with an emergent middle-class common sense about reading/thinking, a common sense that associates knowledge and knowledge production with leisure and consumption (and even disease), rather than with labor or production. Such a collusion renders both reader (Hurstwood) and writer/artist (Carrie) invisible as workers, making the work of the meaning-maker as if "nothing."

When we first see Mr. G. W. Hurstwood, the manager of Fitzgerald and Moy's saloon—a "truly swell saloon, with rich screens, fancy wines, and a line of bar goods unsurpassed in the country" (Dreiser 33)— his appearance is that of a stocky, successful, well-fed, well-respected, upper-middle-class man, "composed in part of his fine clothes, his clean linen, his jewels and, above all, his own sense of his impor-

tance . . . and [he] was altogether a very acceptable individual of our
great American upper class—the first grade below the luxuriously
rich" (33–34). This is a man of appearance, who is also beguiled by
appearance, ripe to become "a victim of the theater" (575); but Dreiser's description of Hurstwood in these early pages gives another indication of why this character will end up as a part of a crowd of impoverished hopeless men, "old men with grizzled beards and sunken
eyes, men who were comparatively young but shrunken by diseases,
men who were middle-aged" (366).

It is not only because Hurstwood is, like Drouet, all flash and no
pan, or because he has no real social power—no financial control over
his work or his home (Kaplan 147)—but also because he is a reader/
writer with an "indifferent nature" (Dreiser 151), who has "the ability
to get off at a distance and see himself objectively— . . . seeing what
he wanted to see in the things which made up his existence" (95).
Objective vision, according to Dreiser's text in this instance, is not
the "objective" sight of a journalist's disinterest. Hurstwood's ability
to distance himself in order to see is, on the contrary, a deeply self-
interested sight: he sees what he wants to see. In this case he sees
himself as a lonely and ardent bachelor who needs young Carrie.
Taken together with his indifferent nature, this ability allows Hurstwood to "read" what he wants and to ignore the rest (of the story).
Hurstwood not only appears to be, by dint of his clean linens, a perfect
specimen of the upper middle class, a "master of appearances" (575) in
a society of the commodified spectacle; his indifferent (self-)interested
vision *necessarily* structures his experience. Thus, for example, he
can't hear any sort of narrative competing with his own: he does not
hear Carrie's repeated desire for marriage, nor does he hear his wife's
story of increasing suspicion, which culminates in divorce papers. All
he can hear is his own (sentimental) story of love, which pours forth
from him in the form of love letters:

> He was not literary by any means but experience of the world and
> his growing affection gave him somewhat of a style. This he exercised
> at his office desk with perfect deliberation. He purchased a box of
> delicately colored and scented writing paper in monogram, which he
> kept locked in one of the drawers. His friends now wondered at the

cleric and very official-looking nature of his position. The five bartenders viewed with respect the duties which could call a man to
do so much desk-work and penmanship.
   Hurstwood surprised himself with his fluency. By the natural law
which governs all effort, what he wrote reacted upon him. He began
to feel those subtleties which he could find words to express. With
every expression came increased conception. Those inmost breathings
which there found words took hold upon him. He thought Carrie
worthy of all the affection he could there express. (108)

Notice the elaborate joke here: because Hurstwood adopts desk work,
his coworkers see him a cleric at his duties. They imagine him a man
of position at work, even though a cleric is not an exalted position,
and penmanship has to do, after all, with the mere form of the letters, absent any content. Nowhere does the text say he is, nor do the
bartenders understand him to be, actually *writing* something of import.
Poking fun at the bartenders for being duped, Dreiser then pokes
fun at Hurstwood as well, asking the reader to ask, What if the bartenders had discovered the delicate, scented *writing* paper Hurstwood
keeps carefully locked in a drawer? The text codifies the image of
working as masculine pen*man*ship, as the idea of a man's duty—"the
five bartenders viewed with respect the duties which could call a *man*
to do so much desk-work and pen*man*ship" (my emphasis)—while
suggesting that writing (love letters) is a conception subject to natural law, thus codified as female (and given what happens to Hurstwood, natural law can be associated as well with brutality, as in the
old saying "nature red in tooth and claw," with the "other," dark and
rapacious side of the female, as traditionally understood in the nineteenth and the early twentieth centuries).
   In fact Hurstwood, when confronted by Fitzgerald and Moy's open
safe, cannot "conceive" the correct story, and this failure begins the
chain of events that will eventuate in his suicide:

He could not bring himself to act definitely. He wanted to think about
it—to ponder it, to decide whether it was best. He was drawn by such
a keen desire for Carrie, driven by such a state of turmoil in his own
affairs that he thought constantly it would be best, and yet he wavered.
He did not know what evil might result from it to him—how soon he
might come to grief. The true ethics of the situation never once occurred to him, and never would have, under any circumstances. (193)

Like the bluecoat who later eyes scab Hurstwood with contempt, Hurstwood cannot see his way to the truth: "In his heart of hearts he [the policeman] hated this 'scab.' In his heart of hearts, also, he felt the dignity and use of the police force, which commanded order. Of its true social significance, he never once dreamed. His was not the mind for that. The two feelings blended in him—neutralized one another and him" (300). Indeed, the text suggests that few men can, for true social significance and true ethics, require real sympathy, a sympathy the novel has rendered natural and female: neither the policeman nor Hurstwood can *ever* see the truth, because neither man has the natural (female) capacity, the "mind" for it. For all his "thinking, thinking, thinking" (240) Hurstwood cannot, nor can the novel, conceive of thinking as doing—"so he read, read, read, rocking in the warm room near the radiator and waiting for dinner to be served" (253).

Indeed, Hurstwood becomes the very sort of (no-)man whose story cannot rouse sympathy: "He lost sympathy for the man that made a mistake and was found out" (Dreiser 67). Since Hurstwood is a sentimental reader/writer, when he sees himself as a character without sympathy—as he repeatedly mutters, a man who has made a mistake and is caught—his own story has been neutralized. Hurstwood, once inspired by Carrie's naturalness to conceive a sympathetic self for himself, the ardent, lonely bachelor, has lost that self, and without it he can no longer dream/work at all.

"She was capital."

Carrie, however, is the stuff of dreams; she is, as Dreiser has a group of gentleman spectators in the novel say, "capital," a prefiguration of the bombshell, the (white) fetishized (female) object of "looking" (133), of pathos and desire.[12] On stage for the first time, in a part secured for her by Drouet, she performs dreadfully until she becomes, with Drouet's helpful enthusiasm and even more helpful glance ("She thought of Drouet looking" [133]), "a cold, white, helpless object" [135]), "one who was weary and in need of protection" (138). After that moment—significantly an acted moment that marks her race (even if the term *white* here is not an intentional race marker) as well as her status as object rather than subject—the audience feels for her, and she has her first success as an American "idol" (Dreiser 140), an actress who is something, a star. Yet, as Rachel Bowlby notes, "to be something means, paradoxically, to imitate passively and minutely gestures which are not her own" (62). Indeed, as the character Robert Ames tells her, Carrie is successful not because she is a good actress but because she naturally reflects the world's longing: her face wears the "natural expression" of the whole world's (universal) desire or "longing" (Dreiser 356), just as Monroe's success as a bombshell was attributed to her naturalness.

In fact, Carrie's success is dependent on her passivity, which is understood in the novel as natural and female: she is "not helplessly tied to the fate of an old-fashioned virtue, the loss of which entails her own decline. Nor is she an active, assertive agent of her own success in the world, rationally assessing each situation or turning point with an eye to the main chance. She makes it, but only to the extent that 'it' makes her" (Bowlby 52). And just like a craft or a vessel, Carrie famously drifts: from conventional morality to being "kept," from man to man, from thing to thing. She thinks of herself as adrift but doesn't really worry about it because, as a woman and a wife, she will drift in whatever direction her man goes. After all, she agrees to run away with Hurstwood, even though he has practically abducted her. After she "marries" her abductor and becomes Mrs. Wheeler, she drifts into near poverty until she makes an important discovery: she isn't actually married. "She had believed it was all legal and binding enough" (Dreiser 266), and as Mrs. Wheeler, neither the Wheelers' impending impoverishment nor Hurstwood's indifference can rouse her to act. Once she discovers the bitter knowledge that whatever else happened up in Montreal, Hurstwood did not legally marry her, Carrie *is* awakened from passivity.

Although few critics take much note of this moment, I would argue that it is crucially important to the way the novel works, because it has been Carrie's status as a wife, as Mrs. Wheeler, that has been the legal fiction that allowed for her passive drift. The role of middle-class wife was one that, at the turn of the century, depended on the idea that woman was a passive vessel; the common sense that a woman would take care of the home while the man went out into the world,

the so-called nineteenth-century "angel in the house" story, has structured Carrie's relationship with Hurstwood. This story has been so
sound a sentimental story for him that he can't read past it. Indeed,
once they are settled in New York and Carrie has made their flat a
domestic haven, Hurstwood begins to drift away from her, now that
she is no longer the dandy little actress of Chicago but rather the ball
and chain, "the wife." Banking on her malleability, Hurstwood mis-
reads her "placid manner" and her "stable good-nature" (Dreiser 231)
as her character:

> He began to imagine that she was of the thoroughly domestic type of
> mind. He really thought, after a year, that her chief expression in life
> was finding its natural channel in household duties. Notwithstanding
> the fact that he had observed her act in Chicago, and that during the
> past year he had only seen her limited in her relations to her flat and
> him by conditions which he made, and that she had not gained any
> friends or associates, he drew this peculiar conclusion. (Dreiser 222)

Dreiser tells us that Hurstwood is misreading Carrie here, calling it a
peculiar conclusion, as it will shortly turn out to be, because it is just
after she discovers she is not legally his wife that Carrie decides to
act again, to seek the stage.

Why is her married status crucial? Because as Mrs. Wheeler, Carrie
works, and she in fact works hard, yet she is unaware that she is
working. She performs domestic service—"Carrie studied the art of
making biscuit, and soon reached the stage where she could show a
plate of light, palatable morsels for her labor" (Dreiser 221)—in return
for the "pay" Hurstwood allows her in the form of rent, food, clothing. She is not simply drifting, she is working; or as Havelock Ellis
would have said of Carrie, as Mrs. Wheeler she *scabs*, because she is,
in effect, "the wife who married for money... the true scab. She is paid
less, gives more in return in labor and care, and is absolutely bound
to her master" (Goldman 183). Indeed, when Hurstwood leaves the
house after the argument in which Carrie finds out she isn't married
to him, the first thing she worries about is money: "She thought, at
first, with the faintest alarm, of being left without money—not of
losing him" (Dreiser 267).

Housework, of course, is still not regarded as work, unless it is paid
for, as in hiring a cleaning service such as Mini Maid. And housework

is still understood by most Americans as "woman's work," which is not-work: the exploited and invisible labor on which capitalism relies.[13] I would argue that this capitalist common sense about "woman's work" *must* follow Carrie onto the stage if she is to remain, for her middle-class audience, feminine and sympathetic. She must not turn into a "working girl," who, like the diarist shirtwaist worker, might understand that she is being exploited. Despite the way in which Dreiser acknowledges that acting is work ("Girls who can stand in a line and look pretty are as numerous as laborers who can swing a pick" [Dreiser 276]), he refuses to let Carrie work at her craft, requiring her to remain as if a craft, to embody the craft of acting as natural: she has "emotional greatness" (271), she's a "born actress" (136), it is her natural endowment, she is a star, as in the heavens. As I've noted before, Carrie's situation prefigures the kind of Hollywood, assembly-line star that Marilyn Monroe would become some five decades later: Monroe, a star who wanted to be seen acting, to have her labor acknowledged as work. Instead, the turn-of-the-century actress was repeatedly treated as "the body," as if making up every day and every night, as Carrie does, is not hard work. If making up should be acknowledged as work, Carrie would come too close to being a working girl. And of course the link between prostitution and acting was a problem for women on the stage; or as Hurstwood says with disgust, "It's not much of a profession for a woman" (272). Still, as the novel shows, the stage, as much as any other industry at the turn of the century, was greatly expanding. More and more young pretty girls, like laborers who can swing a pick, were required to fill out the lines.

Thus Carrie may be capital, "for her looks and her sexuality become a valuable commodity" onstage (Kaplan 157), but as Mrs. Wheeler, she is a scab. Yet, because the gender division of labor under capitalism has rendered her status as a worker (as wife) invisible, which renders the wife a consumer rather than a producer, Carrie can remain capital only if the novel posits her acting as not-work, even if it knows better. When Carrie asks herself with outrage, "Was she going to act and keep house?" (282), or notes that Hurstwood's attitude toward her working "smacked of some one who was waiting to live upon her labor" (282), her attitude marks a buried understanding that not only is keeping house *work* but also a wife is a scab. Carrie was, after all, in

Hurstwood's position before he lost his money; that is, she was stay-
ing home all day, reading, shopping, cooking, and being "paid" to keep
the house in order. Now that he shops, stays in the flat all day, and
reads while she works, she is irritated and cannot recognize that they
have had a "working union" all along and have simply traded *working*
places because the gender division of labor in marriage has made her,
indeed fully as much as Hurstwood, unable to see the truth.[14]

A Working Girl Who Doesn't

Sister Carrie, then, carries from the nineteenth century into the twentieth a commonsense, middle-class, bourgeois story about gender and
labor and still allows a (white) woman to work successfully outside
the home by making a working girl's work invisible. Carrie's success,
in fact, shows readers how an expansion of the workforce to include
women need not revise an older, familiar, nineteenth-century common sense about women. Carrie's work as an actress, rendered as no
work at all by making it a natural talent and thus reliably female and
unthreatening, demonstrated that a girl could become part of the
workforce because she hadn't actually been working (as a wife) and
wasn't actually going to work (as an actress). Thus, despite the way in
which the novel "knows" both George Hurstwood *and* Carrie Madenda
are scabs, it unknows this as well by sticking to a nineteenth-century
script of the feminine as passive. Reading, acting, shopping, writing,
and dreaming become, in the novel, passive, natural, and female,
while real work is codified as active and masculine.

Of course, as Rachel Bowlby argues, a gendered, capitalist logic
that would see work and thinking or work and dreaming or work and
acting or work and reading as dichotomies defined how both acting
and writing came to be understood:

> Women were meant to be consumers not producers, and in so far as
> it was a job of work and a sphere of masculine achievement, the
> profession of writer was unwomanly and a woman attempting to
> enter it was naturally at a disadvantage. But inasmuch as writing was
> perceived as an odd profession—because it often lacked consistent
> rewards of status and money and because it included some socially
> eccentric practitioners—it could also be taken as unmanly, suggest-
> ing the incapacity to hold down a job. (89)

Certainly the way in which reading and writing today are associated with so-called free time attests to an ongoing common sense that reading involves consuming, a common sense that forcefully emerged alongside industrial capitalism around the turn of the century. By reinforcing this ideology, *Sister Carrie* helped to render word making— knowledge production—invisible as labor, despite the way in which authors were increasingly aware of their status as laborers (Bowlby 90–95). Dreiser renders art natural, as natural as, say, labor in birth has also been rendered, since birthing children is one of those wifely domestic duties that appear to be natural but are, in effect, paid for by the husband/man, at least in the traditionally conceived nuclear family.

Thus I would argue that one of the central reasons the shirtwaist striker's vision of a working union—"we are all union people"—did not become the dominant vision is that the *Diary*, unlike *Sister Carrie*, does imagine that thinking, reading, writing, and marriage require work rather than come naturally. For example, it is through the process of her writing, reading, and listening that the diarist awakens to her position as a worker. Watch what happens as a single word changes its meaning and significance for her:

> I was kind of upset by what the last speaker said to us. According to her notion the bosses consider us nothing but hands and don't care what happens to us. It was simply humiliating to listen to her string of words, but when I come to think of it she was right, after all. If I'm out of a job and pick up a newspaper to look for work I go for the page where it says "hands wanted." If I'm delayed and come too late the boss informs me that he has all the hands he needs. And that's exactly what the woman said. It isn't the mother's daughter, or brother's sister or Miss So-and-So that the boss wants, but a good swift pair of hands, and, if they're used up, he looks for others. We don't count at all. (Malkiel 86)

In the process of writing out her experience, the diarist recounts a process of thought. A string of words, once humiliating and mean- ingless, comes into focus and changes the common use of the word *hand*, to show the reader and the diarist how industrial capitalism severs the worker from a web of other relations, mutilating a social and familial identity and rendering the worker a walking wound, a severed hand that doesn't count as a person. After this moment, the diarist says she must listen more closely and find out things for herself rather than rely on what she is told, on common sense. In fact, the girls must forge a new kind of sense in common, for as one of the labor activists in the *Diary* says, the strikers are powerful when they stand together, so they should not back down from the strike, because "it's only lobsters that creep backward. People with common sense move on all the time" (110). This, decides the diarist, does make sense: a socialist common sense (116).

Moreover, in the course of her diary, the shirtwaist worker also awakens to how bad her marriage to her fiancé, Jim, might have been, until he, too, begins to listen and to think. As she says, "And suppose a girl does get married? Does that mean she has to be dead to everything else? To tell the truth, I was never so sure that a working girl gained so very much by getting married" (134). When she tells Jim that she can't marry him unless he'd let her be a "partner to the game" (134), he is stunned and silent. And yet, through listening and talking, Jim, too, wakes up, after which this couple, who had come to a point that they could no longer communicate, now "talked and talked; there seemed to be no end of things to talk about" (190); the diarist even envisions herself and Jim as truly equal. This is a vision of words that work in a world in which *scab* still has a scathing meaning. For the diarist, words can work to change life, and in two months her life has become "a fuller, better" one (211). At the end she declares that she knows she and Jim will find such happiness as Carrie, according to Dreiser, "may never feel" (Dreiser 369). The diarist has, through the agency of words, found a way to live that alters an older common sense about gender, work, and marriage. She has begun the transvaluation Goldman understood as necessary for true social justice, which Carrie's melancholic, consumerist singleness, her loneliness, maintains: "Know, then, that for you is neither surfeit nor content. In your rocking-chair, by your window, dreaming, shall you long, alone" (Dreiser 369). Carrie may have shocked conventional middle-class morality, but she also provided a *very* necessary image for a middle class confronted by the changing shape and nature of labor in the United States—a working girl who doesn't.

FEDERAL
NIGGER HUNTING LICENSE

THIS CERTIFIES THAT _____
Address _____ Sex _____ Wt. _____
_____ Age _____ Ht. _____
City _____ Eyes _____ Hair _____
Having paid the license fee is hereby licensed to hunt & kill NIGGERS during the open season hereof in the United States. This license must be carried on person when hunting NIGGERS and gives the holder permission to hunt day or night, with or without dogs.

Issued at _____ USA, this _____

day of _____ 19 _____

Issued by _____, County Clerk or Warden

Signature of Licensee _____
SEASON OPENS JAN. 1, CLOSES DEC. 31

TAG GOOD FOR ANY NIGGERS
18 19 20 21 22 23 24 25 26 27 28 29 30 31

Circle
Day of
Kill

Name _____
City _____ State _____
Signature _____

NIGGER TAG
1 2 3 4 5 6 7 8 9 10 11 12 13 14 15 16 17

Hunting license purportedly issued in 1995 at a meeting of Alcohol, Tobacco, and Firearms officials. From the Jim Crow Museum in Big Rapids, Michigan.

nigger

The N Word

To take on the word *nigger* at all in my "sampling" of household words may be regarded an act of _____ —you fill in the blank. Who you imagine I am and who you imagine you are will determine, at least in part, how this chapter is read. The power of *nigger* to incite violence, both verbal and physical, has been considerable. Its ability to inflame has leaked across etymological lines, as anyone who has been chastised, or more, for using the word *niggardly* should know, since, despite the etymological disconnect between these two words, controversy over the one has bled onto the other. The linguistic fact that *nigger* and *niggardly* share *no* etymological history is irrelevant. As Derek Attridge argues, "If such coincidences of sound become meaningful parts of the linguistic system for the speakers of the language, they cannot be dismissed as 'illegitimate' or 'historically unfounded'; they simply become facts of language" (187). What counts is the lived experience of racism or "the community's own interpretation of its language's history" (196), for "'when the subject of race is at hand ... the only dictionary that counts is the one that gives meaning to human experience'" (Kennedy 121). The real of experience trumps this coincidence of sound, to change common use and understanding.

Slavery's bloody history and its long, long aftermath have seen to it that *nigger* remains "a familiar and influential insult" (Kennedy 5), the "nuclear bomb of racial epithets, . . . 'the filthiest, dirtiest, nastiest word in the English language'" (28), which may, perhaps, be in a process of renovation, but even Kennedy admits such disarmament continues to involve miscues, anger, and legal battles, particularly with respect to interpretations of the First Amendment.[1] Like the remotivation of the word *queer* or *cocksucker,* any positive remotivation of a historically negative term is rife with ambiguity. Like *sucker, nigger* is a visceral term; melanin and genetics may be the determining factors for skin tone, but the fiction of race to which "color" points is hardly a simple or scientific one. Moreover, like *scab, nigger,* depending on how it is used, can erase or at least put into abeyance the so-called fact of gender.

Given the well-shelled, bloody terrain of linguistic and political conflict this word has sponsored, why enter the fray? Well, how could a book about the politics and defining power of household words in the United States *avoid* this word? The very fact that the word remains in common use, rather than having vanished from a daily lexicon (as *bloomer* has), indicates not only the ongoing power of racism but also how "the common" is as highly valued as it is feared or condemned. To avoid sampling *nigger* simply to dodge conflict would be an act of cowardice, even if my chapter cannot escape the trap of invoking a slur while trying to expose it. Unlike *scab,* which once might have vied for the position of dirtiest, filthiest insult in the English language— at least if we take Jack London's definition to heart—*nigger* remains a dangerous word, a linguistic bomb(shell), inhabited by assumptions about the essence of race. The ability of this word to function, still, as an outrage shows how a common sense about race, inseparable from the commonsense politics of "freedom" in the United States, harbors an ongoing paradox that has, if anything, intensified since the turn of the nineteenth century; this is the paradox that I traced out in the previous chapter, the paradox that words do work—or *wound*—and yet at the same time have the status of *only* words, as if nothing.[2] As both Catharine MacKinnon and Henry Louis Gates have noted, many children are taught to chant "Sticks and stones will break my bones / but names will never hurt me," and yet most children find themselves chanting this piece of household common sense through tears brought on by having been called a supposedly harmless name. And as critic Patricia Hill Collins succinctly notes, "Silencing anyone won't make any of this go away" (94).

Indeed. The underlying paradoxical common sense that words are powerful yet also "just words" not only allows for the ongoing incendiary power of a word such as *nigger* to spark conflict but has also weakened the power of "the" word—the strength of the speech act—altogether. And while the laboring class *had* to expand during the industrial revolution to include not only white (middle-class) women but also a once-enslaved and hence "free" (as in dirt cheap) working population of both men and women, such expansion required an alteration of nineteenth-century commonsense understandings about race; still, such beliefs were necessary to the maintenance of a dominant middle class, which continued to see itself as "white" and to fear interracial contact, despite generations of what was termed, under slavery, miscegenation. Thus, as I argued in the chapter "scab," while prior commonsense knowledge(s) about emotionally charged aspects of social life did change (African-American men did, at last, get the vote, for example) in order to allow for a rapid expansion of an industrialized labor pool as well as for the expansion of commodity consumption, common sense would also see to it that some things would not change *too much*. One way to ensure the continuity between a commonsense picture of the past and one of the future is, as I have argued, to associate knowledge or knowledge production (words) with consumption (even in the sense of the disease) and leisure rather than with labor and production. Such a collusion masks the work words do.

However, while the chapter "scab" focused on how a capitalist, middle-class "story" about the gender division of labor supported this common sense that reading is nothing but leisure, thus prolonging earlier ideological certainties about gender and labor, this chapter will explore a different narrative: one about race and technology. One of the key elements of industrial capitalism at the turn of the century was the way in which technologies of reproduction altered time and space relations. Taylorization was premised on the velocity of the machine age. Indeed, Henry Ford's implementation of Frederick Taylor's *Principles of Scientific Management* (1911) had immediate consequences for the speeding up of American industry, but Ford was not the first to understand and implement Taylor's scientific management. Heightened speed has long been a tool of management to control when and how workers work and how they perceive both time and how much of it they have for "leisure" (such as reading). As Kristin Ross points out in *Fast Cars, Clean Bodies*, Henry Ford's Taylorization of the automobile industry was premised on velocity, both in the production of that consumer durable and in its operation. Moreover, says Ross, Taylorization had a particular impact on the organization of one of the largest American industries to grow after World War I: Hollywood. Or as Ross writes, "Well-capitalized American studios . . . were quick to pick up on the assembly line and scientific marketing techniques worked out in the auto industry" (20). In fact, both the film and the auto industry have depended on an overarching logic that tailors movement and image, mechanization and standardization. Both have used speed to alter modes of perception. And I mention film here because not only did the use of film alter perceptions of time and space, but also film, like the theater and the speed of reproductive technology with respect to printed matter, had a profound impact on the publishing industry, as I pointed out earlier. Yet, as Kristin Ross argues, Taylorization used speed *not* to change the status quo but to "freez[e] time in the form of reconciling past and future— the old ways and the new" (20), in order to install subtly altered modes of desire, tailored to and by the specter of a way of life forever on the horizon: no matter how fast you go, you never arrive at, say, equality? Arriving would spell the end of desire, surely a familiar Hollywood formula. As Antonio Gramsci was to write in 1931, in his *Prison Notebooks* entry "Americanism and Fordism," the "American phenomenon" was "also the biggest collective effort to date to create, with unprecedented speed, and with a consciousness of purpose unmatched in history, a new type of worker and of man" (145).

But what kind of worker? As I've been arguing and as Gramsci's own language suggests, the gender division of labor and its gendered consequences continued to insist that a worker be male, even as women worked in the factories and mills; and what would also matter about this new type of worker and "man" was his color. Thus although Gramsci wrote about Italy and about Fordism in the United States, and Kristin Ross is speaking of postwar France when she claims that "in production, cars had paved the way for film: now, film would help create the conditions for the motorization of Europe: the two technologies reinforced each other" (21), I argue that the same may be said for the speedy transformation and "motorization," if you will, of race and desire as modes of social perception and control that took place alongside both Taylorization and Fordism in the United States—a motorization that froze certain aspects of common sense about race by reconciling past and future, thus altering older, unserviceable logics of white/black racial discrimination (and gender difference) without significant change to the socioeconomic or cultural legacy from which those logics took force. Labor would be reconfigured, and an ideology of difference based on nineteenth-century concepts of physiology and blood would be altered to fit the needs of industrial capital, but the common sense that would emerge from such changes would remain *predominantly* masculinist, racist, and sexist.

Of course, certain modes of thought did change, but to be reductive here, capital needs expanding markets for its own expansion, no matter how conflicted that expansion may be; at the same time, such expansion threatened the middle class with the specter of a more complete version of democracy involving a freedom freer than heretofore imagined. Fordism, of all things, might have produced what Gramsci and other political economists were skeptical of, yet still unsure about, in the 1930s. They asked themselves, would industrial capitalism, fueled by Taylorization and/or Fordism, actually generate *true* democracy? That potential might strike us as ridiculous today, but it once struck a raw nerve: the (undead) understanding that freedom in the United States, because historically conceived in conjunction with raced slavery, *depends* on raced slavery for definition (an observation that serves as one of Toni Morrison's departure points in *Playing in the Dark*). Ideological fictions about racial difference would have to be maintained in order to avert what Morrison might have called the white terror of the potential democratization of bourgeois hierarchies; or to return to Gramsci, if he saw, as he wrote, a "new man" walking out of Fordism, that new working man might no longer be reliably white. To assure a commonsense continuity that would fuse the past to the future without radically altering the picture would be to reconstruct a dominant common sense about race that would focus on *racial* difference in order to efface or neutralize a knowledge about how *class* and *gender* differences secure a phantasmic but all too real color line inscribed by the long-term effects of material poverty and the gender division of labor.[3] In tracing out a common sense about the efficacy of language and the durability of race as a legal fiction embedded in common sense, this chapter will examine how the color line, once fixed by the legal fiction of slavery, was speedily redrawn from the end of the nineteenth century to the middle of the twentieth. Therefore, the term *nigger* will continue to wound, as if in testament to the material suffering inflicted by that early twentieth-century process of (capitalist, middle-class, white) "reconstruction" of common sense, a reconstruction of commonsense certainties about racial difference that continue to haunt the United States.

Politics and the Personal(ity)

In an interview with Ellen Rooney, Gayatri Spivak named the dominant culture in the United States at the close of the twentieth century a "personalist" culture, something akin to the ideology of individualism but predicated on the concept of persons and personality ("In a Word"). Certainly, one of the features of mid- to late nineteenth-century America was the creation of a "celebrity"-oriented culture, the constitution of a trademark persona (evidenced in the later stardom of a figure such as Carrie Madenda), which inaugurated the larger commodification of history itself. For example, the "Victorian" became a commodified historical period and continues to inflect the production of objects such as clothing, architecture, and furniture as well as to describe contemporary modes of behavior that have nothing, really, to do with the nineteenth century or Queen Victoria. Furthermore, the commodity of celebrity serves to advance the commodification of history—and thus what could be a dangerous emptying out of history (of which etymology is a part).

In nineteenth-century America, both Frederick Douglass and Walt Whitman became exemplary cultural celebrity figures, indeed, household names in a national imaginary, where they have remained ever since the Civil War—by which I mean both the historical event and more recently Ken Burns's PBS documentary. Both Douglass and Whitman knew full well how to capitalize on themselves as novel personalities, and they knew they *had* to sell themselves to achieve their goals. Thus, in the 1840s, the slave Frederick Augustus Washington Bailey became an abolitionist speaker whose 1845 *Narrative of Frederick Douglass, an American Slave* would shortly make his newly assumed name internationally famous. At the same time, an unknown composer and sometime schoolteacher became the popular temperance novelist Walter Whitman, whose *Franklin Evans, or The Inebriate: A Tale of the Times* sold over twenty thousand copies, a number that guaranteed reprint.[4]

Fifty years later, both Douglass and Whitman undertook extensive renovations to their "personalities." By 1891, Douglass, an indefatigable orator, newspaper editor, and politician, had not only completed a grand European tour, a middle-class capstone, but had also served, for the nation-state that once enslaved him, as consul general, minister to Haiti. Meanwhile, the popular temperance novelist had changed his name from "Walter" first to "Walt Whitman, an American, one of the roughs, a kosmos," later to "Walt Whitman, a kosmos, of Manhattan the son," and had become a one-man, international poetic industry, complete with novelty sets of photographs, gift books, and autographs.[5]

I recount these sweeping biographical synopses in order to recall here that Douglass and Whitman were long-lived contemporaries, both consummate writers who framed and advertised themselves as exempla of increase. Across their writings, a reader is presented with frequent before-and-after vignettes, a running commentary of self-renewal that spans those decades often identified as culminating in the nadir of American "manifest destiny," the 1830s to the 1890s. Yet most readers rarely see Douglass and Whitman on the same page, in the same venue, critical discussion, syllabus, or advertisement. This isn't to say that it *doesn't* happen; one of the reasons I mentioned

Ken Burns's *Civil War* is that it frequently quoted both writers. Still, the way in which Douglass was offered to a consumer in the 1990s was very different from the way in which Whitman was packaged. It is this packaging of the person, which began in the nineteenth century, that still inflects the way personhood is understood in the United States. I will examine these two nineteenth-century "household names," Douglass and Whitman, in order to raise questions about the constitution of the "novel" person as a form of exportable good and of international capital investment, which point to the ways in which, at the end of the nineteenth century, the emergence of person types or of personality coupled with an insistence on personality as a vehicle for social change—exemplified, for example, in Walt Whitman's poetic behest that "the greater the reform needed, the greater the Personality you need to accomplish it"—shows that the logic of slavery (that persons could be sold as things) wasn't dismantled at all but rather was reconfigured and extended by the shift from an economy in which bodies were bought to one that trades on identity. While slavery was abolished as a legal form, the logic of person ownership within an identitarian economy was transformed into a central and ever-increasingly important tenant of industrial and postindustrial capital. If you want to own a person, it isn't really all that hard. Banks own people all the time, in the form of mortgages, and it is hardly a coincidence of sound that you can hear in *mortgage* the French word for death—*mort*—or a convergence with *mortuary*.

Just how were Douglass and Whitman "sold" to a consumer in the mid-'90s? In the November 1995 *PMLA*, an advertising spread featured *Breaking Bounds: Whitman and American Cultural Studies*. This collection was supposed to "break the bounds of decorum that have separated Whitman's sexuality, politics and poetry," so that "Whitman and his poems are renewed for a new generation."[6] Similarly, in the January 1996 *PMLA*, an advertisement stated that the *Oxford Frederick Douglass Reader* "offers the most complete, diverse and personally revealing account available of nineteenth-century black America's most celebrated writer."[7] In advertising, of course, the use of superlatives or of revelation and novelty is neither surprising nor interesting as a strategy. Whether food or fuel, soaps, smokes, or software, household (brand) names from Maytag to Macintosh to Marilyn Monroe™ have been advertised as new, different or improved, faster, stronger, more powerful or more lifelike: whatever the goods may be, they will be greater, last longer, taste or look better than their previous incarnation. Whitman and Douglass, as literary brand names, likewise have seen frequent renovation; both have been subject to essay collections, new editions, and biography, year after year. Oxford's ads were therefore old in their reliance on the rhetoric of novelty, especially if one considers how both Douglass and Whitman were themselves impresarios of the "new." So Douglass was offered up by Oxford as a classic author, as in venerable, historical, and therefore valuable, despite a long and easily demonstrable history of critical neglect. In the same ad, his work was described as diverse—as in relevant to an interest in "diversity," which might mean everything from his having written in a variety of venues to the way in which he has become a central figure in African-American literature and studies. In the meantime, prospective buyers were assured that what they were getting, above all, was the most personal view available of an outstanding, notable, celebrated figure of black America, a description that both invokes (structurally) and quietly sidesteps a number of *volatile* political issues to which Douglass addressed his work and within which Douglass himself, as a representative of his race, served as a site of contestation. One example? The politics of legitimate citizenship—something the United States, in the early twenty-first century, is in the throes of renegotiating with respect to immigration, illegal resident aliens, and labor issues. Oxford's ad offered Douglass up matter-of-factly as a notable, celebrated black American, although it took the political work of more than fifty years and the legislative work of another century merely to establish firmly that Douglass was a man and not "just a nigger," as he was named in his lifetime. It took all that work and time for America to come to believe that a man like Douglass was (or should be, at any rate) entitled to full citizenship, to the right to participate as an equal in this democracy—a right that is still fraught, at every election, no matter how many times the vision of an already achieved level playing field is put before the public eye.

Similarly, in order to gesture at the kind of bounds broken by the Whitman collection, Oxford made use of two nearly identical, full frontal nude shots of a white-haired, white-bearded Walt Whitman— or perhaps, given the seasonal retail imperatives that publishers always face in December, we were looking at a rather jolly old Saint Nick? Lacking either attribution or caption in the ad, too indistinct for an assured identification, indeed oddly reminiscent of an edited Eadweard Muybridge photograph from *Animal Locomotion* (1883) or *Animals in Motion* (1891)—serial nudes that have been made novel in jewelry and postcards—this illustration was no doubt meant to signify that the corpo*reality* for which *Leaves of Grass* was almost censored in 1882 has finally been fully revealed; the "actual physical presence" that, as Michael Moon has argued, the poet "set himself the problem of attempting to project in a literary text" (5) despite the "impossibility of doing so literally" (50) was now available to you. For only $17.95 in paperback, you could buy what the poetry can never truly offer, the fully exposed, vulnerably naked Whitman, or, if you will forgive the obvious play on "I Sing the Body Electric," Whitman unplugged. The photograph, I should add, is (at least according to Ed Folsom's research) a Thomas Eakins study titled "Old Man" (Erkkila 4). Betsey Erkkila, taking note of the jacket design for *Breaking Bounds*, claims that these photographs may be the most controversial dimension of the volume (3)—an oddly abject claim about a series of essays. Why did Erkkila cede primary importance to photographs of an unknown old man and to the jacket design, when she herself is one of the authors in this collection? Why judge a book by its cover? Because we do it all the time. In effect, it is irrelevant whether the photographs are of Whitman or not; the ad made the photo into Whitman, and thus the consumer was offered a less bound, more organic, and therefore presumably more lip-smacking, tongue-teasing, tasty Walt—the older version was too decorous, too evasive, too bound. The logic of naked revelation that this ad employed bypasses the vexatious politics of representation and democratic form to which the essays in the volume are addressed and in which Whitman's poetry participated, in order to suggest instead that what this collection offers is a Whitman liberated from a prior bondage of decorum.

And so, in a sense, both figures were displayed to a consumer in the 1990s neither as historical contemporaries lodged in the same tumultuous political field nor as contradictory, variable figures, but rather as fully constituted person types: the celebrated Black Writer and the Good Gay Poet, both of whom will be fully revealed, as if the buyer could purchase intimacy with a heretofore unavailable type. It would seem, then, that what was really at a premium was precisely a supposedly unique intimacy or the promise that the purchaser would gain novel, intimate knowledge; in other, less polite, perhaps not poetic but certainly political words, Oxford's strategy was a display ad for the identitarian logic of the late '90s and an identitarian logic that remains still as rock solid and bankable as a rock star. As critic Amy Robinson wrote, the 1990s produced "an academic milieu in which identity and identity politics remain at the forefront of a battle over legitimate critical and/or political acts" (716)—a milieu that produced Douglass as a black classic and Whitman as a queer activist. Such a milieu remains in place.

But if it has become easy for any publisher today to claim that Douglass is, without question, a celebrated "classic" black American, during Douglass's life none of these descriptives, *classic, celebrated, black,* and *American,* was a nomination for him, and others like him, to make or take easily. Moreover, Douglass was deeply engaged in political struggles concerning the disparity between sociopolitical injustices and the Enlightenment precepts that undergird American idealism. He often took conflicted political positions with regard to national, racial, and sexual politics. Before slavery was legally abolished, Douglass was an advocate of assimilation, as his successful effort to create regiments such as the Fifty-fourth Massachusetts shows, yet during the bleakest political retrenchments of Reconstruction, when former abolitionist and suffragette allies worked to defeat the Fifteenth Amendment in favor of women's suffrage, he reconsidered the possibility of black nationalist separatism.[8] Similarly, Whitman was notoriously evasive when it came to pragmatic political questions, and yet establishing precisely where Whitman really "stood" seems to be, still, the ruling obsession of much Whitman scholarship. The poet has been proclaimed everything from a socialist hero and a gay icon to the epitome of nineteenth-century proto-eugenicist racism, an unapologetic imperialist, or, as David Simpson writes, if "in the classroom and in the popular consciousness, Whitman's status as the bard of democracy often remains unchallenged" (179), Whitman also "remains the poet of manifest destiny" (193).

The complexities of Douglass's political allegiances may be nowhere better evidenced than in 1889, when, as President Benjamin Harrison's minister resident and consul general of the United States to the Republic of Haiti, he sought to obtain a naval station at the Môle St. Nicolas, a diplomatic mission that failed for the United States but also, interestingly, resulted in Douglass's "appointment by President Florvil Hippolite to represent Haiti among all the civilized nations of the globe at the World's Columbian Exposition" (Douglass, *Life and Times* 596, 620). Compromised by the threatening presence of the United States Navy in Port-au-Prince, whose commander advocated taking the Môle by intimidation or force; thwarted by prevailing public opinion at home that Haiti should be either annexed or controlled; frustrated by what he called the Haitian government's timidity but fully cognizant that Haiti had good historical and political cause to resist, Douglass was also hampered by Haiti's knowledge that he himself had been a staunch advocate for American annexation attempts in the Caribbean:

> I supported Gen. Grant's ideas on this subject against the powerful opposition of my honored and revered friend Charles Sumner, more than twenty years ago. . . . I said then that it was a shame to American statesmanship that, while almost every other great nation in the world had secured a foothold and had power in the Caribbean Sea, where it could anchor in its own bays and moor in its own harbors, we, who stood at the very gate of that sea, had there no anchoring ground anywhere. (Douglass, *Life and Times* 602–3)

Still, despite these handicaps and cautions, Douglass saw the Môle acquisition as beneficial to both Haiti and the United States. When the terms for the naval station could not be agreed on, Douglass wrote that the blame should be laid not at his feet or at the feet of the U.S. Navy but rather at the doorstep of

> the Government of Haiti itself. It was evidently timid. With every disposition to oblige us, it had not the courage to defy the well-known, deeply rooted, and easily excited prejudices and traditions

of the Haitian people. Nothing is more repugnant to the thoughts and feelings of the masses of that country than the alienation of a single rood of their territory to a foreign power. (*Life and Times* 613–14)

The last statement is quite applicable to the masses of Douglass's own fiercely prejudiced countrymen. Praising Haitian caution and at the same time denouncing it as timid, Douglass's rhetoric plays a prudent diplomatic game that might, in fact, serve as a useful reminder that Haiti's long contentious history with the United States is hardly one bereft of prejudice or even one that has changed tenor substantially, as Haiti's ongoing political instability and outrageous level of poverty attest. This afore-quoted selection from *The Narrative of the Life and Times of Frederick Douglass* shows how Douglass represented his constancy of support for U.S. expansionist politics, because, perhaps too obviously, a view of Douglass both as an imperialist who helped implement a policy toward Haiti—the effect of which remains of political moment—and as Haiti's representative at the World's Columbian Exposition does not involve sides of him that are useful to the composition of a picture of "black America's most celebrated writer." These autobiographical details did not easily fit the shape of the "novel" person being sold as Douglass in 1996. I realize, of course, that I am using the autobiographical to critique the use of the biographic; however, my point is not to criticize the biography per se but rather to raise the following question: Might not critical imperatives to return to "the author" as "real" or demands for personal or autobiographical authenticity deny how shifting and shifty biography can be? And isn't the marketing of identitarian icons, then, less a hopeful sign of some unmediated access to the real and more a site for the production of marketable person goods? That which was at one time unpalatable or difficult to swallow in the popular perception—an African-American writer or a gay poet—became tasty. He who was once rendered no longer legal property, by the abolition of slavery, became a brand spanking new marketable good, a celebrity author. Thus, too, did Whitman stand before us, naked and revealed. Yet Thomas Eakins's uncovered old man also invited the viewer to

> look on this wonder,
> Whatever the bids of the bidder they cannot be high
>   enough for it,

> For it the globe lay preparing quintillions of years without
>   one animal or plant,
> . . .
> Examine these limbs, red, black, or white, they are cunning
>   in tendon and nerve.
> They shall be stript that you may see them. (Whitman,
>   *Complete Poetry* 74)

As do Whitman's oft-quoted words, the ad invoked, without meaning
to do so, the queasy specter of a slave auction, wherein Whit-man—
or perhaps any "man"—can be situated as both the buyer and the
bought, a by-product of a still-expanding identitarian market economy in which everyone, for better or worse, is for sale.

Booking It

But of course Whitman was never *really* sold as a slave in his lifetime,
whereas Douglass was, and I am not arguing that this material difference is of no consequence. Nor was Whitman called a fag, a queer, or
a queen, whereas Douglass had to deflect, dodge, or otherwise defend
himself against the word *nigger* more frequently than any other insult.
Still, both men made their lives out of words and into words; both
men wrote multiple books about the changing self, predicated on autobiography as a potential vehicle for social change. In other words, or
in a word, both writers believed, deeply and fervently, in the power
of the word. To wield the pen was more potent than to wield the
whip; to make a book was to remake the cosmos.

Curiously, in American slang, the word *book* can act as both a
noun and a verb as well as serve in various idiomatic phrases, such as
"I'll throw the book at you." Actors and criminals are booked; trans-
portation can require booking; and then there's "to book it," as in to
make all due haste, to *move*, pick up speed, gain velocity, as in being
on the run or being overbooked or double-booked. Yet this defining,
symbolic object, "the book"—which, for Douglass in particular, served
as a sign of cultural if not humanist legitimacy when it was used
strategically by abolitionists to prove to a middle-class (white) audience that anyone who could write one should be considered a person—this object of most twentieth-century intellectual labor is now

being hailed, with both gusto and despair, as a thing of the past. "We no longer live in a world in which information conserves itself primarily in textual objects" (177), writes Sandy Stone in *The War of Desire and Technology at the Close of the Mechanical Age*. Although she questions the teleology that informs her title, she also resorts to it in order to secure her claim, and she's hardly alone. For many critics, electronic information technology of the so-called post-Fordist era will render forms appropriate to the Fordist industrial era, such as print, obsolete. Books are clumsy and slow, and as Netscape was quick to remind its consumer base, on the Internet slow is dead.

Needless to say, however, both Taylorization and Fordism were also about speed: the velocity of production affected all cultural production, from print to shoes. So here I feel I must shuttle back and forth, without speeding ahead in my argument, because there are competing claims about the effects that may be produced by changes in production and consumption. As previously noted, Gramsci was uncertain whether a new, more democratic man might walk out of the American Fordist period; likewise, the ways in which the social and political fabric of the United States might have been altered remained a source of tension, violence, and debate at the beginning of the twentieth century, as we have seen in the chapter "scab." Since capital expansion did spawn social change, throwing commonsense narratives about important aspects of social and political life into conflict, a very different (working) subject became a possibility, at least as a concept, as the *Diary of a Shirtwaist Striker* makes clear. It isn't surprising, then, that the technological alteration of time and space offered by the computer with respect to twenty-first-century subjects should occasion similar tensions and speculations. Computer technology has made copyright laws that date from the nineteenth century obsolete or, at the very least, difficult to enforce, and publishing, especially book publishing, as is well known, is in crisis. For some, like Stone, if "the hoary... methods of representation that have worked... for so long are breaking down" (177), then this crisis is an occasion for promising, if dangerous, speculation about change: a radically altered subject for a radically altered future. For others, such as critics Kristin Ross and Evan Watkins, the telos of breakdown, no matter how strenuously ironized as Stone would have it, seems more a symptomatic necessity for the continued production of newness than speculative or even descriptive. To quote Ross once again, Taylorization used speed not for change but to "freez[e] time in the form of reconciling past and future." If *Sister Carrie*'s narrative outcome is any indication, more and more women might go to work, but because much of women's work is still rendered invisible as labor, then "woman," no matter what color, is not going to get to equal pay, or even equality, any time soon, even *with* the vote. Likewise, the commodification of persona, as discussed previously, allowed parts of nineteenth-century race logic to become imbedded in a new identitarian common sense about labor and race, which raced along on the speed of new technologies of reproduction. The meaning of the word *nigger*, then, as an incendiary, wounding insult was frozen—to steal from Ross—in time, and its meaning as objectifying insult was carried forward with only mild alteration, a word "booking" nowhere incredibly fast.

A brief look at two books from the so-called Fordist period, which, like *Sister Carrie*, have labor disputes as pivotal textual moments, will show how a (racist) desire to be "white" is manufactured and installed as if it were a universal desire and one that could deflect class conflict, thus continuing to reinstall racial (and indeed gender) difference as central to the domestic economy of the mid-twentieth century. A caveat: I am well aware that *nigger* as it appears in literature—as opposed to print more generally, for example—has remained an issue in education. Frequent attempts to silence the word by censorship or attempts to expunge the word from the dictionary altogether have been and will no doubt continue to be made. In fact, it might be taken as common sense that this chapter should revisit so-called important literary contributions with respect to the use or abuse of this "sampled" word. However, in keeping with my alternate logic of sampling and to disrupt a common sense about the literary and how a literary analysis ought to look, I will instead examine two novels that are rarely, if ever, read together, given the supposedly vast commonsense differences, literary and aesthetic, ascribed to them: George S. Schuyler's *Black No More* (1931) (an account of the strange and wonderful workings of science in the land of the free in AD 1933–1940) and F. Scott Fitzgerald's *The Last Tycoon* (1941).[9] These two books, produced a decade apart, might seem worlds apart with respect to genre, audience, and value. They are certainly noncanonical in the traditional sense, even if Fitzgerald, as a celebrity, is as much an American literary object as either Whitman or Douglass. But instead of returning to the frozen ideological battleground of literary value, what I will demonstrate is how these books are thematically bound together in their representation of technological devices that could and would "install" a common sense about race tailored to the needs of industrial capital. Such a common sense worked against unionization and allowed for an expansion of the workforce that did not entail drastic social change.

In January 1931, a well-known journalist for the *Pittsburgh Courier*, the *Nation*, and the *American Mercury* published his first satiric novel, *Black No More*. Schuyler was then, and has remained, a controversial figure; he was a member of Marcus Garvey's Universal Negro Improvement Association, which he would later denounce, and a self-identified socialist who turned, in his own word, conservative. His work has generated some critical attention but also plenty of denunciation. *Black No More* boldly takes on "the nigger question," to use Thomas Carlyle's deliberately inflammatory title,[10] and chronicles the fortunes of a mechanism that electrochemically turns black folks white. Dr. Junius Crookman, who invents what he thinks of as his instant uplift machine, is wildly successful, since "the only way for a Negro to solve his problem in America" is, as he says himself, "'to either get out, get white, or get along'" (Schuyler 27). Since the doctor was not getting out and was getting along only indifferently, he began to put his mind to thinking about how to get white. Soon, he came up with a device that would accomplish the change of black to white through "electrical nutrition and glandular control" (27), a device that, with financial backing, allows for the "great and lucrative experiment of turning Negros into Caucasians" (30). Here is Dr. Junius Crookman's advertising strategy:

> They were near the Crookman Sanitarium. Although it was five
> o'clock on a Sunday morning, the building was brightly lighted from
> cellar to roof and the hum of electric motors could be heard, low and
> powerful. A large electric sign hung from the roof to the second floor.
> It represented a huge arrow outlined in green with the words BLACK-
> NO-MORE running its full length vertically. A black face was depicted

at the lower end of the arrow while at the top shone a white face to
which the arrow was pointed. First would appear the outline of the
arrow; then, BLACK-NO-MORE would flash on and off. Following that
the black face would appear at the bottom and beginning at the
lower end the long arrow with its lettering would appear progressively
until its tip was reached, when the white face at the top would blazon
forth. After that the sign would flash off and on and the process
would be repeated. (43)

The Black-No-More device is made of "sparkling nickel" and
"resembled a cross between a dentist's chair and an electric chair,"
which eerily prefigures the Optic White paint factory's odd, man-
changing machine in Ralph Ellison's *Invisible Man* ("Well, boy, it
looks as though you're cured. . . . You're a new man" [235]). A canny
satirization of American ingenuity and technology, this sparkling
nickel gadget electrically displaces black with white but only to have
this new sort of whiter than whiteness redraw racial difference. Rather
than erasing race, the machine causes the population, both black
and white, to fear those who appear to be too white because whites
might then be taken to be Crookman-altered blacks, and blacks might
be caught out as altered—although seeing that particular difference
is as tough as seeing blackness in a character who "could pass for white
which would have been something akin to a piece of anthracite coal
passing for black" (Schuyler 44). This device, as well as the story itself
as a narrative device, transforms race and yet at the same time leaves
the social relations in the culture static. For if some of the individual
whited "Negros" change their economic status in the course of the
story, overall the status quo, in which poor white and black populations remain fixed in poverty and fixated by what Schuyler terms "colorophobia," is not altered. One of the most wickedly satiric and eventually violent upshots of this stasis is that the once-black Max
Disher/now-white Matthew Fisher ends up as the grand exalted giraw
of the Knights of Nordica, a white supremacist group. Writing for this
group, Matthew publishes *The Warning*, which "painted terrifying pictures of the menace confronting white supremacy and the utter necessity of crushing it. Very cleverly he linked up the Pope, the Yellow
Peril, the Alien Invasion and Foreign Entanglements with Black-
No-More as devices of the Devil. He wrote with such blunt sincerity

that sometimes he almost persuaded himself that it was all true" (106). Using such rhetoric and the fear of the "white nigger" (128) to inflame poor white southerners, Matthew manages to quell that which Schuyler understands as the real problem: labor activism. The labor organizer, having been rendered a white nigger (a Jewish man who lives in Harlem who believes "in dividing up property, nationalizing women and was in addition an atheist" [128]), doesn't even get to speak to the workers, who chase him out of town. Max/Matthew's propaganda works so well that

> the working people were far more interested in what they considered, or were told was, the larger issue of race. It did not matter that they had to send their children into the mills to augment the family wave; that they were always sickly and that their death rate was high. What mattered such little things when the very foundation of civilization, white supremacy, was threatened? (131)

In its satiric intent, then, the novel might be said to argue in concert with W. E. B. Du Bois, who wrote in 1931:

> Present organization of industry for private profit and control of government by concentrated wealth is doomed to disaster. It must change and fall if civilization survives. The foundation of its present world-wide power is the slavery and semi-slavery of the colored world including the American Negroes. Until the colored man, yellow, red, brown and black, becomes free, articulate, intelligent and the receiver of a decent income, white capital will use the profit derived from his degradation to keep white labor in chains. (409)

However, the novel (unlike Du Bois, with whom Schuyler often found himself at odds) is profoundly skeptical of any device—whether it be ideological, political, or industrial, as the electrical advertising sign spoofs—designed to produce a new (working) man. Science and technology would *not*, in fact, succeed where the Civil War had failed (Schuyler 25). The device might turn a Max into a Matthew, but Matthew replicates the very ideological grounds that drove Max to the Crookman Sanitarium in the first place, including assumptions about heterosexuality that render the pretty women in the book "ignorant" and about homosexuality that situate it beyond the pale (as it were). Racial prejudice is reinvented by the very person who has suffered from it, and by the end of the novel Americans have become so frightened of being white, lest they be taken to have been black, that everyone who can afford it flocks to new "devices," new commodity products such as Egyptienne Stain and Zulu Tan, and so "it was a common thing to see a sweet young miss stop before a shop window and dab her face with charcoal" (Schuyler 222). The social fabric that depends on a common sense about race (sexuality and class) hasn't been altered for the majority: the rich remain rich, the poor, poor, women are women, men are men, and the battle over "colorophobia" goes on.

Ten years after the publication of Black No More, at what was to be the end of his life, a harried, underpaid (at least by his own lights) screenwriter, who had worked on the screenplay for Gone With the Wind in 1938–39 and who, like Schuyler, was a pen-for-hire magazine contributor, wrote about work in the Hollywood industry. The resulting book, The Last Tycoon, stars Monroe Stahr, a Jewish film producer whose hectic pace is causing him heart trouble.[11] Like Black No More, this unfinished novel's plot is driven by a device: if Max Disher is motivated to become white because of his desire for "a tall, slim, titian-haired girl who had seemingly stepped from heaven or the front cover of a magazine" (Schuyler 20)—and the novel assumes that Disher's desire for this white woman is a universal desire, that is, no man could resist—then Monroe Stahr is obsessed by a young woman whose glowing white face uncannily replicates that of his dead, white, movie-star wife, Minna Davis, whose "haunting jollity...had fascinated a generation"—as if Minna had been Marion Davies, Jean Harlow, or a prefiguration of Monroe (Fitzgerald 79). "Smiling faintly at him not four feet away was the face of his dead wife, identical even to the expression" (33). "It was Minna's face—the skin with its peculiar radiance as if phosphorous had touched it" (79). Stahr is both attracted to and repelled by the specter of Minna reanimated, back from the grave: "An awful fear went over him and he wanted to cry aloud. Back from the still sour room, the muffled glide of the limousine hearse, the falling concealing flowers, from out there in the dark—here now warm and glowing" (33). The person who possesses this face, an Irish woman named Kathleen Moore, is and is not his wife on several levels: she is engaged to the American, as he is called; she has lived with a man—a king, in fact—from whom she ran away; she herself is not

American, and above all she is not of Hollywood, unlike Minna, who was tied to pictures, which Stahr notes are his true love. On the only evening he and Kathleen spend together, they encounter "a Negro man...collecting grunion quickly" (112), small silver fish that beach themselves annually on the same day at the same time of the night, 10:16 p.m., on the California coast. Stahr calls them "very punctual fish," as if they were bound, like factory workers, to the punch clock (112). In the course of this scene, Stahr and the stranger with his pails of fish talk about something few characters in American literature ever do much of, even if most Americans spend most of their lives engaged in it: work.

> "What's your work?" the Negro asked Stahr.
> "I work for the pictures."
> "Oh." After a moment he added, "I never go to movies."
> "Why not?" asked Stahr sharply.
> "There's no profit. I never let my children go." (113)

When the man leaves the beach, he leaves unaware that he has, in this short conversation, "rocked an industry" (113). For the rest of Stahr's unfinished textual life and romance, which was halted by Fitzgerald's own fatal heart attack in December 1941, he obsessively returns to the man's dismissal of his work, gripped by a feverish desire to make pictures that will change the stranger's mind. He imagines the man

> waiting at home for Stahr with his pails of silver fish, and he would be waiting at the studio in the morning. He had said that he did not allow his children to listen to Stahr's story. He was prejudiced and wrong and he must be shown somehow, some way. A picture, many pictures, a decade of pictures, must be made to show him he was wrong. (116)

What, one is left to wonder, would Stahr show to this man, whom the text names as "Negro" rather than "nigger," a curious shift for Fitzgerald, who had no trouble using racial epithets like *buck* and *nigger* in his 1925 novel *The Great Gatsby*, which also features a conversation about Tom Buchanan's faith in white supremacy. However, by 1941, Fitzgerald's Stahr—significantly Jewish and thus the only ethnic protagonist Fitzgerald ever attempted to compose—knows something

Nick Caraway, in 1925, did not: that the older story about race, the "nigger" story if you will, won't fly easily anymore.[12] Unless stories for the Negro, as opposed to the nigger, were made, a growing literate, working audience—a demographic that was already middle-class and lucrative—would be lost. Of course, one of the other significant things that Stahr knows only too well, which Caraway cannot know, is the leveling economic impact of the Great Depression. *Tycoon* is only too aware that the Depression has thrown the United States into so-cial and political turmoil; for example, several characters fear that a "revolution" might have happened or might still happen: "It was in the lowest time of the depression, and the young actress kept staring out of the window in such a way that the stewardess was afraid she was contemplating a leap. It appeared though that she was not afraid of poverty, but only of revolution" (Fitzgerald 7).

The Last Tycoon never makes clear what sort of picture Stahr would give to the Negro man, who is, incidentally, a reader: "I really come out to read some Emerson," he says when asked if the grunion is worth the trip all the way out to Santa Monica (112). What would Stahr, who clearly has never read Emerson (unlike Kathleen, who has), show this serious Negro family man to make him change his mind about the profitability of film for his children? The novel doesn't know, except to say that Stahr imagines the picture he will make for this man must be "serious" in some way that his Hollywood pictures gen-erally are not. This dilemma over good and bad pictures runs through-out the novel, and it situates Stahr in the vexed position of author-producer whose work has been rendered in commodity culture as if of no consequence, to be consumed like candy (like cotton candy Carrie? like ice cream Monroe?) and forgotten as swiftly as Minna Davis was forgotten. For although her face entertained a generation, within three years Hollywood has already forgotten her (Fitzgerald 38), even if Stahr can't. Stahr's dilemma also indicates how Hollywood, as an industrialized commodity-production machine, knew perfectly well it would have to "grow" the audience to include—or persuade—an increasingly literate, working African-American population.

What both Schuyler's novel and Fitzgerald's know is that capital-ism doesn't care, particularly, about race. Capitalism cares about cap-ital, commodity production, and novelty; at the same time, capital expansion requires exploitation, and thus the specter of racial (and sexual) differences, which common sense assumes are less malleable than class, had to be maintained in order to keep working people— the growing labor force—from recognizing themselves as an exploited *class*, irrespective of race, ethnicity, sexuality, or gender. In *Black No More*, the way in which poor white labor is managed by the rhetoric of racial intolerance shows how this strategy of containment works through a racist appeal to emotion and fear: if no one is visibly "the nigger," someone has to be made over into the exploited, "the bottom rail" in Civil War–era slang, without jarring the economic system too much. In *The Last Tycoon*, the Depression has taught Stahr (for which read Hollywood as an industry) that the Negro is the future: a soon-to-be middle-class audience just waiting to be tapped. The only other person of color in *Tycoon* is Stahr's doctor's assistant, a "colored" man who is in charge of the portable cardiograph (130), as if to signify that technology-as-futurity will be a future in which *nigger* has been replaced by less charged terms such as *Negro* and *colored*. Significantly, of course, Stahr is dying. This once "technological virtuoso" (150) has become frail and sick. Stahr's Fordist Hollywood, the Hollywood of Minna Davis, in which pictures have nothing to say to the Negro, will have to be transformed if, like any capitalist industry, it is to expand. In fact, Stahr's last act is to play "the wicked overseer to a point he would have called trash if he had watched it on the screen" (150), a role that could have put Stahr in a pre–Civil War plantation scene, like one of the various historical costume dramas that parade across the lot where Stahr works. In fact, since he thinks of writers as children, he is, in effect, an overseer of the "niggers" of Hollywood, and it is not a frivolous choice, on Fitzgerald's part, to have Stahr's visitor, one Prince Agge, upset to see Mr. Lincoln, in stovetop and shawl, shove a triangle of pie into his (reanimated) mouth. Thus it is not surprising to find Stahr overplaying a (nineteenth-century?) overseer in order to goad a *writer's* union organizer, a man named Brimmer. Brimmer, a socialist, tells Stahr,

> "At the bottom of your heart, you know I'm right."
> "No," said Stahr, "I think it's a bunch of tripe."
> "—you think to yourself, 'He's right,' but you think the system will last out your time."

"You don't really think you're going to overthrow the government."
"No, Mr. Stahr. But we think perhaps you are." (147)

Brimmer's comment about moving pictures overthrowing the government far more easily than any union can is a canny one, as is Fitzgerald's sense that the Hollywood Fordist machine, a racist machine in which the power of writing has been broken down into piecework and rendered as if nothing, would not last unchanged; it would have to deal not only with labor issues but also with the changed face of labor and an increasingly middle-class African-American audience who was literate.

Why do I keep stressing reading and literacy? Why is it so important that the man catching grunion reads Emerson? Because at that time literacy still signified *as* an important device for the constitution of an African-American middle class. Literacy was still associated with social uplift, and reading, for that population, was still regarded as useful labor. In *Sister Carrie*—in which, by the way, not a single person of color ever appears, even though the novel takes the reader to both Chicago and New York—reading is leisure to a white, consumerist middle class; for the Negro man on the beach, reading is profitable work, even as late as 1941. Certainly for him and his children, absent as "they" are from the majority of pre-Depression Hollywood films, reading was more socially and politically profitable than spending a nickel on the movies.

Devices and Desire

Significantly, two years after Fitzgerald's 1941 meditation on Hollywood's (frivolous) work and its irrelevancy to the new "Negro" (reading) man, Loews, Inc., released its first musical comedy with an "all black cast," called *Cabin in the Sky*. Arthur Freed (a Jewish man) produced it; and it was Italian American director Vincente Minnelli's first credited work. The film, among other things, is *not* the serious one that Stahr thought necessary to reach the man with his silver grunion. No. Hollywood was simply going to make a "white" musical with black actors. Casting Lena Horne as one of the lead actresses only confirms this point, since she spent a long career balanced on the line of color that Hollywood both appeared to broach and yet maintained.

But more important for my argument, the film as a *film*, as a technological device you could access for a nickel, like Schuyler's nickel machine, seems oddly aware of itself as this *device*, a technological device able to reinscribe racial difference through commodification and the family-romance plot (device) of (heterosexual) desire. One of the film's central plot devices is a big white consumer durable, a washing machine. This white labor-saving machine, a sign of modernity (speed) and domesticity, is a gift from an erring (black) husband to his faithful (black) wife. Everyone, the film presumes, desires such a thing—just as the invention of "Marilyn Monroe" presumed that *everyone* must desire her or desire to be her, that she was, as Sister Carrie is, capital, the ultimate object of (white, middle-class) desire. The African-American couple in *Cabin in the Sky* behave in every way like a middle-class heterosexual couple of their time, 1943, and yet they still live in a (slave) cabin, which has not been wired for electricity. So the labor-saving machine that husband has given wife— an emblem of white, middle-class domesticity—can't be used. Yet. Not until the cabin can be, and the film suggests will be, wired. Someday. Desired then, or at least the film presumes everyone wants a washing machine, the machine is disabled in the domestic diegesis, a filmic context still visually tied to the past (slavery) and to the ideological common sense that dates back to *Uncle Tom's Cabin*, that is, only in heaven ("in the sky," as the film suggests) can the "nigger" find relief from his or her earthly condition as such. Although the long sequences about heaven and hell in this film are meant to be funny, not only does the humor depend on now-obsolete minstrelsy jokes, but also the film repeatedly suggests, in the same manner that Uncle Tom's death is "heroic," that the only way for this particular type of couple to be happy together is in heaven.

So here is the first of its kind Hollywood moving picture made with an all-black cast—progress, or so Hollywood thought. But the film depicts an African-American community still too rural and poor to even *have* a movie theater, and the characters in the film don't seem to know what a moving picture might be. In each case, the technological "device" (either the white washing machine or the film itself) seems, on the face of things, unusable to the people for whom it was made and intended. But the device also sits there, waiting, as it still

does, since you can always rent the video, waiting for the correct historical, ideological moment for the desire it represents—a commodified desire codified through technology as white, middle-class,
and heterosexual—to be activated, to go off (like a bombshell?). For
the juice, as it were, to be turned on, as if to electrocute and thus
neutralize ideological dissent, racial strife, and social conflict, as if,
through the installation of desire by technology, to turn black into
white.

Typewriters, the word initially used to name the workers, eventually referred to the machines.

cyber

A Real Live Wire

As we roll into the twenty-first century, another technological device, the personal computer—and a new language of computerization—has deeply infiltrated the household and everyday speech. "If *the Internet* isn't a household word in your household, you may be behind the times," warned CNN, on Friday, March 14, 1997. In the United States, and for most Americans, the word *Internet* also means cyberspace, also means virtual reality, also means the Web, all of which designate futurity in some way, the prodigious promise of tomorrow. But the cyberific Tomorrowland promised by the computer is also the "now," unlike those distant fabulous tomorrows imagined by pulp magazines of the 1930s, such as *Wonder Stories* and *Amazing Stories*. Even the tomorrow presented to the American public during the heady days of the space race—when "Life in the Year 2000," at least according to the Ford Motor Company prophecy, would include routine commuter flights to a Moonport (as if the Fordist period would last forever)—has not come to pass. Science fiction as a genre in the twenty-first century may continue to imagine the future for us, yet the Web has already woven futurity into the weft of daily life. Futurity, it seems, is no longer about tomorrow. The future is *now*. Advertisements for everything from Transitions eyeglasses to insurance to cars remind us of this. Yes, that once-upon-a-time fiction of science, the computer, has also changed our everyday language: *dot* is no longer a simple nickname for Dorothy (who has certainly left Kansas far behind by now), and *e* is no longer a mere vowel. Neither *DNA* nor *http* are random sets of letters. *Online* has become one word rather than two, and it no longer means what you do at the post office or the grocery store, although you can access both "online." Home is just a click or two (of your crimson heels?) away. The marketing possibilities that have arisen from the making of fictions into science have been profound indeed: not only is the Internet the world's biggest mall, but just look what you can buy! Clonaid offers a "range of services like creating personal stem cells, INSURACLONE™, OVULAID™ and CLONAPET™" (www.clonaid.com). DreamTech's Clones-R-Us offers custom cloning of ourselves and family members or a supermodel's DNA, and so one day you can have a beautiful . . . slave? . . . all your own. As Donna J. Haraway's "Manifesto for Cyborgs" declared in the mid-1980s, we are all already cyborgs, as in engineered and constructed beings, living in a real-live wired, genetically altered world.

For Haraway, of course, it was the cyborg—not the clone or the computer, although the cyborg is arguably both at once—that was the quintessential icon of the postmodern condition. Haraway's cyborg, unlike the clone or the computer, is a politically savvy polymorph, a "bad girl . . . a shapechanger whose dislocations are never free, who's trying to remain responsible to women of many colors and positions" while also committed to gender-blending or even transgender politics ("Promises" 308)—a meet emblem of "bleshing," to use a much older and far less successfully disseminated science-fiction neologism of the 1970s. Haraway's celebration of the cyborg led to a profusion of scholarly and semischolarly book titles devoted to the cyborg, such as *Cyborg Citizen: Politics in the Posthuman Age* (Chris Hables Gray, 2002); *The Cyborg Handbook* (Heidi J. Figuroa-Sarriera and Chris Hables Gray, 1996); *The Gendered Cyborg* (Gill Kirkup, ed., 1999); *Cyborg Babies* (Robbie Davis-Floyd and Joseph Dumit, eds., 1998); *Machine Dreams: Economics Becomes a Cyborg Science* (Philip Mirowski, 2001); and *Cybersexualities* (Jenny Wolmark, 2000). The manifesto also prompted a rather telling Web site spoof: at http://cyborgmanifesto.org, readers were asked to either agree or disagree with an *Adbuster* text of a "cyborg manifesto" (not Haraway's document, although several respondents purported to be Donna Haraway, the "Real" Donna Haraway, and the "Real Real" Donna Haraway). This particular online manifesto spoof advocates a postbiological future. Richard DeGrandpre of *Adbusters* was surprised by the results of posting the site. As he says,

> Of the thousand or so readers who commented on The Cyborg Manifesto online, only a small few recognized it for what is was—a spoof. The vast majority took it at face value. What does this tell us? Perhaps most importantly, and surprisingly, it tells us that people have little difficulty imagining a future in which nature is abandoned for a total cybernetic existence. Some are against it, some are for it, but many or most can imagine it.[1]

So, Toto, we truly aren't in Kansas anymore! Dorothy can in fact "click" her way back "home." And although I admit readily that *The Wizard of Oz* is a playful reference point, then again, if we are all already cyborgs and have been for years now—whether Scarecrow, Cowardly Lion, or Tin Man—as cyborgs, we also share the past, even as we are propelled forward away from (into) it.[2] Critic N. Katherine Hayles notes that the hybrid neologism "cyborg . . . is both a product of this process and a signifier" for how the past/old is both displaced by, yet retained in, the future/new. "The linguistic splice that created its name (*cyb* ernetic *org* anism)," writes Hayles, "metonymically points toward the simultaneous collaboration and displacement of new/old, even as it instantiates this same dynamic."[3] Of course, even the cyborg itself was not a novelty when Haraway wrote the manifesto, if you consider how deeply she/he's indebted to both the robot and to that other, once popular machine-human hybrid, the android. Polish author Stanislaw Lem did not have Haraway's version of the cyborg in mind when he wrote *The Cyberiad* (1974 in English translation), nor did Michael Caidin when he wrote his 1972 novel *Cyborg*.

Furthermore, if we disassemble *cyborg* into its component linguistic parts, we find that neither *cybernetic* nor *cyber* is a meet emblem of the future. *Cyber* is very old word whose literal meaning, "pilot," derives from ancient Greek. Thus, for all its futuristic spin, *cybernetic* is a far older word than either *cyborg* or *cyberspace*, another science-fictional coinage attributed to Canadian author William Gibson's *Neuromancer*, published in that once-upon-a-time impossibly futuristic year 1984.[4]

What I find most significant about *cyber*, however, and why I chose it as the after*word* is that it not only manages to hang on to its ability to signify the future but also continues to grow the English language as a prefix. Cyber signals novelty, futurity, and a connection, however tenuous, to technological innovation. One might call the cyberindustry a sign of resource enhancement in the face of increasing resource scarcity. In other words, when annexed or prefixed to another word, *cyber* seems to give older words a spin, a forward-looking pizzazz—a promise that the new will replace or enhance or expand the old, even as the old is retained, if at times diminished to a ghost in the machine. As Evan Watkins remarks, "Common sense tells you that what capitalism does for a living is produce more, and newer, and different, and interesting economic resources" (7), a common sense at work in the explosion of cybridity. And so the mass markets of television, radio, magazines, and newspapers, not to mention similarly conceived venues mounted as Web pages, are inundated with all manner of cybrids, cybervenues, and cyberproducts, cyber, cyber, cyber, ad nauseam. Cyberterrorism seems here to stay.

Indeed, cybrids are popular signifiers of an as-yet-to-come, even if "the future" is increasingly the "now." History—or more properly, perhaps, a traditional concept of the past—is over, even as it is, as Hayles notes, retained. History, then, would seem to have little value when the future is at stake, while the present is forever being evacuated. Time, "booking it" since the nineteenth century, hits warp speed. At this velocity, time will be altered yet again. Hayles articulates some of that alteration by taking note of how the nineteenth-century, industrial-age binary machine/human (170–71) has been gradually rearticulated as a continuum, particularly since the 1950s, "when the idea that human beings might not be the end of the line was beginning to sink in" (172). The concept of replication, taken from mass production, has come to mean nearly the same thing as human generation. Thus, she argues, "when humans can no longer be distinguished from androids, the life-cycle and dis/assembly zone occupy the same space" (171).

For good or ill, then, we are marched forward into "elsewhen,"[5] the era of the posthuman, in which any clearly definable difference between machine and human or human and nonhuman is in the process of collapse, even if some boundaries remain. There are those who seek, of course, to stave off the posthuman. President George W. Bush frequently remarked that human cloning should be legally banned as immoral: "The use of embryos to clone is wrong. . . . We should not as a society grow life to destroy it."[6] Imagined scenarios of a nightmare future, in which humans, like pigs, are mass produced in order to harvest organs, remains a grim fantasy, even if it, too, has been culled, in part, from the pages of popular (science) fiction.[7] At the same time and at the other end of the spectrum, animal rights activists seek to save animals from their current (mass-market) fate as food and organ donors.

In the meantime, as political debates intensify with respect to human cloning, scientists at Texas A&M, funded by biotech company Genetic Savings & Clone, announced in March 2002 that their "Operation CopyCat" project was successful at cloning a cat—CC, for Carbon Copy—whose cute little furry self was splashed briefly across the news. But CC came with a hitch. She didn't look like the "original" cat. She may have been the first cat's genetic twin, but, as the Johns Hopkins Newsletter remarked, "Not everything is determined by genetics. In this case, a cat's calico pattern is, in fact, partially determined by the mother's (or surrogate mother's) womb. . . . There's no clear-cut answer as to whether an animal—or a human for that matter—is more a product of its genes or its environment." CC is a copy on the "inside," but on the outside she is not identical to her "parent," or, more genetically speaking, twin.[8]

I hasten to add here that cloning as a scientific endeavor, sometimes referred to as therapeutic cloning, and cloning as a bio-reproductive endeavor are not the same "animal" either, even if, like CC and her predecessor, they are presumed to be identical processes. The former is an experimental search for genetic knowledge (i.e., science); the latter involves a market that trades on the emotional truth of fiction. Biotech concerns and companies such as Clonaid, DreamTech, Genetic Savings & Clone, and PerPETuate represent profit-oriented endeavors, and what they promise is not, strictly speaking, science. What they promise is a fiction of life everlasting. With cloning, or so the story goes, you will never have to say good-bye. These companies will allow people to harvest, store, and clone the DNA of their beloved pets so that at the instant of death they can snap their fingers and have a new, supposedly identical pet appear on their doorstep.[9] The same goes for your lost child, dead mother, murdered brother. No matter that cloning is, at best, still a long-long-shot gamble or that the current chances of Fluffy2 either (a) actually surviving or (b) looking anything like Fluffy1 are more than simply remote. We nonetheless book ahead to the moment when death will be vanquished by science. Biotech companies know their audience, and that audience, by and large, doesn't focus on the inconvenient details of actual science. That audience would rather hear a (fictional) promise: that we might turn back time and skip the trauma of loss.[10] To live forever. To see Gramma—or Fluffy—again, and thus extend the past forever into the future. Or, as Clonaid's Web site claims, "Thus today, man's ultimate dream of eternal life, which past religions only promised after death in mythical paradise, becomes a scientific reality."

This is a very old story, but one that has been dislodged from the realm of the past and rendered new or "now" by technological innovations in genetic engineering. Thus the fantasy (of eternal life) gains the illusion of reality (in a purchasable material service). Of course, as with all consumer desires made flesh-on-demand, the price tag is steep. But people are willing to pay for what is, after all, the (il)logical consequence of an old cultural promise, that haunting phantasmic dream that the story of America itself signifies: to be a "space" where "time" (historical antecedents, genealogy, class) has no meaning, where the past (the history of class, race, and gendered positionality) has been displaced by a new freedom (future) from all boundaries.

Paradoxically, of course, this version of everlasting life rests squarely on the invocation of fatality, as I have argued in various chapters throughout this book: a vampire can live forever only after dying; a bombshell is fatal(e); a scab may stem the tide, but it is the site of a wound—the wound of a history, buried like a live wire within the currency of ordinary household words. The Western (Judeo-Christian/

science) fiction of life everlasting rests on an invocation of apocalypse (revelation), where only a few (the chosen) will live, while the
many (most of us) cannot "be" at all.

"On the inside, it's a whole different story—"

Yet I, too, have just invoked apocalypse. To explain how I've arrived
at the narrative doorstep of mass destruction, I will turn back the
clock or take a look backward at a fiction from the nineteenth century,
Herman Melville's *Billy Budd*. But wait a minute, isn't the past, like,
um, *so* over? Didn't we say, a few pages back, that history is of little
value? Arguably, the answer is yes. Herman Melville's nineteenth-
century "inside narrative," *Billy Budd*, is a relic of the past, a canon-
ized, classical American fiction. It would seem to have nothing to do
with contemporary science, politics, or ethics. Common sense surely
indicates that a nineteenth-century fiction is, by now, really, *really*
old. Yet, curiously enough, whenever I teach the novel, the title character gets diagnosed according to present-day medical standards. All
the indications, I'm told, point to the diagnosis that Billy suffers from
a genetic disorder—far more of a visceral inside narrative than Melville
might ever have imagined.[11] In this genetic interpretation, Billy's vocal
defect, that "his voice . . . was apt to develop an organic hesitancy, in
fact more or less a stutter or even worse"(*Budd* 53), points to a cognitive
disorder. So does his illiteracy and his degree of self-consciousness, of
which "he seemed to have little or none, or about as much as we may
reasonably impute to a dog of Saint Bernard's breed" (52), so that "to
deal in double-meanings and insinuations of any sort was quite foreign to his nature" (49). All of these characteristics are evidence of a
cognitive disorder—usually autism. Budd's abandonment by his biological parents is only icing on this cake, because his parents must
have also been "challenged" themselves and would have known their
child would be "defective." So they left him "in a pretty silk-lined
basket hanging one morning from the knocker of a good man's door
in Bristol" (51). A beautiful boy to look at, but "on the inside, it's a
whole different story," a story about defective genes, as this section's
heading suggests.[12]

Gone is the notion of irony. Gone, deadpan sarcasm. Gone, the history of narrative itself, that is, the tried-and-true narrative of mysterious but noble heritage, which Melville invokes when he says, "Yes, Billy Budd was a foundling, a presumable by-blow and evidently, no ignoble one. Noble descent was as evident in him as in a blood horse" (52). Gone, too, is the logic of naturalized distinctions that accompanied the class fantasy of noble blood, distinctions that would later subtend the logic of twentieth-century eugenics, a "science" that gave rise to genetics. But the troubling historical lineage of genetics is not at issue for this kind of "genetic" interpretation, in part because invoking a genetic disorder as the source of the problems presented by the inside narrative appears to resolve the dilemmas of this text in one fell swoop. Made over into a case that would, today, have proper medical remediation, Billy can be pitied; his murder of Claggert, mitigated. Claggert's resemblance to Billy—his unknown origins, his "natural" but unnamed depravity—can also be assigned to bad genes. Even Billy's execution can be softened: since genetics had not yet been discovered, how could Captain Vere have known he'd condemned a disabled person?

While such interpretative energy erases the literary past, it is not misplaced energy. After all, genetic evidence is often invoked as a final, ideal, irrefutable truth: in the courtroom, DNA puts to rest doubt about guilt, sometimes decades after the crime; in disasters, lost relatives can be identified using DNA evidence from the smallest of fragments. If cyberspace is a household reality, genetics is in the criminal justice system, and genetic engineering is on the dinner table, even if large-scale cloning is still somewhere over the rainbow. Although the idea called genetic engineering can still make people think of Nazi Germany, genetics itself is a promising science rather than a scary fiction, because whatever fears Americans have about human cloning, the science of genetics promises a cure; the Human Genome Project promises to prolong life; DNA evidence promises to free the innocent and find the dead. So the synonymy of genetics and eugenics as essentially the same science isn't readily called to mind. Or if the history of genetics is recalled, it often comes out as an act of disavowal, as in No, no, genetics is *not* eugenics! The Nazis practiced

eugenics! Of course, the American Eugenics Society had popular support before World War II, and it isn't as if the logic of eu/gen(et)ics
doesn't operate in animal breeding, whether the animal is bred to glow,
win racing purses, or represent the standards of the American Kennel
Club or the American Cat Fancier Association.

Certainly the importance of "blood"—a concept (like the word
cyber) far older than the discourses made available by genetics, as
Melville's wry comparison of Billy Budd to a blood horse shows—
hasn't vanished into the past. Family law valorizes blood relations;
parents seek to conceive their own offspring. This desire is sometimes
couched in the language of love: being the biological child of one's
parents can only help a child, say, in the event of illnesses associated
with DNA or should a transfusion or organ donation become necessary. Princeton geneticist Lee Silver once said to me that all parents
seek the best for their child because such a desire is part of the genetic
script of parenting.[13] But how, then, to understand child labor, tor-
ture, murder, prostitution, abuse, abandonment, and the marketing
of babies? Do all parents of abused children suffer from a flaw in their
parenting gene? And if they do have a genetic flaw, should they be
allowed to reproduce? Isn't this the logic of sterilization programs?

At this juncture it might be prudent to note that "the idealization
of genetic ties is intertwined with the most profound racist fantasies,
including the desire for racial purity," to quote Drucilla Cornell.[14]
Yet, by law and custom, we still valorize blood and understand DNA
as the "master molecule" capable of endless good.[15] Which is also to
overlook the way genetics underwrites genocide: eugenics is not simply the past; and genetics, the future. Ethnic cleansing is a contemporary political euphemism for genocide, besides which any number
of bloody conflicts are being fought and political policies made to fit
recalcitrant myths and fictions about race, ethnicity, and gender. For
example, a persistent story (science fiction?) about AIDS claims that
"having" a virgin (girl) will both cure men of the disease and protect
them from it. Such stories contribute to kidnapping, child prostitution, and infant rape. They deepen the worldwide AIDS epidemic.

Still, the idealization of genetics and the potential for that idealization to lend itself to genocide don't involve an awareness that is

particularly stressed when profit is at stake. Genetics is, rather, the real, the authentic, and the good. For example, on May 27, 1992, the FDA gave its unconditional approval to the production and distribution of genetically engineered fruits and vegetables.[16] No labeling or disclosure of said engineering by a parent company need be offered the consumer. The FDA understands genes as "natural" and therefore not in need of oversight, because genes are "organic," not artificial, like an additive or a controlled substance. As if nature, being natural, cannot also and always spell death. Yet recent research suggests that a particular genetically altered strain of corn that produces its own natural pesticide might be able to quietly kill off the monarch butterfly in addition to the corn pests that the introduced gene was intended to target. The monarch has no deleterious effect on corn whatsoever; and besides being lovely, it is vitally necessary to other pollination processes. Thus, if the monarch dies out, so too will other forms of plant life, even if those who wrote the script, as it were, for this strain of corn never intended it to kill the monarch, let alone other flora or fauna. And while this potential for the monarch to vanish altogether remains in dispute, the mere possibility seems worth mentioning.

Indeed, the idealization of genetics as natural and therefore good forgets that genetics is a body of knowledge expressed through a code and, as such, is subject to slippages, duplicities, reversals, and complications, depending upon how DNA sampling is done, who is doing it, and what the goal of the sampling is, among a whole range of other variables. According to semiotician Thomas Sebeok, the genetic code is the most fundamental of all semiotic networks, and certainly genetics and linguistics share this: a field of interpretation. While both are scientific, insofar as both genetics and linguistics represent a body of codified knowledge, from the Latin *scientia*, neither is foolproof. So if nature must perforce "speak" through a (linguistic) code, and if what she says is mediated by that code, how can she be reliably programmed? Few stop to wonder whether she might just as soon speak in tongues.

Biotech corporations, however, continue to "rewrite" DNA in both medical and agricultural research. The Human Genome Organization (HUGO) has produced a masterscript of DNA sequencing that spells out the overarching category of the "human" in a universally understood biological "language." Yet the standardized one-size-fits-all model that HUGO has employed has been criticized from within the scientific community. The Human Genome Project, first proposed in 1991 by an alliance of geneticists in the United States, was a counterorganization. So if, as Jacques Derrida has noted, when "the contemporary biologist speaks of writing and *pro-gram* in relation to the most elementary processes of information within the living cell," he or she also should indicate that the processes of interpretation are vital.[17] DNA is a mode of inscription, and, as with all forms of inscription or mediation, what is expressed by the code may not, in the end, ever be coterminous with the good intention of the author, no matter how ethical, moral, or righteous that intention may have been. Moreover, despite all the popular, profit-oriented promises that a genetic story will always be a happy one, fatality is embedded in the most idealized of these stories, something that *Billy Budd*, oddly enough, seems to comment on, as if it were as culturally prescient as any "science fiction." For what is at issue, in the last stages of Melville's inside narrative, are the following questions: Just what is fiction as opposed to fact? What is knowledge? How is truth—or justice—determined? Doesn't the way a story is told affect its truth value? And isn't it fair to take note that an event, once "expressed" or represented in narrative, is never precisely coterminous with the event itself?

These questions may, perhaps, seem to morph Melville into Derrida, but toward the end of this novel, a curious conversation between the purser and the surgeon takes place. The purser demands that the surgeon, who sees himself as a scientific man, explain why the invariable muscular spasm (i.e., orgasm) of a hanged man's body did not occur in Budd's case. The purser believes this a "testimony to the force lodged in will power" (124), but the surgeon ridicules the idea that Budd could've willed such a thing. He bridles, then dodges the question until the purser asks instead: "Was the man's death effected by the halter, or was it a species of euthanasia?" (125). The surgeon says he doubts the scientific authenticity of the term *euthanasia*, which he calls "something like your will power.... It is at once imaginative and metaphysical—in short, Greek" (125). But the surgeon's own "scientific" authority has been breached, thus leaving the purser's questions open: Could the peculiarities surrounding Budd's hanging have been effected by the operation of an "inside" narrative such as willpower?

As Eve Kosofsky Sedgwick argues, one answer would be a deadly yes. According to Sedgwick, *Billy Budd* turns on a Western cultural fantasy that the world can be purged of "perversity":

> Following both Gibbon and the Bible, moreover, with an impetus borrowed from Darwin, one of the few areas of agreement among modern Marxist, Nazi, and liberal capitalist ideologies is that there is a peculiarly close, though never precisely defined, affinity between same-sex desire and some historical condition of moribundity, called "decadence," to which not individuals or minorities but whole civilizations are subject. (*Epistemology* 130)

Read this way, *Budd* does have the chilling implications she narrates: that "the trajectory toward gay genocide was never clearly distinguishable from a broader, apocalyptic trajectory toward something approaching omnicide" (128). And, if we extend the genetic logic with which I opened this section—the idea that Billy suffers from an unnamed genetic disorder—then surely he can also be read as "flawed," either by autism or by the so-called gay gene? Whether autistic child or gay man, Billy becomes his own worst enemy. Questions about the morality of social laws, the ethics of military tribunals, the misuse of power, these social and political questions fall away in the face of biology-as-ideology.[18] Billy was designed from the inside out to self-destruct—a truly despairing vision, but then again no one can be blamed for his death. DNA done it.

Infamously, of course, the questions about Budd—who he was, how and why and if he should have died—are never resolved by the narrative itself, for, as Barbara Johnson notes, the story has not one ending but four conflicting ones.[19] Captain Vere claims, at the drumhead court he convenes, to be warding off the possibility of mutiny or mass revolt among his men. But Vere then dies murmuring, "Billy Budd, Billy Budd" (*Budd* 129), not in "the accents of remorse" (129), but rather in an accent (of desire?) left unnamed, although one provocative enough to make the *Bellipotent*'s senior officer uneasy. Meanwhile, according to a naval chronicle, Budd was "no Englishman but one of those aliens adopting English cognomens" who "vindictively" stabbed the master-at-arms, John Claggert, to death (130). Yet to his fellow sailors, Budd is the Handsome Sailor, incapable of crime, and their (homosocial) love for him, their identification with him, is recorded in a ballad, "Billy in the Darbies" (132).

Melville's voice, of course, is not absent from these endings, for he insists of his "inside narrative" that it is "truth uncompromisingly told" and will therefore "always have its ragged edges; hence the conclusion of such a narration is apt to be less finished than an architectural finial" (*Budd* 128). One can never say which ending is "the" end, nor easily resolve the question: Is the narrative truth (science?) or a tissue of lies (fiction)? The author makes what one might call a knowledge claim or a truth claim for this novel—the authorial voice calls the fiction, fact. Of course most readers read *Budd* as an antiquated fiction, and certainly it is marketed as fiction, not fact.

Moreover, it is a notoriously unfinished tale, fact or fable, because "the manuscript was in a heavily revised, still 'unfinished' state when [Melville] died on September 28, 1891" (*Budd* 12), a state of such disarray that the first editor of the manuscript, Raymond Weaver, wrote in 1928, "Such is the state of the *Billy Budd* manuscript that there can never appear a reprint that will be adequate to every ideal" (12). Yet the sparkling promise of a reprint adequate to an ideal, one with a "genetic" truth, was unveiled in 1962, when editors Harrison Hayford and Merton Sealts Jr. produced the Genetic Text of this unfinished story. They say their text represents "the most obvious editorial ideal...to put before the reader precisely what the author would have published" (12–13). Through painstaking forensic-detective editorial work, these editors have deciphered the "genesis" of production, teasing out Melville's revisionary process so that one "text" emerged from another in the seamless genetic sequencing of stages A, B, C, D, X, E, F, G, with substages such as Bc. This editorial genetics was not a new process in the 1950s, but it does reflect a perceived need for a viable, stable, accurate, pure "text," an ideal text, representing what the author intended: messy, unruly, unfinished, "defective" or stuttering texts such as *Billy Budd* require editorial gene therapy.[20]

Since 1962 and the advent of the so-called postmodern, such editorial practices have been called into question;[21] even Hayford and

Sealts understood their project as a multivalent one, given that the Phoenix edition is an abridged "reading text" separate from the full, scholarly Genetic Text, which allows any interested party to see the "genetic" manuscript in fragments. Besides, depending on the publisher's interest, the 1928 Weaver version and the 1948 F. Barron Freeman version, as well as the Hayford and Sealts Phoenix edition, are all still in circulation. Given this situation, the fungible, fragile complexities of the narrative remain visible and, I would argue, demonstrate that language *is* as complex as genetics, and since genetics is also a language, language is as much a part of the structure of who we understand ourselves to be as our DNA is. Language, like genetics, can radically alter reality—but not always in happy, comforting, even predictable ways. One must keep on "reading" and "writing"; for example, those who "wrote" the pesticidal corn into existence never intended genocide for the lovely monarch butterfly. Nor does the process of such reading and writing ever quite end, except, perhaps, in death. And yet there remains a cultural fantasy that sees genetics as "real," while language is "unreal," a fantasy that refuses to acknowledge the link between the two, for fear that such an acknowledgment might—what?

Generation(s)

Alter perception? But perception is always in flux. Time, a keyword of anxiety for the twentieth century, was altered as industrialization, the railroad, photography, and film altered how time was used, measured, perceived. Space, too, has been altered—and space is a keyword of concern for the twenty-first century. However, such alterations do not affect everyone simultaneously or in precisely the same manner. Still, the malleability of time/space may offer another reason for the almost obsessive twenty-first-century focus on the "inside narratives" of both genetics and cyberspace, the virtual space of the Internet.

Not surprisingly, among the veritable forest of cyberspace products, cybersex in all its forms may be both the most expansive and the most expensive. "Lust motivates technology," reports one enthusiast,[22] and it is difficult to deny that sexual innuendo, sexual puns, and sexualized products have overdetermined the most popular and widespread narratives about cyberspace. Indeed, pornography and the PC share a terrain of jokes, legal ambiguity, and anxiety. As for jokes, well, there are very bald and basic jokes about wet software and hardware or hardwiring, about joysticks, touch pads, drives, and viral infections; the personal computer may be composed of silicon, but the way it has been narrated has made it seem a carbon-based carbon copy of the (post)human. From the explosion of reproductive services available online to the possibility of transferring "live" DNA electronically, cybersex dominates the Internet. And as a word, *cybersex* has been used to designate anything from pornography to genetic engineering. A brief trip to Google (May 24, 2002) turned up around 227,000 sites that claim to hail under the rubric "cybersex," from cybersex .com, which claims to be the oldest, most extensive of online porn sites, to Clones-R-Us, which, after all, offers reproductive technology as an alternative (designer) method for getting with child.

What to make of this cornucopia of cybersex, if anything? It is my contention that the sexualized language of cyberspace indicates how the past—or fictions that subtend ideological structures supposedly *lodged* in the past—is reanimated and extended into the present/ future, in both an extension and an intensification of what Foucault called "biopower," which also demonstrates, as Hayles argues, that the past is both displaced and retained by fictions, with interesting consequences for the concept of "humanity," consequences that again take us into the realm of the posthuman.[23] Cybersex is an extension of popular, pseudopsychological inside narratives about the person inside you, first disseminated during the late 1960s through such practices as EST. Many of these popular venues have focused on "intimacy" or the lack thereof and, I would argue, have helped to narrow and recodify boundaries both between and within public and private realms, thus altering how the public and the private are understood. In other words, it is my contention that cybersex is an extension of a broader popular cultural discourse that has systematically redefined the boundary between public and private as *uniform* across cultural, economic, and geographical distances. The result? The realm of the intimate becomes, more and more, a matter of public record. What can, or cannot, be understood as strictly personal or private is often, in fact, reduced to predictable sets of prescripted narrative, applicable to everyone and therefore readable by, or accessible to, all. For example, Americans often feel they have an absolute right to know another's sexual orientation. Indeed, it is considered one's political and personal duty, since the 1960s sexual revolution, to be "open." The categories of orientation have been diversified as of the twenty-first century: you can be homo, hetero, bi, transgendered. Not that claiming any one of these marks of identity doesn't come with a social or political price tag. It does, as I have argued in the chapter "sucker." Nevertheless, the idea that being open is a good thing is widespread. Inside narratives, it would seem, have to come out or be outed. Accessibility, sometimes also now called transparency, has been touted as a human right, associated with democracy and individual freedom. Yet at the same time and in the name of transparency, the level of an American citizen's right to privacy has been legally curtailed, particularly with respect to the recent politics of terrorism, and by terrorism I also mean domestic terrorism. We may all have a right to be unique and different, but differences must be clearly legible; that is, difference must be something everyone can understand and have access to. If there's a difference on the inside, it must be a familiar difference to ensure that, if we are all different, we are also all the same.

But this, too, is a venerable narrative pattern, and, as I've argued across several of the preceding chapters, whether that pattern is one that stresses the universal or one that stresses diversity, it comes to us bearing a dialectical history. To understand the centrality of the universal is also to understand the claims of the diverse and vice versa. And one must be well-versed in that dialectical history in any attempt to critique, alter, or intervene in the human story. To put this another way: it has been useful, and in recent years critically fashionable, to attack the ideology of universalism as essentialist. And I am broadly sympathetic to the aims of such critiques, given their roots in the sociopolitical movements of the 1960s. However, it would do well to remember also the potential uses of universalist models; after all, it was in the name of the category "human" that slavery was abolished. Universalism did offer a means by which to call into question those problematic historical separations of public and private spheres, which gave rise to heightened modes of gender inequality and can still be said to undergird the uneasy legal discourses and police practices.

That is, contrary to the liberatory expectations that gave rise in the United States to the 1970s feminist slogan "The personal is political," what has happened since that time has not been as liberatory as many had hoped. Instead of an increased politicization of the private, we've seen an increasingly commodified, depoliticized, individuated personal. And this new personal is made increasingly available for public consumption, if not, as Foucault might say, available for inspection and regulation. That which might once have been considered inviolably intimate—let's just say, one's own genetic makeup? or that you've had a miscarriage? an abortion? cancer?—is in the process of going public. At the risk of being called both elitist and old-fashioned, I'll just quote the poet and essayist Wallace Stevens here, who lamented the invasion of radio into the home in the 1940s when he wrote, "Now we are intimate with total strangers and unhappily they are intimate with us."[24]

In fact, the model of the personal in which the personal is part of the public sphere structures an increasingly atomized regime of commodity normalization in the name of so-called personal choice and freedom. Cyberspace is a venue distinctly suited to this depoliticized, anticollective model of the public personal, as cyberspace enthusiast Howard Rheingold points to in his claim that cyberspace produces an "online hyperpersonal effect."[25] Cybersex, if we adopt his sense of the hyperpersonal, is an ecstatic promise to take us past all the impediments of embodiment—no mess, no disease, no fuss, no need for foreplay, safe sex, or extended conversation. But I'm not arguing that something inherent in either genetic engineering as a science or the computer as a technological tool is to blame for this state of affairs, whether one finds in them technophilic ecstasy or technophobic agony. A computer is both no more and no less than a prosthesis, like many other such devices—say, a pencil—devised to enhance communication. Rather, what I am arguing is that this hyperhomogeneity of the personal is tied to a predominant, late-capitalist economic logic that depends on the generation of supposedly individuated, diversified, but nevertheless structurally homogeneous consumer groups; these groups, in turn, allow for what is hailed as unmediated interactivity or transparency. Both similar and different, these groups are perceived to have "intimacy needs" that have been tailored by, and to, a product line, and soon, if Clones-R-Us has its way, the product line will include humans as well. Cybersex assumes that everyone desires the same thing: just as the film I discussed in the chapter "nigger" assumes everyone wants a washing machine (everyone loves a Hollywood movie), even those who don't have electricity (yet). Advocates, of course, vow that cyberspace and cybersex will abolish "distance" altogether. Apparently they have forgotten that both face-to-face and online communication is *always* mediated by language; blissfully inattentive to the possibility that going beyond all boundaries into endlessness might not be nirvana, advocates seem to respond only to the pleasures of volume and velocity. So, why worry about human cloning? Cybersex ensures that we are clones: our desires are plugged in. We are already replicants, reliable (consumers), available (online), and always accessible, both already read and all ready.

In Conclusion: A Moment of Intimacy, Please?

What I hope is evident by this point is that cyberadvocates assume we humans are all the same on the inside: we have the same dreams, same desires, same hope, same despair. And yet this story doesn't seem to have had much appeal in the sociopolitical domain. No matter how politically naive, this fantasy of transparent connection based on humanness doesn't go away; we, it is assumed, all want to go beyond flesh, time, space, death to achieve pure intimacy. Indeed, since the late 1970s, the word *intimacy* has been used in a public discourse about contemporary American life that plays itself out in everything from state policy to school prayer in furious debates over identity politics, diversity, economic policy, violence, and the democratic process.

But if you will allow me to, let me pause here to ask a disingenuous question: When you've been intimate with someone, what have you done? When I asked one of my colleagues this, she laughed and said, "Sure, I know. Intimate means heterosexual intercourse," by which my friend meant we all just know that *intimate* means "sex." But I think this commonsense definition might have surprised people in the 1940s, when *intimacy* meant "the core of a person's private sphere, which by law, tact, and convention is shielded from intrusion." In fact, since the 1970s at least, the definition of *intimacy* has broadened so much, the promise of it can sell just about anything. Personal growth, a genre of popular psychology that has been burgeoning since the 1970s, tells us, as in the 1987 best-selling *Art of Intimacy*, that being intimate is an "experience of connectivity" and the "central energizer of life" (Malone and Malone 25). The general message of this intimacy is that humanness is intimacy, or as the *Art of Intimacy* puts it, intimacy "is crucial to . . . our preparation for, our capacity for, societal intimacy and closeness, national intimacy and closeness, international intimacy and closeness, human and nonhuman intimacy and closeness" (75).

Profound, vast, vital, intimacy begins to sound like the very "stuff" of life—a description that has, of course, been used to characterize the master molecule, DNA. So, when proponents of electronic communications promise to give us intimacy, it's no wonder there's a rush. Here and only here do all the improper, recalcitrant impediments to "true" intimacy, true humanness, and truth *tout court* vanish. Gender, race, ethnicity, nationality, class, and eventually species will, some enthuse, disappear. Here we enter once again the realm of the human-nonhuman hybrid. Back in 1992, for example, two Macintosh designers wrote what became a Web document called "On the Road to Intimacy," in which they predicted we would one day all have an intimate digital assistant, or a "helpful friend you could carry in your pocket" (Dunham and Shwarts). They understand intimacy as a friendly, familiar device like a telephone, which, we are told,

> is an intimate device. You don't have to think about using it, and probably don't consider yourself to be using high technology when you do. When you talk on the phone, you frequently forget that you are. An intimate computer should be equally transparent. Ideally, you shouldn't know you're using a computer until it does something wonderful.

Of course one wants to ask: Now, really, who can forget they're on the telephone? More interesting is the syntax of the statement "When you talk on the phone, you frequently forget that you are."

What might it mean to forget that you *are*?

On the lighter side of this question, I hope those on the cell behind the wheel of a car remember that they are, please. On the darker side of this question, I would say that this is a most acute form of intimacy indeed, where all barriers, including the barrier of one's self and psyche, vanish. Of course, this is an old nineteenth-century New England transcendentalist philosophical ideal, but such liberating human transparency and "freedom" for and from all hasn't been, after all, simple to achieve. There remain untidy economic facts that stay the fantasy; it is also clear that violent, sexualized behavior hasn't been substantially altered; and to buy life everlasting in the form of a silicon friend who will never die or age or in the form of a DNA license is not just expensive but also borders on silly. In other words, too often what is new out on the Web is just another version of an old, old fairy tale. Meanwhile, radical conservative collectives, such as the racist, anarchist, Ku Klux Klan affiliate Stormfront, are turning more and more to the Net to extend their old message of divisiveness, hatred, and justifiable murder. And mass murder, whether nuclear or biological, is frequently invoked, by pundits and politicians, as a potential terrorist outcome of worldwide bloodsucking terrorists, but of course "we" aren't terrorists ourselves, ever.

History is hardly over. The past, encoded within one simple word such as any of the "household words" in my sampling of plain speak, shapes how stories can be told and received; history steers perception and the funding of far more of our lives than is sometimes readily apparent. And while I may be called alarmist to take such notice of the subtle historical shifts in a single word's meaning—the movement, say, of *bloomers* from politics to playground—these shifts suggest to me that we may revise our language, but the story doesn't always change as much or as radically as might be either feared by some or hoped by others. And so always keeping in mind that history not only *matters* but also shapes, we also need to listen for other words and other narratives than those of the past-as-future—new (science) fictions or idioms—in order to understand difference as more than yet another version of the same, a story truly "other" than the one(s) offered by the posthuman tale of the cyberclone, that fiction of science that appears, at least at the moment, to prevail.

Notes

Introduction

1. One thinks, as Sinfield did, of Gramsci.
2. And as Mencken points out, *horse sense* itself is a compound Americanism, and "these compounds (there must be thousands of them) have been largely responsible for giving the language its characteristic tang and color" (95).
3. Raymond Williams's *Keywords* is, in part, a model for this study.
4. See Freud, *Interpretation*.
5. For other accounts of common sense, see, for example, "the strength of ideology derives from the way it gets to be common sense" (Sinfield 806).

Any discussion of common sense and ideology takes us, for example, to Immanuel Kant on *the sensus communis* in *The Critique of Judgment;* to Gramsci's discussion of common sense in *The Prison Notebooks;* and certainly to Althusser. See also Belsey.

6. Or as Mencken wrote, "Slang originates in an effort, always by ingenious individuals, to make the language more vivid and expressive" (52).
7. Mencken once famously quipped that this magazine was so bad it might go over, to which he added his famous line: There's no underestimating the intelligence of the American public. Quips of this cranky nature make for both Mencken's piquancy and his unpopularity in some circles.
8. One thinks of the Sokol-Ross debates.

bloomers

1. As Gayle V. Fischer remarks in "'Pantalets' and 'Turkish Trowsers,'" dress reform occupied a number of women, for different and often conflicting reasons.

2. On the general preferability of male attire, see Fischer; and Coon; see also Steele, *Paris*.

3. Stanton 201. See also Kesselman.

4. See also Kelley.

5. As Fischer remarks, Lady Mary Wortley Montague famously wore trousers in her travels in Turkey (see "Costumes of All Nations" 45). For a more extensive history of trousers as underwear, see also Ewing, *Dress*.

6. In any history of the Bloomer costume, the question of decency is raised, generally with regard to the relationship between trousers and gender and trousers and undergarments. Bloomers also became associated with any social upheaval in general; for discussions of eroticism and trousers, see Steele *(Paris)*; Ewing *(Dress)*; Fischer; and Kesselman; see also: Steele, *Fashion*; Craik; Gaines and Herzog; and Byrde.

7. See also Peiss; Garber; Barnes and Eicher; and Lurie.

8. See Coon 12–14; see also Stanton et al. 890; and Lerner 335.

9. According to Lerner, "It soon became a symbol of revolt against all the senseless restrictions imposed on women and was worn with grim persistence in the face of ridicule, abuse and public censure" (335–36). But women like the Grimké sisters finally gave it up: "Sarah gave the costume up gladly, for she had worn it only from conviction; Angelina did so with the understanding that in time a better and more attractive dress for women would be developed and accepted" (336). See also Birney.

10. See Worrell. As Worrell notes, "How a nation's children are treated and educated reveals much about its attitudes towards its citizens.... Evidence shows that American children's clothing utilized new European styles and daring or even 'shocking' new ideas sooner than did the fashions of adults. Apparently we dress our children in new styles that we ourselves are not always ready to accept. In recent history, young children wore bikini bathing suits before their parents did. The same was true with pantaloons at the beginning of the nineteenth century.... Girls wore trousers or pantalets before their mothers did and made bloomers part of their regular wardrobe before their mothers did" (4).

11. Mabel Lee's memoirs are detailed and articulate about the battle she and others like her waged for the acceptance of women in sports (199).

12. See Ewing, *History* 81–82; and Green 26–27.

13. Such questions are reflected in incidents such as the blue jean scandal in Italy, 1998, when the courts ruled that a woman who wore blue jeans could not legally be raped.

14. See also Martin.

15. See Ewing, *History*. See also Baines; and Gattey.

16. These particular definitions were taken from *The Random House Dictionary of the English Language*, the unabridged edition; other dictionaries consulted were *The American Heritage Dictionary*, *Webster's Dictionary*, and *The Dictionary of American Slang*.

17. The linkage to childhood is evidenced in a 1993 children's book, *Bloomers!* by Rhoda Blumberg, an illustrated children's guide to the suffragette movement.

18. Reprinted in Franklin 435–40.

19. Although Catharine Beecher is often seen as more conservative than her sister, Harriet Beecher Stowe, she was passionate about the need for girls to take exercise; see, for example, her book *Physiology and Calisthenics*.

20. The story of the Bloomer's genesis has been recounted both by the participants themselves and by various histories of the movement, as cited above; see Coon's Introduction; Kesselman; Stanton; and Lerner.

21. As Gayle Fischer notes, even the women of the Oneida Community gave up wearing it outside the confines of their own community walls.

22. As quoted by Barry, 82. Barry is quoting a letter from Elizabeth Cady Stanton to Susan B. Anthony, February 19, 1854, Library of Congress.

23. Elizabeth Cady Stanton, "The Degradation of Disfranchisement," *Woman's Tribune* (February 7, 1891), as quoted by L. Newman (64).

24. As quoted in Martin (100–101), Miss Ada S. Ballin thought the Bloomer died because it was "too violent" a change.

25. See also Gattey; and Steele, *Paris*.

26. See Ewing, *Dress* and *History*; and Garber.

27. This kind of eroticism, especially the eroticization of little girls, is evident in popular American culture in figures such as Little Eva, Shirley Temple, Lolita, and JonBenet Ramsey. Part of Marilyn Monroe's appeal was her combination of childlike innocence and overt sexuality. Humbert Humbert is borrowed from Vladimir Nabokov's *Lolita*. See also Dyer.

28. As Anne C. Coon notes, the so-called bra burners also suffered the same kind of ridicule as Bloomerites. The press seized upon dress as the issue and thus dismissed the other, more radical and political claims of feminism; see 35 fn. 4.

29. See also Lurie, *The Language of Clothes*, in which she insists that bloomers did not enjoy any widespread attention until the 1890s.

30. As I have written elsewhere (*Conceived by Liberty* 54), abolitionists such as Lydia Maria Child often referenced other cultural practices to which they took exception when attempting to talk about the condition of women. Chinese foot binding was a favorite example; so was the seraglio. Despite the evident and often virulent racism that ran through the women's movement, it is unlikely that these commentators were unaware of the irony they invited

by wearing something like Turkish trowsers or were uninterested in the suffering of their "sisters," particularly given the following poem that Gayle V. Fischer quotes, noting how it "compares the 'inhuman' 'Turkish' harem with the 'inhuman' Western practice of wearing physically restrictive clothing: Talk of Turkish women / In their harem-coop,— / Are we less inhuman, / Hampering with a hoop?" (123).

    31. See Garber. See also Chauncey.

sucker

    1. I cite these two novels because each is interested in the politics of the so-called average person. *Sucker* as a term for those who end up on the wrong fiduciary end of economic and political developments has also migrated, as evidenced in the publication of Anne Billson's 1993 vampire farce about Prime Minister Thatcher's economic policies, *Suckers.*

    2. For a short history of breast-feeding, see Hoffert. See also Copjec.

    3. Attempts to remotivate a derogatory term as positive are a familiar strategy. A contemporary dramatic example of such usage can be found in Tony Kushner's play *Angels in America,* part 2: *Perestroika,* which demonstrates as well the ambivalent effect of a physical insult. In this play, Belize, "a former drag queen," and Roy M. Cohn, "a successful New York lawyer," argue over a stash of illegal AZT, which Cohn has procured for himself. In one scene, these two characters trade heated insults that traverse an American lexicon of sex, class, race, ethics, ethnicity, and etiquette, beginning with *nigger,* alighting upon *cocksucker,* and ending in *kike.* But Cohn's response to this exchange is, paradoxically, admiration. Once he has gotten Belize to call him everything from a cocksucker to a kike, he says, "Now you're talking! . . . Now you can have a bottle" of the AZT (Kushner 61). The scene's drama depends on ambivalence: if Cohn's delight is presented to the audience through Belize as disgusting, the part itself, as written, is full of gusto. The heart of my argument is that the provocation of Cohn's gusto produces a tour de force of abusive naming that, in the end, will benefit the one person for whom Cohn claims to have only contempt: Belize. Turn this around, and Belize will get the AZT from the one person who embodies all he abhors: Cohn. Disgust and desire, pleasure and pain: the defining characteristics of most physical, bodily insults.

    4. The play and the film *M. Butterfly* (1996) as well as the films *The Ballad of Little Jo* (1993) and *The Garden of Good and Evil* (1997) feature central characters who, like the television talk-show host RuPaul, cross-dress in such a way as either to live as the so-called opposite sex or to fool the people around them, including their lovers—a "game" that the film *The Crying Game* (1992) also capitalized upon.

5. Florida's vampires, on and off the Internet, are legion, it would seem. For examples, see the Miamian who claimed to be driven to kill and drink blood ("Records Show Killer Drank Women's Blood") and the case of Rod Ferrell ("Cult Head Wants New Trial"). Seventeen-year-old Floridian Rod Ferrell, who has been dubbed a vampire cult leader, was sentenced to death in February 1998 for the November 1996 bludgeoning deaths of Richard Wendorf and Naoma Queen. At his trial, Ferrell's lawyers attempted to show that the young man had been a victim of satanic child abuse and was not of sound mind.

6. *Buffy the Vampire Slayer*, in its use of a tongue-in-cheek version of vampirism, comes to mind.

7. Incidentally, the press corps of Marilyn Monroe's time gave her the nickname "the Body."

8. The association of the vampire with the cinema is so common almost every critic cited in this chapter comments on it.

9. As White says, "Automobiles could be made to perform dreadful tasks. In Western Kenya in 1968, travelers feared accepting rides because the *wazimamoto* had cars with specially designed backseats that could automatically drain the blood of whoever sat there" (33).

10. Apologies to Benedict Anderson for borrowing his title.

11. For example, according to Lora Romero, the critical endeavors of those progressives whose intellectual pursuits were shaped by the "ethnic separatisms of the 60s and 70s" (129), whatever their liabilities, were more attuned to "their organic intellectual traditions" (134) and certainly more engaged in actual social movements than proponents of what she names as the post-structuralist enterprise of "difference criticism"—in this case, Barbara Johnson, Henry Louis Gates, and Donna Haraway. These critics, says Romero, attempted to "apply the poststructuralist concept of 'difference' to minority culture" in order to "delineate a purely formal theory of ethnic literary expression . . . in an attempt to transform what might be seen as a political liability into a cognitive asset" (129)—the political liability being the logic of separatism. "Difference criticism," writes Romero, "represents itself as politically progressive or even radical, despite the fact that it lacks a social movement with which to identify" (129). For Romero, then, post-structuralism in toto represents a return to abstract formalism, which she defines as a methodological attention to language that equates "literary value with textual obscurity" as an aspect of naturalizing class distinctions—or what she calls "the middle-class fantasy of transcending class and ideology" (131) that merely serves to consolidate both. This configuration, in Romero's estimation, undermines any effort to reconceive the shape of intellectual labor, since it must posit anomie as a cognitive advantage, a sign of intellectual mastery. Validating obscurity and professional jargon over clarity and immediacy, elevating

anomie over intimacy, difference critics, in mounting a debate about the logic
of essentialist separatist movements, have evidently given the go-ahead to
right-wing collectivities such as the National Association of Scholars, "whose
anti-ethnic studies platform," says Romero, "should make difference critics
reflect upon the efficacy of their critiques of separatism" (141). While I agree
with Romero's alarm at the NAS and share her desire to locate an effective left-
wing methodology, I am not as sure about the efficacy of immediacy as she
was, at least in this argument.

12. According to Michael Bérubé it is not the cultural left but, rather,
the new right of the 1990s that has sought most aggressively alternate rhetorics
and an "alternate credentializing" that "will allow them to avoid meeting
academic standards for the production of knowledge" (95).

13. For a different argument regarding the remotivated use of the word
queer, see also Morton.

14. Tammy Watts, as quoted in *Time*, July 3, 1995, speaking out against
the ban of a late-term abortion procedure called an intact D and E by physicians but dubbed "brain-sucking" by the radical right. The ban was approved.

15. An intact D and E is a late-term abortion procedure pioneered by
Dr. James McMahon; it terminates the fetus inside the womb through a
series of injections and then delivers it intact, although the brain is suc-
tioned out to make delivery easier.

16. I have written about the rhetoric of reproduction, culture, and the
nation-state in my first book. I am indebted there, and here, to Kristen Luker,
for her fine work in *Abortion and the Politics of Motherhood*, and to Barbara
Johnson, "Apostrophe, Animation, and Abortion." See also K. Newman,
Fetal; and Condit.

17. Gayatri Spivak has commented on strategic essentialism numerous
times, not only in *Outside in the Teaching Machine*, but also in interviews, in
The Spivak Reader, and *In Other Worlds*; see also Diana Fuss's *Essentially
Speaking*.

18. Travers 101. Quips Travers, "It's a twist on Oliver that Dickens never
imagined" (102).

19. See also Diana Fuss's *Identification Papers*.

bombshell

1. *New York Post*, December 18, 1998. The *Daily News* ran an editorial
the same day entitled "Of Bombs and Bombshells."

2. Despite political activism about or cultural flirtations with androg-
yny, drag, unisex, bisexuality, and/or transgendering, traditional heterosexual
arrangements remain dominant and privileged—as evident in most social
arrangements, in advertising, law, medicine. Take for example, the persistence
of the term the *opposite sex*. Or the popular book that became a board game

in the late 1990s, *Men Are from Mars; Women Are from Venus.* See also: Warner, *Fear of a Queer Planet;* Califia; and Patton, *Fatal Advice.*

3. Common sense often also insists that sex is better left a private matter, although how it can be considered a private matter at all is questionable, given the numerous public legalities, political restrictions, religious disciplines, and discursive practices that are produced in relation to it (hourly if you are on the Internet), as Michel Foucault was at pains to demonstrate in volume 1 of *The History of Sexuality*

4. Whether such an association with JFK hurt or helped Clinton's "image" remains debatable.

5. All of these descriptions were given of Monroe at one time or another by those to whom she was close or with whom she worked, including husband Arthur Miller, Laurence Olivier, Lauren Bacall, Jane Russell, Billy Wilder, Nunally Johnson, and Jack Paar, among others. See Mills.

6. The phrase is from photographer Cecil Beaton, as quoted by Arnold (32). In regard to the ambiguity of the bombshell's identity, it's worth remembering, for example, that Monroe was one of the few people Nikita Khrushchev asked to meet on his goodwill tour of the United States in 1959; later, in 1992, photographs from this meeting were used by tabloid newspapers to prove that Monroe was a spy for the KGB. For the most reliable biographical information on Monroe, see McCann; Spoto; Leming; and Baty.

7. The quoted phrase is from the *Star,* October 20, 1998.

8. In regard to the enabling amnesia, see also Caruth.

9. As my colleague John Murchek reminds me, French has two terms that can be translated as *knowledge: savoir* and *connaissance.* English makes no such distinction.

10. See Toby Miller.

11. A pattern of the Light Lady/Dark Lady literary pairing, inherited from the nineteenth century. See also my argument in *Conceived by Liberty* 11.

12. See Dyer 42–44.

13. See Brumberg.

14. See Sullivan, *Bombshells* and *Va Va Voom!*

15. Or the famous quote in *My Story:* "Yes, there was something special about me, and I knew what it was. I was the kind of girl they found dead in a hall bedroom with an empty bottle of sleeping pills in her hand" (66).

16. Regarding Monroe's commodification, her name has been multiply trademarked by her estate as Marilyn,™ Marilyn Monroe,™ and Marilyn Monroe (signature).™ For her restaging of Harlow, Dietrich, and Bow, see Richard Avedon's sequence of Monroe stills in *Life* magazine, December 11, 1958. For her identification with bombs, see, for example, a popular novel of the 1960s, Alvah Bessie's *The Symbol,* which is a fictionalized account of Monroe's life. Here, she is called the S-X Bomb. Indeed, according to the novel's description, "Sometimes her picture was superimposed over the mushroom

cloud itself, and the montage provoked editorial writers on the *Worker* and the *West Coast People's World* to mild paroxysms of rage at this display of vulgar and corrupt capitalist ideology, which Spectacular executives thought quite amusing until the *San Francisco Chronicle* wrote: "To couple the blatant exploitation of sex with the horror of the bomb that destroyed Hiroshima and Nagasaki—as a Hollywood movie company is doing in advance advertisements for a forthcoming feature film—strikes us as the height of mindless vulgarity" (169).

17. Variations on the theme of the incongruence between the Bombshell and the Brain fascinated the popular press and imagination at the time of their marriage; Fox Studios considered floating a story that linked Jayne Mansfield to Charles Van Doren as a publicity stunt, and the rumor that Monroe once slept with Albert Einstein continues to circulate. That brains and bodily attributes are opposite continues to run as a topos through contemporary popular forms, as in Nicholas Roeg's film *Insignificance,* in which the Monroe-DiMaggio marriage is triangulated through Albert Einstein and the creation of the theory of relativity. The film attempts to link sex and violence through the invocation of the atomic bomb, although it also manages to suggest that the Monroe figure deserves to be blown away, for reasons that remain obscure.

Famously, although Art Miller was targeted by the House Un-American Committee, it was the announcement of his upcoming marriage, made publicly to the press on the steps of the Senate even before he'd proposed, that helped to defang the committee's prosecution. The marriage revised Miller's public persona so that the left-wing, Jewish, one-time Communist intellectual vanished in the bright flashbulb light of his new role as famous, presumably virile husband. Thus the potential version of Miller as an alien Communist or national traitor was replaced by a version of Miller as heroic national treasure, both artistic and moral: a very different public fate from the one faced by Miller's friend, director, and one-time Monroe bedmate Elia Kazan after his testimony (Leming 9–11, 77).

18. See also Dinnerstein.

19. One thinks, for example, of Governor Jesse "the Body" Ventura's popular voter appeal as someone who was more "real" than most politicians.

20. Recalling F. Scott Fitzgerald's *The Beautiful and the Damned,* a narrative of doomed beauty into which biographies about F. Scott Fitzgerald himself so often fall, as if he had become his own *Great Gatsby.*

21. Curiously, one of Norma Jeane Baker's caretakers repeatedly likened the child to the character Christina Light in Henry James's *Princess Casamassima.*

22. *Vogue,* September 15, 1962.

23. Or a valiant "victim of . . . a society that professes dedication to the relief of the suffering, but kills the joyous," as Ayn Rand wrote in the *Los Angeles Times* of August 19, 1962.

24. "Candle in the wind" comes from Elton John/Bernie Taupin, "Candle in the Wind," 1974. The song was revised in August 1997 as an elegy and tribute to Princess Diana. For "a mind out of the ordinary," see Sandburg 91; for "her quick wit and native intelligence," see Mills 14.

25. See Gregory and Speriglio; and Wolfe.

26. With apologies and thanks to my colleague Susan Hegeman ("Taking Blondes Seriously"). Critics have taken the idea of the blonde seriously, particularly with regard to questions about race, but Monroe herself is often featured as the site of a breakdown in anything like serious significance.

27. Crane 29: "The girl, Maggie, blossomed in a mud-puddle."

28. Prostitution, of course, is not gender specific. See also Chapkis.

29. The conflicting testimonies of Anita Hill and Clarence Thomas regarding his sexual harassment are a case in point, given the reluctance of the all-male Senate committee to lend any credibility to Anita Hill.

30. See Gourevitch; and Poniewozik.

31. Miller insistently and repeatedly claimed the play was not autobiographical. See also Savran 57; A. Miller, Timebends 532.

32. Capote's In Cold Blood is often cited as the first best-selling creative nonfiction. Capote wrote Breakfast at Tiffany's with Monroe in mind and was reputedly furious when Audrey Hepburn was given the film role. Mailer's Executioner's Song is also considered to have furthered this genre, although one might also call his book Marilyn as well as his On the Elegance of Women and stage play Strawhead versions of creative nonfiction. On Mailer's writing about Monroe, see also A. Miller, Timebends 532–33.

33. It is well known that Adolf Hitler admired Henry Ford. And as Michel Foucault writes about Nazism, it was "doubtless the most cunning and the most naive . . . combination of the fantasies of blood and the paroxysms of a disciplinary power" (History 149).

34. I make this connection, too, through Dyer's argument, in "Monroe and Sexuality," that Monroe was being used to locate a "new" understanding of female sexuality that arose in the 1950s—the concept of the vaginal versus the clitoral orgasm, represented as "oceanic."

scab

1. See also Brumberg.

2. Alabama became the first state to revive chain gangs, under Governor Fob James, who took office in January 1995. Florida and Arizona followed suit in 1997. The four hundred men on Alabama's gangs are mostly repeat offenders and those with discipline problems. Jones said similar criteria would be used in picking women inmates. Shackled women will be ordered to cut grass, pick up trash, and plant a large vegetable garden behind the prison, officials said. It is not known yet if they will be shackled in groups of five, as men are.

3. See www.iamawlodge1426.org/scab.htm.

4. As I took note of in *Conceived by Liberty*, chapter 1. See particularly Fitzhugh.

5. See "The Traffic in Women" in Goldman's *Red Emma Speaks*.

6. At least Marilyn Monroe's million might have bought something besides the kind of press Darva Conger set herself up to receive, although that, I admit, is a somewhat risible claim.

7. As Françoise Basch notes in her preface to Malkiel's text, it is not clear how widely this narrative circulated.

8. I choose here to use the term *realist/naturalist* because, as Rachel Bowlby notes, following in Fredric Jameson's footsteps, realist narrative precedes the "realist" period in the United States; moreover, much critical ink has been spilled over just exactly what a "naturalist" novel, as opposed to a realist narrative, might be. See Bowlby; and Jameson.

9. See Bowlby 83–98. See also Peiss.

10. That the novel was, as editor Claude Simpson says, "considered a scandal" is evident both in early reviews and in Doubleday's refusal to give the novel circulation. See Dreiser, *Sister Carrie*, ed. Simpson, v–xix.

11. All citations to Dreiser's *Sister Carrie* are to the Norton Critical Edition, 1991, unless Claude Simpson's edited edition is specified.

12. See also Hochman.

13. As Angela Davis, in *Women, Race and Class*, argues.

14. Here I disagree with Rachel Bowlby, who argues that "acting remains a real job" in the novel (63).

nigger

1. See also Matsuda et al.; and Collins. Cross burning, for instance, spurred a U.S. Supreme Court deliberation late in 2002: is it or is it not a speech act protected by the First Amendment?

2. See also MacKinnon's *Only Words*.

3. Angela Davis's work has heavily influenced my thinking here. See her *Women, Race and Class*.

4. *Franklin Evans* was first published in the *New World* 2, no. 10, extra series no. 34, November 1842, 1–31, and sold twenty thousand copies.

5. On Whitman's name changes, see Whitman, *Portable* 56, stanza 24; and Whitman, *Complete Poetry* 41, stanza 24. On his poetic industry, see Sedgwick, *Between Men* 206; and Kazin, "Introduction" to *Specimen Days*, where Kazin calls Whitman "a nearly mythic figure" of international reach, "the poet of 'democracy' not limited to Americans. During the 1914–18 war, fallen French and German soldiers alike were found in the trenches with Whitman's poems in their uniforms" (xix).

6. See *PMLA* (New York: Modern Language Association) (November 1995): 1314.

7. See *PMLA* (January 1996): 171.

8. See Foner.

9. This book also exists with the title form *The Love of the Last Tycoon*, as edited by Matthew J. Bruccoli.

10. See August. Famously, Thomas Carlyle and John Stuart Mill debated the question of race in England in public editorials that represent "a clear-cut conflict between...two former friends who went their separate ways" in regard to "the crucial question of what is a just relationship between white men and black men in modern society" (x).

11. See Fitzgerald.

12. Another telling example of this shift can be seen in a children's book called *Ten Little Niggers*, originally published in 1875 and reprinted numerous times (1890, 1900, 1910) in the early part of the twentieth century. However, the 1942 edition is called *Ten Little Negros* and attempts, in what now seems a pathetic way, to correct for the scalding racism of the earlier editions. Many thanks to Michelle Martin for this piece of evidence.

cyber

1. Richard DeGrandpre, at http://cyborgmanifesto.org, seems taken aback by the respondents to the *Adbusters* hoax.

2. Or to quote the last line of F. Scott Fitzgerald's *The Great Gatsby*, "So we beat on, boats against the current, borne back ceaselessly into the past."

3. Hayles, "Life Cycle" 159. See also Hayles, *How We Became Posthuman;* and Hayles and Hansen.

4. As many noted at the time of *Neuromancer's* publication, George Orwell's classic science-fiction novel *1984* had not—or had it?—come true.

5. From Stephanie A. Smith, "Dispatches from Elsewhen," talk delivered at the University of California, Berkeley, Women's Studies Forum, 1987.

6. See the *Gainesville Sun*, Tuesday, November 27, 2001.

7. The idea that people might be used as an organ resource is part of an ongoing urban legend about black-market kidneys and stolen livers. A number of Web sites are devoted to tracking urban legends. For one of these sites, see www.urbanlegends.com/medical/organ.theft/organ_theft_unos.html. This legend has also surfaced in mass-market novels, such as Robin Cook's *Coma* (1977).

8. CC's story appeared in a slew of reports, on television and radio, in the newspaper, and online (www.jhunewsletter-CC, accessed March 1, 2002).

9. To "make" CC, the researchers cloned eighty-seven embryos into eight surrogate mother cats just to get one healthy cat. While this may have

been a step up from the 277 attempts made before Dolly was cloned, it was still a long shot.

10. Apologies to Cher for borrowing from her song title "If I Could Turn Back Time."

11. In the title *Billy Budd (an Inside Narrative)*, the subtitle was settled on by editors Hayford and Sealts as a result of their "genetic" editorial work. Prior to their 1962 version of this story, the title was not "as the author gave it," because previous editors had failed "to recognize Mrs. Melville's hand in the manuscript. . . . For the title of the story two versions survive. One occurs in pencil draft on a slip attached to a separate leaf: 'Billy Budd / Foretopman / What befell him / in the year of the / Great Mutiny / &c.' The other occurs as a penciled addition at the top of the first leaf of the story proper: 'Billy Budd / Sailor / (An inside narrative).' That the second of these was in fact Melville's final intention for the title is made clear by all *genetic* evidence" (19, my emphasis).

12. From the advertisement for *Inside Edition*, see also www.insideedition .com.

13. In a lively debate at the Einstein Forum, Potsdam, Germany, June 4–6, 1999, for the forum "Genetics and Genealogy." See also Silver.

14. Cornell is paraphrasing Roberts in *The Genetic Tie*; see Cornell 110.

15. On the DNA as considered the master molecule, see Keller. See also Haraway, "Modest."

16. See Smith, "Cyber(genetics)."

17. Derrida, *Grammatology* 9. See also Butler's analysis of the "master gene" regarding DNA XY chromosomes in *Gender Trouble* 106–11.

18. I am following on Lewontin's reasoning in *Biology as Ideology*.

19. And that the novel is an elaborate commentary about reading itself is addressed by Johnson in "Melville's Fist."

20. See, for example, Bowers; and Greg.

21. See, for example, McGann.

22. See Milstead and Milhon.

23. See Foucault, *History*, for his construction of the concept of biopower, as used in this chapter.

24. Or so mourns Stevens (18).

25. See www.well.com/user/hlr/tomorrow/hyperpersonal.html. See also Rheingold, *The Virtual Community*, either at www.rheingold.com/vc/book or in print.

Bibliography

Adorno, Theodor. *The Jargon of Authenticity.* Chicago: Northwestern University Press, 1973.

Agamben, Giorgio. *The Coming Community.* Translated by Michael Hardt. Theory Out of Bounds series, vol. 1. Minneapolis: University of Minnesota Press, 1993.

Alterman, Eric. "Losing the Right to Choose." *Rolling Stone* 716, September 7, 1995, 39–43.

Anderson, Benedict. *Imagined Communities: Reflections on the Origin and Spread of Nationalism.* London: Verso Books, 1991.

Ariès, Philippe, and Georges Duby, gen'l. eds. *A History of Private Life,* vol. 5: *Riddles of Identity in Modern Times,* ed. Antoine Prost and Gerard Vincent, trans. Arthur Goldhammer. Cambridge, MA: Harvard University, Belknap Press, 1991.

Arnold, Eve. *Marilyn Monroe: An Appreciation.* New York: Alfred A. Knopf, 1987.

Attridge, Derek. "Language as History/History as Language: Saussure and the Romance of Etymology." In *Post-Structuralism and the Question of History,* ed. Derek Attridge, Geoff Bennington, and Robert Young, 183–211. Cambridge: Cambridge University Press, 1987.

Auerbach, Nina. *Our Vampires, Ourselves.* Chicago: University of Chicago Press, 1995.

August, Eugene R., ed. *Carlyle, The Nigger Question / Mill, The Negro Question.* New York: Appleton-Century-Crofts, 1971.

Austin, J. L., Marina Sbisa, and J. O. Urmsson, eds. *How to Do Things with Words*. Cambridge, MA: Harvard University Press, 1975.

Baines, Barbara Bruman. *Fashion Revivals: From the Elizabethan Age to the Present Day*. New York: Drama Book Publishers, 1981.

Banta, Martha. *Imaging American Women: Idea and Ideals in Cultural History*. New York: Columbia University Press, 1987.

———. *Taylored Lives: Narrative Productions in the Age of Taylor, Veblen, and Ford*. Chicago: University of Chicago Press, 1993.

Barker, Francis. *The Tremulous Private Body: Essays on Subjection*. London: Methuen, 1984.

Barnes, Ruth, and Joanne B. Eicher, eds. *Dress and Gender: Making and Meaning*. New York: Berg Publishers (St. Martin's), 1992.

Barrett, Michèle. *The Politics of Truth: From Marx to Foucault*. Stanford, CA: Stanford University Press, 1991.

Barry, Kathleen. *Susan B. Anthony: A Biography of a Singular Feminist*. New York: Ballantine, 1988.

Barthes, Roland. *The Fashion System*. Translated by Matthew Ward and Richard Howard. New York: Hill and Wang, 1983.

Baty, S. Paige. *American Monroe: The Making of a Body Politic*. Berkeley: University of California Press, 1995.

Beecher, Catharine. *Physiology and Calisthenics for Schools and Families*. New York: Harpers, 1856; revised 1867.

Belsey, Catherine. *Critical Practice*. London: Routledge, 1991.

Bérubé, Michael. "Bite Size Theory." *Social Text* 36 (1993): 84–97.

Bessie, Alvah. *The Symbol*. New York: Random House, 1966.

Billson, Anne. *Suckers*. New York: Atheneum, 1993.

Birney, Catherine. *The Grimké Sisters: Sarah and Angelina Grimké: The First Women Advocates of Abolition and Woman's Rights*. Boston: Lee and Sheppard, 1885.

Blumberg, Rhoda. *Bloomers!* New York: Bradbury Press, 1993.

Bordo, Susan. *Unbearable Weight: Feminism, Western Culture and the Body*. Berkeley: University of California Press, 1993.

Boston Globe. Mickey Mantle obituary. August 14, 1995, 2.

Bowers, F. *Textual and Literary Criticism*. Cambridge: Cambridge University Press, 1959.

Bowlby, Rachel. *Just Looking: Consumer Culture in Dreiser, Gissing and Zola*. New York: Methuen, 1985.

Brumberg, Joan Jacobs. *The Body Project: An Intimate History of American Girls*. New York: Random House, 1997.

Butler, Judith. *Bodies That Matter: On the Discursive Limits of "Sex."* New York: Routledge, 1993.

———. *Excitable Speech: A Politics of the Performative*. New York: Routledge, 1997.

————. *Gender Trouble*. New York: Routledge, 1990.

Byrde, Penelope. *Nineteenth-Century Fashion*. London: B. T. Batsford, 1992.

Califia, Pat. *Public Sex: The Culture of Radical Sex*. San Francisco: Cleis Press, 1994.

Carr, Karen, and England, Rupert, eds. *Simulated and Virtual Realities*. London: Taylor and Francis, 1995.

Caruth, Cathy. *Unclaimed Experience: Trauma, Narrative and History*. Baltimore: Johns Hopkins University Press, 1996.

Case, Sue-Ellen. "Tracking the Vampire." *differences: A Journal of Feminist Cultural Studies* 3, no. 2 (1991): 1–20.

Chapkis, Wendy. *Live Sex Acts: Women Performing Erotic Labor*. New York: Routledge, 1997.

Chauncey, George. *Gay New York: Gender, Urban Culture, and the Making of the Gay Male World, 1890–1940*. New York: HarperCollins, 1994.

Collins, Patricia Hill. *Fighting Words: Black Women and the Search for Justice*. Minneapolis: University of Minnesota Press, 1998.

Condit, Celeste Michelle. *Decoding Abortion Rhetoric*. Urbana: University of Illinois Press, 1990.

Coon, Anne C, ed. *Hear Me Patiently: The Reform Speeches of Amelia Jenks Bloomer*. Westport, CT: Greenwood Press, 1994.

Copjec, Joan. "Vampires, Breast-Feeding, and Anxiety." *Read My Desire: Lacan against the Historicists*. Cambridge, MA: MIT Press, 1994.

Corkin, Stanley. "*Sister Carrie* and Industrial Life: Objects and the New American Self." *Modern Fiction Studies* 33, no. 4 (1987).

Cornell, Drucilla. *At the Heart of Freedom: Feminism, Sex and Equality*. Princeton, NJ: Princeton University Press, 1998.

"Costumes of All Nations: The Toilette in Turkey." *Godey's Magazine and Lady's Book* 44 (January 1852): 45.

Cottom, Daniel. *Text and Culture: The Politics of Interpretation*. Minneapolis: University of Minnesota Press, 1989.

Craft, Chris. "Kiss Me with Those Red Lips: Gender and Inversion in Bram Stoker's *Dracula*." In *Speaking of Gender*, ed. Elaine Showalter, 216–42. New York: Routledge, 1984.

Craik, Jennifer. *Faces of Fashion: Cultural Studies in Fashion*. New York: Routledge, 1994.

Crane, Stephen. *Maggie: Girl of the Streets*. New York: Fawcett, 1960.

Cronon, William, ed. *Uncommon Ground: Toward Reinventing Nature*. New York: W. W. Norton, 1995.

"Cult Head Wants New Trial." *Gainesville Sun*, March 26, 1998.

Davis, Angela Y. *Women, Race and Class*. New York: New Vintage Books, 1983.

Derrida, Jacques. *The Archeology of the Frivolous: Reading Condillac*. Translated by John P. Leavey Jr. Lincoln: University of Nebraska Press, 1980.

―――. "Eating Well." In *Points . . .*, ed. Elisabeth Weber, 255–87. Stanford, CA: Stanford University Press, 1995.

―――. *Of Grammatology*. Baltimore: Johns Hopkins University Press.

Dickens, Charles. *David Copperfield*. New York: Penguin, 1971.

Dinnerstein, Dorothy. *The Mermaid and Minotaur*. New York: Harper Colophon Books, 1977.

Djilas, Aleksa. "A Collective Madness." *New York Times Book Review*, June 22, 1997.

Dolar, Mladen. "I Shall Be with You on Your Wedding Night: Lacan and the Uncanny." *October* 58 (1991): 5–23.

Douglass, Frederick. *The Narrative of Frederick Douglass, an American Slave*. Edited by Henry Louis Gates. New York: Penguin, 1995; originally published 1845.

―――. *The Narrative of the Life and Times of Frederick Douglass*. New York: Bonanza Books/Crown, 1962.

Dreiser, Theodore. *Sister Carrie: An Authoritative Text, Backgrounds, and Sources Criticism*. Edited by Donald Pizer. Norton Critical Editions. New York: W. W. Norton, 1991.

―――. *Sister Carrie*. Edited by Claude Simpson. Boston: Houghton Mifflin's Riverside Press Cambridge, 1959.

Dresser, Norine. *American Vampires: Fans, Victims, Practitioners*. New York: Vintage Books, 1989.

Du Bois, W. E. B. "The Negro and Communism." In *The Oxford W. E. B. Du Bois Reader*. Edited by Eric J. Sundquist. New York: Oxford University Press, 1996.

Dunham, David, and Scott Shwarts. "On the Road to Intimacy." www .pensee.com/pensee/intimacy.html.

Dyer, Richard. "Monroe and Sexuality." *Heavenly Bodies: Film Stars and Society*. Cinema/bfi/series. New York: St. Martin's, 1986.

Ellison, Ralph. *Invisible Man*. New York: Vintage International, 1980.

Enstad, Nan. *Ladies of Labor, Girls of Adventure: Working Women, Popular Culture and Labor Politics at the Turn of the Century*. New York: Columbia University Press, 1999.

Erkkila, Betsy. "Introduction." In *Breaking Bounds: Whitman and American Cultural Studies*, ed. Betsy Erkkila and Jay Grossman, 1–20. New York: Oxford University Press, 1996.

Eurydice. "Scar Lovers: Sex in the U.S.A., Part One." *Spin*, August 1995, 60–66, 111.

Ewing, Elizabeth. *Dress and Undress: A History of Women's Underwear*. London: Bibliophile, 1981.

―――. *History of Twentieth-Century Fashion*. London: B. T. Batsford, 1974.

Fern, Fanny [Sara Parton]. *Folly as It Flies: Hit at by Fanny Fern*. New York: G. W. Carleton, 1868.

————. *Fresh Leaves*. New York: Mason Brothers, 1857.

Fischer, Gayle V. "'Pantalets' and 'Turkish Trowsers': Designing Freedom in the Mid Nineteenth-Century United States." *Feminist Studies* 23, no. 1 (Spring 1997): 111–39.

Fitzgerald, F. Scott. *The Last Tycoon*. Edited by Edmund Wilson. New York: Penguin, 1977 (originally published 1941).

Fitzhugh, George. *Cannibals All! Or Slaves without Masters*. Richmond, VA: A. Morris, 1857.

Flugel, J. C. *The Psychology of Clothes*. International Psycho-Analytical Library series, no. 18. London: Hogarth Press and the Institute of Psycho-Analysis, 1966.

Folsom, Ed. "Whitman's Calamus Photographs." In *Breaking Bounds: Whitman and Cultural Studies*, ed. Betsy Erkkila and Jay Grossman, 193–219. New York: Oxford University Press, 1996.

Foner, Philip S., ed. *Frederick Douglass on Women's Rights*. Westport, CT: Greenwood Press, 1976.

Foucault, Michel. *The History of Sexuality*. Vol. 1: *An Introduction*. New York: Vintage Books, 1980.

————. "Nietzsche, Genealogy, History." *Language, Counter-Memory, Practice: Selected Essays and Interviews*. Ithaca, NY: Cornell University Press, 1977.

Franklin, Wayne, ed. *American Voices, American Lives*. New York: W. W. Norton, 1997.

Fraser, Nancy. "Rethinking the Public Sphere: A Contribution to the Critique of Actually Existing Democracy." In *The Phantom Public Sphere*, ed. Bruce Robbins, 1–32. Minneapolis: University of Minnesota Press, 1993.

Freud, Sigmund. *The Interpretation of Dreams*. New York: Avon, 1983.

————. *The Three Essays on the Theory of Sexuality*. 1905. Vol. 7 of *The Standard Edition of the Complete Psychological Works of Sigmund Freud*. 24 vols. Translated and edited by James Strachey. London: Hogarth, 1953; 1953–74.

Friedan, Betty. *The Feminine Mystique*. New York: Dell, 1963.

Fuller, Margaret. *Woman in the Nineteenth Century*. New York: W. W. Norton, 1971.

Fulton, Ben. "Interviews with Vampires." *Private Eye Weekly* (Salt Lake City), December 1, 1994, 8–10.

Fuss, Diana. *Essentially Speaking: Feminism, Nature and Difference*. New York: Routledge, 1989.

————. *Identification Papers*. New York: Routledge, 1995.

Gaines, Jane, and Charlotte Herzog. *Fabrications: Costume and the Female Body*. New York: Routledge, 1990.

Garber, Marjorie. *Vested Interests: Cross-Dressing and Cultural Anxiety*. New York: HarperPerennial, 1992.

Gates, Henry Louis. *Speaking of Race, Speaking of Sex: Hate Speech, Civil Rights and Civil Liberties*. New York: New York University Press, 1994.

Gattey, Charles Nelson. *The Bloomer Girls*. New York: Coward-McCann, 1967.

Gelder, Ken. *Reading the Vampire*. New York: Routledge, 1994.

Ginsberg, Merle. "Interview with the Vampire Author." *TV Guide*, October 22, 1994, 24–27.

Goldman, Emma. *Red Emma Speaks: An Emma Goldman Reader*. Compiled and edited by Alix Kates Shulman. Amherst, NY: Humanity Books, 1998.

Gourevitch, Philip. "The Memory Thief." *New Yorker*, June 14, 1999, 48–68.

Gramsci, Antonio. *Selections from the Prison Notebooks*. Edited and translated by Quintin Hoare and Geoffrey Nowell Smith. New York: International Publishers, 1995.

Green, Nancy L. *Ready-to-Wear, Ready to Work: A Century of Industry and Immigrants in Paris and New York*. Durham, NC: Duke University Press, 1997.

Greg, W. W. *The Editorial Problem in Shakespeare: A Survey of the Foundations of the Text*. Oxford: Clarendon Press, 1951.

Gregory, Adela, and Milo Speriglio. *Crypt 33, the Saga of Marilyn Monroe: The Final Word*. New York: Birch Lane Press, 1993.

Grimké, Charlotte L. Forten. *The Journals of Charlotte L. Forten Grimké*. Edited by Brenda Stevenson. New York: Schomburg Library of Nineteenth-Century Black Women Writers, Oxford University Press, 1988.

Halley, Janet. "The Construction of Heterosexuality." In *Fear of a Queer Planet*, ed. Michael Warner, 82–104. Minneapolis: University of Minnesota Press.

Hanson, Ellis. "Undead." In *Inside/Out*, ed. Diana Fuss, 324–40. New York: Routledge, 1991.

Haraway, Donna J. "A Manifesto for Cyborgs: Science, Technology and Socialist Feminism in the 1980s." *Socialist Review* 80 (1985).

———. "Modest_Witness@Second_Millennium" (1995). *Modest-Witness@Second Millennium. FemaleMan© Meets OncoMouse™*. New York: Routledge, 1997.

———. "The Promises of Monsters." In *Cultural Studies*, ed. Lawrence Grossberg, Cary Nelson, and Paula Treichler, 295–337. New York: Routledge, 1992.

Hayles, N. Katherine. *How We Became Posthuman: Virtual Bodies in Cybernetics, Literature, and Informatics*. Chicago: University of Chicago Press, 1999.

———. "The Life Cycle of Cyborgs: Writing the Posthuman." In *Cybersexualities*, ed. Jenny Wolmark, 157–73. Edinburgh: Edinburgh University Press, 1999.

Hayles, N. Katherine, and Mark Hansen. *Embodying Technesis: Technology beyond Writing*. Studies in Literature and Science. Ann Arbor: University of Michigan Press, 2000.

Hegeman, Susan. "Taking *Blondes* Seriously." *American Literary History* 7, no. 3 (1995): 525–54.

"Hidden Message Put in State Budget." *Gainesville Sun*, June 12, 1995, 2.

Hochman, Barbara. "The Portrait of the Artist as a Young Actress: The Rewards of Representation in *Sister Carrie*." In *New Essays on Sister Carrie*, ed. Donald Pizer, 43–64. Cambridge: Cambridge University Press, 1991.

Hoffert, Sylvia D. *Private Matters: American Attitudes toward Childbearing and Infant Nurture in the Urban North, 1800–1860*. Chicago: University of Illinois Press, 1989.

Hunt, Lynn, ed. *The New Cultural History*. Berkeley: University of California Press, 1999.

Jameson, Fredric. *The Political Unconscious: Narrative as a Socially Symbolic Act*. Ithaca, NY: Cornell University Press, 1981.

Johnson, Barbara. "Apostrophe, Animation, and Abortion." *Diacritics* 16 (1986): 29–47.

———. "Melville's Fist: The Execution of *Billy Budd*." *Studies in Romanticism* 18 (Winter 1979): 567–99.

Jones, Jacqueline. *American Work: Four Centuries of Black and White Labor*. New York: W. W. Norton, 1998.

Kant, Immanuel. *The Critique of Judgement*. Translated by James Creed Meredith. Oxford: Clarendon Press, 1982.

Kaplan, Amy. *The Social Construction of American Realism*. Chicago: University of Chicago Press, 1988.

Kazin, Alfred. *Specimen Days*. Boston: Godine, 1971.

Keller, Evelyn Fox. "Master Molecules." In *Are Genes Us? The Social Consequences of the New Genetics*, ed. Carl F. Cranor, 89–98. New Brunswick, NJ: Rutgers University Press, 1994.

Kelley, Mary. *Private Woman, Public Stage: Literary Domesticity in Nineteenth-Century America*. New York: Oxford University Press, 1984.

Kennedy, Randall. *nigger: The Strange Career of a Troublesome Word*. New York: Pantheon Books, 2002.

Kesselman, Amy. "The 'Freedom Suit': Feminism and Dress Reform in the United States, 1848–1875." *Gender and Society* 5 (December 1991): 495–510.

Kipnis, Laura. "Adultery." *Critical Inquiry* 24, no. 2 (Winter 1998): 289–327.

Kushner, Tony. *Angels in America*, part 2: *Perestroika*. New York: Theatre Communications Group, 1993–1994.

Lacan, Jacques. *The Four Fundamental Concepts of Psycho-analysis*. New York: W. W. Norton, 1981.

Laqueur, Thomas. *Making Sex: Body and Gender from the Greeks to Freud*. Cambridge, MA: Harvard University Press, 1990.

Le Blanc, Paul. *A Short History of the U. S. Working Class: From Colonial Times to the 21st Century*. Amherst, NY: Humanity Books, 1999.

Lee, Mabel. *Memories of a Bloomer Girl*. Washington, DC: American Alliance for Health, Physical Education and Recreation, 1977.

Leming, Barbara. *Marilyn Monroe*. New York: Crown 1998.

Lerner, Gerda. *The Grimké Sisters from South Carolina: Pioneers for Woman's Rights and Abolition*. New York: Shocken Books, 1971.

Lewontin, Richard C. *Biology as Ideology: The Doctrine of DNA*. New York: HarperPerennial, 1993.

Lincoln, Abraham. Address given to the Wisconsin State Agricultural Society, September 30, 1859. In *The Portable Abraham Lincoln*, 150–61. Edited by Andrew Delbanco. New York: Penguin, 1993.

Lockwood, Scammon. "She Didn't Have Any Sense." *McClure's*, June 1922.

Lohof, Bruce. *American Commonplace: Essays on the Popular Culture of the United States*. Bowling Green, OH: Bowling Green State University Popular Press, 1982.

London, Jack. "The Scab," a speech first given before the Oakland Socialist Party Local, April 5, 1903, collected in *War of the Classes*. http://sunsite.berkeley.edu/London/Writings/WarOfTheClasses/scab.html.

Lord, M. G. *Forever Barbie: The Unauthorized Biography of a Real Doll*. New York: Avon, 1995.

Luker, Kristen. *Abortion and the Politics of Motherhood*. Berkeley: University of California Press, 1984.

Lurie, Alison. *The Language of Clothes*. New York: Random House, 1981.

Lyotard, Jean-François. *The Differend: Phrases in Dispute*. Minneapolis: University of Minnesota Press, 1988.

———. "The Sign of History." In *Post-Structuralism and the Question of History*, ed. Derek Attridge, Geoff Bennington, and Robert Young. Cambridge: Cambridge University Press, 1987.

MacKinnon, Catharine. *Only Words*. Cambridge, MA: Harvard University Press, 1995.

Malkiel, Theresa. *The Diary of a Shirtwaist Striker*. New York: ILR Press, 1909; republished, Cornell University, 1998.

Malone, Thomas Patrick, and Patrick Thomas Malone. *The Art of Intimacy*. New York: Simon and Schuster, 1988.

Martin, Linda. *The Way We Wore: Fashion Illustrations of Children's Wear 1870–1970*. New York: Scribner's, 1978.

Marx, Karl. *Capital: A Critique of Political Economy*. Edited by Friedrich Engels. Modern Library Facsimile Edition. New York: Charles H. Kerr, 1906.

Matsuda, Mari J., Charles R. Lawrence III, Richard Delgardo, and Kimberlè Williams Crenshaw. *Words That Wound*. Boulder, CO: Westview Press, 1993.

Matthiessen, F. O. *American Renaissance*. Chicago: University of Chicago Press, 1990.

McCann, Graham. *Marilyn Monroe*. New Brunswick, NJ: Rutgers University Press, 1987.

McGann, J. J. A Critique of Modern Textual Criticism. Chicago: University of Chicago Press, 1983.

Melville, Herman. Billy Budd (an Inside Narrative). Edited by Harrison Hayford and Merton M. Sealts Jr. Chicago: University of Chicago Press, 1962.

————. "Misgivings." In Battle-Pieces and Aspects of the War: Civil War Poems. Edited by Lee Rust Brown. New York: Da Capo Press, 1995.

Mencken, H. L. The American Language: An Inquiry into the Development of English in the United States. New York: Alfred A. Knopf, 1921.

Meryman, Richard. "Fame Can Go By." Interview with Marilyn Monroe. Life, August 3, 1962, 32–38.

Miller, Arthur. After the Fall: A Play by Arthur Miller. New York: Viking Press, 1964.

————. Timebends. New York: Grove Press, 1987.

Miller, D. A. The Novel and the Police. Berkeley: University of California Press, 1988.

Miller, Jacques-Alain. "Extimité." Prose Studies 2, no. 3 (1988): 121–31.

Miller, Toby. Technologies of Truth: Cultural Citizenship and the Popular Media. Minneapolis: University of Minnesota Press, 1998.

Mills, Bart. Marilyn on Location. London: Sidgwick and Jackson, 1989.

Milstead, Jeff, and Jude Milhon. Interview with Mike Saenz. Mondo 2000 (Berkeley) 4 (1991): 4.

Monroe, Marilyn. My Story. New York: Stein and Day, 1974.

Moon, Michael. Disseminating Whitman. Cambridge, MA: Harvard University Press, 1991.

Morrison, Toni. Playing in the Dark: Whiteness and the Literary Imagination. New York: Vintage, 1993.

Morton, Donald. "Birth of the Cyberqueer." PMLA 110, no. 3 (1995): 369–79.

Moses, Gavriel. The Nickel Was for the Movies: Film in the Novel. Berkeley: University of California Press, 1995.

Murray, R. Emmett. The Lexicon of Labor: More Than 500 Key Terms, Biographical Sketches, and Historical Insights concerning Labor in America. Foreword by Thomas Geoghegan. New York: New Press, 1998.

"NAACP Will Invite Farrakhan to Meeting." New York Times, January 12, 1994; reprinted in Gainesville Sun, January 15, 1994, 3.

Newman, Karen. "Directing Traffic: Subjects, Objects and the Politics of Exchange." differences: A Journal of Feminist Cultural Studies 2, no. 2 (1990): 41–54.

————. Fetal Positions: Individualism, Science, Visuality. Stanford, CA: Stanford University Press, 1996.

Newman, Louise. White Women's Rights: The Racial Origins of Feminism in the United States. New York: Oxford University Press, 1999.

Paine, Thomas, Common Sense. London: Penguin, 1976.

Patton, Cindy. *Fatal Advice: How Safe-Sex Education Went Wrong*. Durham, NC: Duke University Press, 1996.

———. "Tremble Hetero Swine." In *Fear of a Queer Planet*, ed. Michael Warner, 143–77. Minneapolis: University of Minnesota Press, 1993.

Peiss, Kathy. *Cheap Amusements: Working Women and Leisure in Turn-of-the-Century New York*. Philadelphia: Temple University Press, 1986.

Peplow, Michael W. *George S. Schuyler*. Boston: Twayne Publishers (G. K. Hall), 1980.

Perelman, Michael. *The Invention of Capitalism: Classical Political Economy and the Secret History of Primitive Accumulation*. London: Duke University Press, 2000.

Pizer, Donald, ed. *New Essays on "Sister Carrie."* Cambridge: Cambridge University Press, 1991.

Poniewozik, James. "Rigoberta Menchu Meets the Press." Salon Magazine, www.salonmagazine.com/news/1999/02/12newsa.html.

Rabinowitz, Paula. *Labor and Desire: Women's Revolutionary Fiction in Depression America*. Chapel Hill: University of North Carolina Press, 1991.

"Records Show Killer Drank Women's Blood." *Gainesville Sun*, February 19, 1995.

Rheingold, Howard. *The Virtual Community*. Cambridge, MA: MIT Press, 2000.

Roberts, Dorothy. "The Genetic Tie." *University of Chicago Law Review* 62, no. 1 (Winter 1995).

Robinson, Amy. "It Takes One to Know One: Passing and Communities of Common Interest." *Critical Inquiry* 20, no. 4 (Summer 1994): 715–36.

Rollyson, Carl E., Jr. *Marilyn Monroe: A Life of the Actress*. Ann Arbor, MI: UMI Research Press, 1986.

Romero, Lora. "'When Something Goes Queer': Familiarity, Formalism and Minority Intellectuals in the 1980's." *Yale Journal of Criticism* 6, no. 1 (1993): 121–41.

Roof, Judith. *Reproductions of Reproduction: Imaging Symbolic Change*. New York: Routledge, 1996.

Rose, Jacqueline. *The Haunting of Sylvia Plath*. Cambridge, MA: Harvard University Press, 1992.

Ross, Kristin. *Fast Cars, Clean Bodies: Decolonization and the Reordering of French Culture*. Boston: MIT/October Press, 1996.

Rubin, Gayle. "The Traffic in Women: Notes on the Political Economy of Sex." In *Towards an Anthology of Women*, ed. Rayna R. Reirer, 157–210. New York: Monthly Review Press, 1975.

Sandburg, Carl. "Tribute to Marilyn." *Look*, September 1962, 90–94.

Sanders, Barry. *A Is for Ox: The Collapse of Literacy and the Rise of Violence in an Electronic Age*. New York: Random House, Vintage Books, 1995.

Savran, David. *Communists, Cowboys, and Queers: The Politics of Masculinity in the Work of Arthur Miller and Tennessee Williams*. Minneapolis: University of Minnesota Press, 1992.

Schuyler, George. *Black No More*. Boston: Northeastern University Press, 1989 (originally published 1931).

Searle, John R. *Speech Acts: An Essay in the Philosophy of Language*. Cambridge: Cambridge University Press, 1970.

Sebeok, Thomas. *Global Semiotics*. Bloomington: Indiana University Press, 2001.

Sedgwick, Eve Kosofsky. *Between Men: English Literature and Male Homosocial Desire*. New York: Columbia University Press, 1985.

———. *Epistemology of the Closet*. Berkeley: University of California Press, 1990.

———. *Tendencies*. Durham, NC: Duke University Press, 1993.

Seltzer, Mark. "Serial Killers (I)." *differences: A Journal of Feminist Cultural Studies* 5, no. 1 (Spring 1993): 92–127.

Shakespeare, William. *Henry V*. New York: Arden 1983.

Shulman, Robert. "Dreiser and the Dynamics of American Captialism." In *Theodore Dreiser, Sister Carrie: An Authoritative Text, Backgrounds, and Sources Criticism*, ed. Donald Pizer, 560–75. Norton Critical Editions. New York: W. W. Norton, 1991.

Silver, Lee M. *Remaking Eden: Cloning and Beyond in a Brave New World*. New York: Avon, 1997.

Simpson, David. "Destiny Made Manifest: The Styles of Whitman's Poetry." In *Nation and Narration*, ed. Homi Bhabha, 177–96. New York: Routledge, 1990.

Sinfield, Alan. "Cultural Materialism, *Othello*, and the Politics of Plausibility." In *Literary Theory: An Anthology*, ed. Julie Rivkin and Michael Ryan, 804–26. Edinburgh: Blackwell, 1998.

Smith, Stephanie A. *Conceived by Liberty: Maternal Figures and 19th-Century American Literature*. Ithaca, NY: Cornell University Press, 1995.

———. "Cyber(genetics)." In *Genealogie und Genetik*, ed. Sigrid Wiegel. Einstein-Bücher series. Berlin: Akademie Verlag, 2002.

———. "Suckers." *differences: A Journal of Feminist Cultural Studies* 10, no. 1, special issue, "Eating and Disorder" (1998): 175–208.

Spillers, Hortense. "Notes on an Alternative Model—Neither/Nor." *The Difference Within: Feminism and Critical Theory*, ed. Elizabeth Meese and Alice Parker, 165–88. Philadelphia: John Benjamin, 1989.

Spivak, Gayatri Chakravorty. "In a Word: Interview." In *The Second Wave: A Reader in Feminist Theory*, ed. Linda Nicholson. New York: Routledge, 1997.

———. *In Other Worlds: Essays in Cultural Politics*. New York: Methuen, 1987.

———. *Outside in the Teaching Machine*. New York: Routledge, 1993.

————. "A Response to 'The Difference Within: Feminism and Critical Theory.'" In *The Difference Within: Feminism and Critical Theory*, ed. Elizabeth Meese and Alice Parker, 207–20. Philadelphia: John Benjamin, 1989.

————. *The Spivak Reader*. Edited by Donna Landry and Gerald Maclean. New York: Routledge, 1996.

Spoto, Donald. *Marilyn Monroe: The Biography*. New York: HarperCollins, 1993.

Stanton, Elizabeth Cady. *Eighty Years and More—Reminiscences 1815–1897*. New York: T. Fisher Unwin, 1898; reprint, New York: Shocken Books, 1971.

Stanton, Elizabeth Cady, Susan B. Anthony, and Matilda J. Gage. *History of Woman Suffrage*. 6 vols. New York: Fowler and Wells, 1881–1922.

Steele, Valerie. *Fashion and Eroticism: The Ideals of Feminine Beauty from the Victorian Era to the Jazz Age*. New York: Oxford University Press, 1985.

————. *Paris Fashion: A Cultural History*. New York: Oxford University Press, 1988.

Stein, Leon, and Annette K. Baxter, eds. *Dress Reform: A Series of Lectures Delivered in Boston, on Dress as It Affects the Health of Women* (with illustrations), ed. Abba Goold Woolson. Boston: Roberts Brothers, 1874. Reprinted in facsimile in the series Women in America: From Colonial Times to the 20th Century, ed. Leon Stein and Annette K. Baxter. New York: Arno Press, 1974. (Cited page numbers refer to the facsimile reprint edition.)

Steinem, Gloria. *Marilyn/Norma Jeane*. Photos by George Barris. New York: Signet, 1986.

Stevens, Wallace. "The Noble Rider and the Sound of Words." *The Necessary Angel: Essays on Reality and the Imagination*, 1–36. New York: Vintage Books, 1951 (essay originally published 1942, Princeton University Press).

Stone, Alluquere Rosanne. *The War of Desire and Technology at the Close of the Mechanical Age*. Cambridge, MA: MIT Press, 1996.

Street, Bryan V. *Literacy in Theory and Practice*. Cambridge: Cambridge University Press, 1984.

Sullivan, Steve. *Bombshells: Glamour Girls of a Lifetime*. New York: St. Martin's–Griffin, 1998.

————. *Va Va Voom! Bombshells, Pin-Ups, Sexpots, and Glamour Girls*. Toronto: Stoddart Press, 1995.

Summers, Anthony. *Goddess: The Secret Lives of Marilyn Monroe*. New York: Onyx, division of Penguin, 1985.

Trachtenberg, Alan. *The Incorporation of America: Culture and Society in the Gilded Age*. New York: Farrar, Strauss and Giroux, Hill and Wang, 1982.

Travers, Peter. "The Dying Game." Review of *Interview with the Vampire*, dir. Neil Jordan. *Rolling Stone*, December 15, 1994, 101–2.

Warner, Michael. "Something Queer about the Nation-State." *States of Culture* 3 (1993): 14–16.

———, ed. *Fear of a Queer Planet*. Minneapolis: University of Minnesota Press, 1993.

Watkins, Evan. *Everyday Exchanges: Marketwork and Capitalist Common Sense*. Stanford, CA: Stanford University Press, 1998.

Weatherby, W. J. *Conversations with Marilyn*. New York: Mason/Charter, 1976.

Weston, Kath. "Do Clothes Make the Woman? Gender, Performance Theory, and Lesbian Eroticism." *Genders* 17 (Fall 1993): 1–21.

White, Luise. "Cars Out of Place: Vampires, Technology, and Labor in East and Central Africa." *Representations* 43 (1993): 27–50.

Whitman, Walt. *Complete Poetry and Selected Prose*. Edited by James E. Miller Jr. Boston: Houghton Mifflin, 1959.

———. *The Portable Walt Whitman*. Edited by Mark Van Doren. New York: Penguin, 1977.

Whitman, Walter. *Franklin Evans or The Inebriate: A Tale of the Times*. Edited by Jean Downey. New Haven, CT: Yale University Press, 1967.

Williams, Raymond. *Culture and Society, 1780–1950*. London: Chatto and Windus, 1958.

———. *Keywords*. New York: Oxford University Press, 1983.

Wolfe, Donald H. *The Last Days of Marilyn Monroe*. New York: William Morrow, 1998.

Worrell, Estelle Ansley. *Children's Costume in America, 1607–1910*. New York: Scribner's, 1980.

Žižek, Slavoj. *For They Know Not What They Do*. London: Verso, 1994.

Index

Stephanie A. Smith, associate professor of English at the University of Florida, examines the intersections of science, fiction, politics, race, and gender. Her books include *Conceived by Liberty, Other Nature, The-Boy-Who-Was-Thrown-Away,* and *Snow-Eyes.*